PRAYERS AND MEDITATIONS
BY BAHÁ'U'LLÁH

PRAYERS AND MEDITATIONS

BY BAHÁ'U'LLÁH

Translated by SHOGHI EFFENDI
from the original Persian and Arabic

BAHÁ'Í PUBLISHING TRUST
WILMETTE, ILLINOIS

ISBN 0-87743-024-1
Library of Congress Catalog Card Number 53-10767

PRINTED IN THE UNITED STATES OF AMERICA

PRAYERS AND MEDITATIONS
BY BAHÁ'U'LLÁH

PRAYERS AND MEDITATIONS
BY BAHÁ'U'LLÁH

I

Glorified art Thou, O Lord my God! Every man of insight confesseth Thy sovereignty and Thy dominion, and every discerning eye perceiveth the greatness of Thy majesty and the compelling power of Thy might. The winds of tests are powerless to hold back them that enjoy near access to Thee from setting their faces towards the horizon of Thy glory, and the tempests of trials must fail to draw away and hinder such as are wholly devoted to Thy will from approaching Thy court.

Methinks, the lamp of Thy love is burning in their hearts, and the light of Thy tenderness is lit within their breasts. Adversities are incapable of estranging them from Thy Cause, and the vicissitudes of fortune can never cause them to stray from Thy pleasure.

I beseech Thee, O my God, by them and by the sighs which their hearts utter in their separation from Thee, to keep them safe from the mischief of Thine adversaries, and to nourish their souls with what Thou hast ordained for Thy loved ones on whom shall come no fear and who shall not be put to grief.

II

Unto Thee be praise, O Lord my God! I entreat Thee, by Thy signs that have encompassed the entire creation, and by the light of Thy countenance that hath illuminated all that are in heaven and on earth, and by Thy mercy that hath surpassed all created things, and by Thy grace that hath suffused the whole universe, to rend asunder the veils that shut me out from Thee, that I may hasten unto the Fountain-Head of Thy mighty inspiration, and to the Day-Spring of Thy Revelation and bountiful favors, and may be immersed beneath the ocean of Thy nearness and pleasure.

Suffer me not, O my Lord, to be deprived of the knowledge of Thee in Thy days, and divest me not of the robe of Thy guidance. Give me to drink of the river that is life indeed, whose waters have streamed forth from the Paradise (Riḍván) in which the throne of Thy Name, the All-Merciful, was established, that mine eyes may be opened, and my face be illumined, and my heart be assured, and my soul be enlightened, and my steps be made firm.

Thou art He Who from everlasting was, through the potency of His might, supreme over all things, and, through the operation of His will, was able to ordain all things. Nothing whatsoever, whether in Thy heaven or on Thy earth, can frustrate Thy purpose. Have mercy, then, upon me, O my Lord, through Thy gracious providence and generosity, and incline mine ear to the sweet melodies of the birds that warble their praise of Thee, amidst the branches of the tree of Thy oneness.

Thou art the Great Giver, the Ever-Forgiving, the Most Compassionate.

steadfastness

III

Glorified art Thou, O Lord my God! I beseech Thee by Him Who is Thy Most Great Name, Who hath been sorely afflicted by such of Thy creatures as have repudiated Thy truth, and Who hath been hemmed in by sorrows which no tongue can describe, to grant that I may remember Thee and celebrate Thy praise, in these days when all have turned away from Thy beauty, have disputed with Thee, and turned away disdainfully from Him Who is the Revealer of Thy Cause. None is there, O my Lord, to help Thee except Thine own Self, and no power to succor Thee save Thine own power.

I entreat Thee to enable me to cleave steadfastly to Thy Love and Thy remembrance. This is, verily, within my power, and Thou art the One that knoweth all that is in me. Thou, in truth, art knowing, apprised of all. Deprive me not, O my Lord, of the splendors of the light of Thy face, whose brightness hath illuminated the whole world. No God is there beside Thee, the Most Powerful, the All-Glorious, the Ever-Forgiving.

IV

Magnified be Thy name, O Lord my God! Thou art He Whom all things worship and Who worshipeth no one, Who is the Lord of all things and is the vassal of none, Who knoweth all things and is known of none. Thou didst wish to make Thyself known unto men; therefore, Thou didst, through a word of Thy mouth, bring creation into being and fashion the universe. There is none other God except Thee, the Fashioner, the Creator, the Almighty, the Most Powerful.

I implore Thee, by this very word that hath shone forth above the horizon of Thy will, to enable me to drink deep of the living waters through which Thou hast vivified the hearts of Thy chosen ones and quickened the souls of them that love Thee, that I may, at all times and under all conditions, turn my face wholly towards Thee.

Thou art the God of power, of glory and bounty. No God is there beside Thee, the Supreme Ruler, the All-Glorious, the Omniscient.

V

Lauded be Thy name, O my God! Thou beholdest me in the clutches of my oppressors. Every time I turn to my right, I hear the voice of the lamentation of them that are dear to Thee, whom the infidels have made captives for having believed in Thee and in Thy signs, and for having set their faces towards the horizon of Thy grace and of Thy loving-kindness. And when I turn to my left, I hear the clamor of the wicked doers who have disbelieved in Thee and in Thy signs, and persistently striven to put out the light of Thy lamp which sheddeth the radiance of Thine own Self over all that are in Thy heaven and all that are on Thy earth.

The hearts of Thy chosen ones, O my Lord, have melted because of their separation from Thee, and the souls of Thy loved ones are burnt up by the fire of their yearning after Thee in Thy days. I implore Thee, O Thou Maker of the heavens and Lord of all names, by Thy most effulgent Self and Thy most exalted and all-glorious Remembrance, to send down upon Thy loved ones that which will draw them nearer unto Thee, and enable them to hearken unto Thine utterances.

Tear asunder with the hand of Thy transcendent power, O my Lord, the veil of vain imaginings, that they who are wholly devoted to Thee may see Thee seated on the throne of Thy majesty, and the eyes of

such as adore Thy unity may rejoice at the splendors
of the glory of Thy face. The doors of hope have
been shut against the hearts that long for Thee, O my
Lord! Their keys are in Thy hands; open them by the
power of Thy might and Thy sovereignty. Potent
art Thou to do as Thou pleasest. Thou art, verily, the
Almighty, the Beneficent.

VI

Praise be to Thee, O Lord my God! I swear by Thy
might! Successive afflictions have withheld the pen
of the Most High from laying bare that which is
hidden from the eyes of Thy creatures, and incessant
trials have hindered the tongue of the Divine Ordainer from proclaiming the wonders of Thy glorification and praise. With a stammering tongue, therefore, I call upon Thee, O my God, and with this my
afflicted pen I occupy myself in remembrance of Thy
name.

Is there any man of insight, O my God, that can
behold Thee with Thine own eye, and where is the
thirsty one who can direct his face towards the living
waters of Thy love? I am the one, O my God, who
hath blotted out from his heart the remembrance of
all except Thee, and hath graven upon it the mysteries of Thy love. Thine own might beareth me

witness! But for tribulations, how could the assured be distinguished from the doubters among Thy servants? They who have been inebriated with the wine of Thy knowledge, these, verily, hasten to meet every manner of adversity in their longing to pass into Thy presence. I implore Thee, O Beloved of my heart and the Object of my soul's adoration, to shield them that love me from the faintest trace of evil and corrupt desires. Supply them, then, with the good of this world and of the next.

protection for the believers

Thou art, verily, He Whose grace hath guided them aright, He Who hath declared Himself to be the All-Merciful. No God is there but Thee, the All-Glorious, the Supreme Helper.

protection from self
purpose of tribulations

VII

Fast

Praise be to Thee, O Lord my God! I beseech Thee by this Revelation whereby darkness hath been turned into light, through which the Frequented Fane hath been built, and the Written Tablet revealed, and the Outspread Roll uncovered, to send down upon me and upon them who are in my company that which will enable us to soar into the heavens of Thy transcendent glory, and will wash us from the stain of such doubts as have hindered the suspicious from entering into the tabernacle of Thy unity.

I am the one, O my Lord, who hath held fast the cord of Thy loving-kindness, and clung to the hem of Thy mercy and favors. Do Thou ordain for me and for my loved ones the good of this world and of the world to come. Supply them, then, with the Hidden Gift Thou didst ordain for the choicest among Thy creatures.

These are, O my Lord, the days in which Thou hast bidden Thy servants to observe the fast. Blessed is he that observeth the fast wholly for Thy sake and with absolute detachment from all things except Thee. Assist me and assist them, O my Lord, to obey Thee and to keep Thy precepts. Thou, verily, hast power to do what Thou choosest.

There is no God but Thee, the All-Knowing, the All-Wise. All praise be to God, the Lord of all worlds.

VIII

Glorified be Thy name, O Lord my God! Thou beholdest my dwelling-place, and the prison into which I am cast, and the woes I suffer. By Thy might! No pen can recount them, nor can any tongue describe or number them. I know not, O my God, for what purpose Thou hast abandoned me to Thine adversaries. Thy glory beareth me witness! I sorrow not for the vexations I endure for love of Thee, nor

acquiescence

feel perturbed by the calamities that overtake me in Thy path. My grief is rather because Thou delayest to fulfill what Thou hast determined in the Tablets of Thy Revelation, and ordained in the books of Thy decree and judgment.

My blood, at all times, addresseth me saying: "O Thou Who art the Image of the Most Merciful! How long will it be ere Thou riddest me of the captivity of this world, and deliverest me from the bondage of this life? Didst Thou not promise me that Thou shalt dye the earth with me, and sprinkle me on the faces of the inmates of Thy Paradise?" To this I make reply: "Be thou patient and quiet thyself. The things thou desirest can last but an hour. As to me, how- ever, I quaff continually in the path of God the cup of His decree, and wish not that the ruling of His will should cease to operate, or that the woes I suffer for the sake of my Lord, the Most Exalted, the All- Glorious, should be ended. Seek thou my wish and forsake thine own. Thy bondage is not for my protec- tion, but to enable me to sustain successive tribula- tions, and to prepare me for the trials that must needs repeatedly assail me. Perish that lover who discerneth between the pleasant and the poisonous in his love for his beloved! Be thou satisfied with what God hath destined for thee. He, verily, ruleth over thee as He willeth and pleaseth. No God is there but Him, the Inaccessible, the Most High."

IX

Magnified be Thy name, O Lord my God! I know not what the water is with which Thou hast created me, or what the fire Thou hast kindled within me, or the clay wherewith Thou hast kneaded me. The restlessness of every sea hath been stilled, but not the restlessness of this Ocean which moveth at the bidding of the winds of Thy will. The flame of every fire hath been extinguished except the Flame which the hands of Thine omnipotence have kindled, and whose radiance Thou hast, by the power of Thy name, shed abroad before all that are in Thy heaven and all that are on Thy earth. As the tribulations deepen, it waxeth hotter and hotter.

Behold, then, O my God, how Thy Light hath been compassed with the onrushing winds of Thy decree, how the tempests that blow and beat upon it from every side have added to its brightness and increased its splendor. For all this let Thee be praised.

I implore Thee, by Thy Most Great Name, and Thy most ancient sovereignty, to look upon Thy loved ones whose hearts have been sorely shaken by reason of the troubles that have touched Him Who is the Manifestation of Thine own Self. Powerful art Thou to do what pleaseth Thee. Thou art, verily, the All-Knowing, the All-Wise.

X

O Thou Whose face is the object of the adoration of all that yearn after Thee, Whose presence is the hope of such as are wholly devoted to Thy will, Whose nearness is the desire of all that have drawn nigh unto Thy court, Whose countenance is the companion of those who have recognized Thy truth, Whose name is the mover of the souls that long to behold Thy face, Whose voice is the true life of Thy lovers, the words of Whose mouth are as the waters of life unto all who are in heaven and on earth!

I beseech Thee, by the wrong Thou hast suffered and the ills inflicted upon Thee by the hosts of wrongful doers, to send down upon me from the clouds of Thy mercy that which will purify me of all that is not of Thee, that I may be worthy to praise Thee and fit to love Thee.

Withhold not from me, O my Lord, the things Thou didst ordain for such of Thy handmaidens as circle around Thee, and on whom are poured continually the splendors of the sun of Thy beauty and the beams of the brightness of Thy face. Thou art He Who from everlasting hath succored whosoever hath sought Thee, and bountifully favored him who hath asked Thee.

No God is there beside Thee, the Mighty, the Ever-Abiding, the All-Bounteous, the Most Generous.

XI

Lauded be Thy name, O Lord my God! Darkness hath fallen upon every land, and the forces of mischief have encompassed all the nations. Through them, however, I perceive the splendors of Thy wisdom, and discern the brightness of the light of Thy providence.

They that are shut out as by a veil from Thee have imagined that they have the power to put out Thy light, and to quench Thy fire, and to still the winds of Thy grace. Nay, and to this Thy might beareth me witness! Had not every tribulation been made the bearer of Thy wisdom, and every ordeal the vehicle of Thy providence, no one would have dared oppose us, though the powers of earth and heaven were to be leagued against us. Were I to unravel the wondrous mysteries of Thy wisdom which are laid bare before me, the reins of Thine enemies would be cleft asunder.

Glorified be Thou, then, O my God! I beseech Thee by Thy Most Great Name to assemble them that love Thee around the Law that streameth from the good-pleasure of Thy will, and to send down upon them what will assure their hearts.

Potent art Thou to do what pleaseth Thee. Thou art, verily, the Help in Peril, the Self-Subsisting.

XII

Praised be Thou, O Lord my God! This is Thy servant who hath quaffed from the hands of Thy grace the wine of Thy tender mercy, and tasted of the savor of Thy love in Thy days. I beseech Thee, by the embodiments of Thy names whom no grief can hinder from rejoicing in Thy love or from gazing on Thy face, and whom all the hosts of the heedless are powerless to cause to turn aside from the path of Thy pleasure, to supply him with the good things Thou dost possess, and to raise him up to such heights that he will regard the world even as a shadow that vanisheth swifter than the twinkling of an eye.

Keep him safe also, O my God, by the power of Thine immeasurable majesty, from all that Thou abhorrest. Thou art, verily, his Lord and the Lord of all worlds.

trials

XIII

Lauded be Thy name, O my God! Thou beholdest how the tempestuous winds of tests have caused the steadfast in faith to tremble, and how the breath of trials hath stirred up those whose hearts had been firmly established, except such as have partaken of the Wine that is life indeed from the hands of the

Manifestation of Thy name, the Most Merciful. These are the ones whom no word except Thy most exalted word can move, whom nothing whatever save the sweet smelling fragrance of the robe of Thy remembrance can enrapture, O Thou Who art the Possessor of all names and the Maker of earth and heaven!

I implore Thee, O Thou Who art the beloved Companion of Bahá, by Thy name, the All-Glorious, to keep safe these Thy servants under the shadow of the wings of Thine all-encompassing mercy, that the darts of the evil suggestions of the wicked doers among Thy creatures, who have disbelieved in Thy signs, may be kept back from them. No one on earth, O my Lord, can withstand Thy power, and none in all the kingdom of Thy names is able to frustrate Thy purpose. Show forth, then, the power of Thy sovereignty and of Thy dominion, and teach Thy loved ones what beseemeth them in Thy days.

Thou art, verily, the Almighty, the Most Exalted, the All-Glorious, the Most Great.

XIV

All praise be to Thee, O my God! Thou beholdest my helplessness and poverty, and bearest witness unto my woes and trials. How long wilt Thou abandon me among Thy servants? Suffer me to ascend into

Thy presence. The power of Thy might beareth me witness! Such are the tribulations with which I am encompassed that I am powerless to recount them before Thy face. Thou, alone, verily, hast through Thy knowledge reckoned them.

I beseech Thee, O Thou Who art my Companion in my lowliness, to rain down upon Thy loved ones from the clouds of Thy mercy that which will cause them to be satisfied with Thy pleasure, and will enable them to turn unto Thee and to be detached from all else except Thee. Ordain, then, for them every good conceived by Thee and predestined in Thy Book. Thou art, verily, the All-Powerful, He Whom nothing whatsoever can frustrate. From everlasting Thou hast been clothed with transcendent greatness and power, with unspeakable majesty and glory. There is no God beside Thee, the Almighty, the All-Glorious, the Ever-Forgiving.

Glorified be Thy name, Thou in Whose hand are the kingdoms of earth and heaven.

XV

O Thou Who art the Ruler of earth and heaven and the Author of all names! Thou hearest the voice of my lamentation which from the fortress-town of 'Akká ascendeth towards Thee, and beholdest how my captive friends have fallen into the hands of the workers of iniquity.

We render Thee thanks, O our Lord, for all the troubles which have touched us in Thy path. Oh, that the span of my earthly life could be so extended as to embrace the lives of the former and the latter generations, or could even be so lengthened that no man on the face of the earth could measure it, and be afflicted every day and every moment with a fresh tribulation for love of Thee and for Thy pleasure's sake!

Thou well knowest, however, O my God, that my wish is wholly dissolved in Thy wish, and that Thou hast irrevocably decreed that my soul should ascend unto the loftiest mansions of Thy Kingdom, and pass into the presence of my all-glorious Companion.

Hasten, by Thy grace and bounty, my passing, O my Lord, and pour forth upon all them that are dear to Thee what will preserve them from fear and trembling after me. Powerful art Thou to do whatsoever may please Thee. No God is there except Thee, the All-Glorious, the All-Wise.

Thou seest, O my Lord, how Thy servants have left their homes in their longing to meet Thee, and how they have been hindered by the ungodly from looking upon Thy face, and from circumambulating the sanctuary of Thy grandeur. Pour out Thy steadfastness and send down Thy calm upon them, O my Lord! Thou art, in truth, the Ever-Forgiving, the Most Compassionate.

XVI

mercy

Praise be to Thee, O Lord my God! Thou seest my tears and lamentations, and hearest my sighing, my cry and bitter wailing. I am the one, O my Lord, that hath held fast the cord of Thy mercy which hath surpassed the entire creation. I am the one that hath clung to the hem of Thy loving-kindness, O Thou in Whose hand is the empire of all names!

Have mercy upon me and upon all them that are in my company, through the wonders of Thy grace and power. Shield us, then, O my God, from the mischief of Thine enemies, and assist us to help Thy Faith, and to protect Thy Cause, and to celebrate Thy glory. Thou art, verily, He Who from everlasting hath inhabited the inaccessible heights of His unity, and will continue to remain the same for ever and ever. Nothing whatsoever escapeth Thy knowledge, nor is there anything that can frustrate Thee. No God is there beside Thee, the Almighty, the Ever-Faithful, the Most Exalted, the All-Glorious, the Best-Beloved.

Lauded and glorified art Thou, in Whose hand is the empire of all things!

XVII

Magnified be Thy name, O God, the Lord of heaven! Attire my head with the crown of martyrdom, even as Thou didst attire my body with the ornament of tribulation before all that dwell in Thy land. Grant, moreover, that they whose hearts yearn over Thee may draw nigh unto the horizon of Thy grace, above which the Day-Star of Thy beauty sheddeth its radiance. Ordain, also, for them what will make them rich enough to dispense with aught else except Thee, and rid them of all attachment to such as have repudiated Thy signs.

There is none other God but Thee, the Guardian, the Self-Subsisting.

XVIII

Praised be Thou, O my God! How can I thank Thee for having singled me out and chosen me above all Thy servants to reveal Thee, at a time when all had turned away from Thy beauty! I testify, O my God, that if I were given a thousand lives by Thee, and offered them up all in Thy path, I would still have failed to repay the least of the gifts which, by Thy grace, Thou hast bestowed upon me.

I lay asleep on the bed of self when lo, Thou didst waken me with the divine accents of Thy voice, and didst unveil to me Thy beauty, and didst enable me to listen to Thine utterances, and to recognize Thy Self, and to speak forth Thy praise, and to extol Thy virtues, and to be steadfast in Thy love. Finally I fell a captive into the hands of the wayward among Thy servants.

Thou beholdest, therefore, the exile which I suffer in Thy days, and art aware of my vehement longing to look upon Thy face, and of mine irrepressible yearnings to enter the court of Thy glory, and of the stirrings of my heart under the influences of the winds of Thy mercy.

I entreat Thee, O Thou Who art the Ruler of the kingdoms of creation and the Author of all names, to write down my name with the names of them who, from eternity, have circled round the Tabernacle of Thy majesty, and clung to the hem of Thy loving-kindness, and held fast the cord of Thy tender mercy.

Thou art, in truth, the Help in Peril, the Self-Subsisting.

XIX

Praised be Thou, O Lord my God! I implore Thee, by Thy Most Great Name through Which Thou didst stir up Thy servants and build up Thy cities, and by

Thy most excellent titles, and Thy most august attributes, to assist Thy people to turn in the direction of Thy manifold bounties, and set their faces towards the Tabernacle of Thy wisdom. Heal Thou the sicknesses that have assailed the souls on every side, and have deterred them from directing their gaze towards the Paradise that lieth in the shelter of Thy shadowing Name, which Thou didst ordain to be the King of all names unto all who are in heaven and all who are on earth. Potent art Thou to do as pleaseth Thee. In Thy hands is the empire of all names. There is none other God but Thee, the Mighty, the Wise.

I am but a poor creature, O my Lord; I have clung to the hem of Thy riches. I am sore sick; I have held fast the cord of Thy healing. Deliver me from the ills that have encircled me, and wash me thoroughly with the waters of Thy graciousness and mercy, and attire me with the raiment of wholesomeness, through Thy forgiveness and bounty. Fix, then, mine eyes upon Thee, and rid me of all attachment to aught else except Thyself. Aid me to do what Thou desirest, and to fulfill what Thou pleasest.

Thou art truly the Lord of this life and of the next. Thou art, in truth, the Ever-Forgiving, the Most Merciful.

XX

Lauded be Thy name, O Thou Who beholdest all things and art hidden from all things! From every land Thou hearest the lamentations of them that love Thee, and from every direction Thou hearkenest unto the cries of such as have recognized Thy sovereignty. Were their oppressors to be asked: "Wherefore have ye oppressed them and held them in bondage in Baghdád and elsewhere? What injustice have they committed? Whom have they betrayed? Whose blood have they spilled, and whose property have they plundered?" they would know not what to answer.

Thou knowest full well, O my God, that their only crime is to have loved Thee. For this reason have their oppressors laid hold on them, and scattered them abroad. Aware as I am, O my God, that Thou wilt send down upon Thy servants only what is good for them, I nevertheless beseech Thee, by Thy name which overshadoweth all things, to raise up, for their assistance and as a sign of Thy grace and as an evidence of Thy power, those who will keep them safe from all their adversaries.

Potent art Thou to do Thy pleasure. Thou art, verily, the Supreme Ruler, the Almighty, the Help in Peril, the Self-Subsisting.

Protection from adversaries

XXI

mercy

Praised be Thou, O Lord my God! I am Thy servant and the son of Thy servant. I have set my face towards Thy Cause, believing in Thy oneness, acknowledging Thy unity, recognizing Thy sovereignty and the power of Thy might, and confessing the greatness of Thy majesty and glory. I ask Thee, by Thy name through which the heaven was cleft asunder, and the earth was rent in twain, and the mountains were crushed, not to withhold from me the breezes of Thy mercy which have been wafted in Thy days, nor to suffer me to be far removed from the shores of Thy nearness and bounty.

I am he who is sore athirst, O my Lord! Give me to drink of the living waters of Thy grace. I am but a poor creature; reveal unto me the tokens of Thy riches. Doth it beseem Thee to cast out of the door of Thy grace and bounty such as have set their hopes on Thee, and can it befit Thy sovereignty to hinder them that yearn after Thee from attaining the adored sanctuary of Thy presence and from beholding Thy face? By Thy glory! Such is not my belief in Thee, for I am persuaded that Thou art the God of bounteousness, Whose grace hath encompassed all things.

I beseech Thee, O my Lord, by Thy mercy that hath surpassed the entire creation, and Thy generosity that hath embraced all created things, to cause me to turn my face wholly towards Thee, and to seek

Thy shelter, and to be steadfast in my love for Thee. Write down, then, for me what Thou didst ordain for them who love Thee. Powerful art Thou to do what Thou pleasest. No God is there beside Thee, the Ever-Forgiving, the All-Bountiful.

Praised be God, the Lord of the worlds!

XXII

steadfastness

Endurement

Exalted art Thou, O Lord my God! I am the one who hath forsaken his all and set his face towards the splendors of the glory of Thy countenance, who hath severed every tie and clung to the cord of Thy love and of Thy good-pleasure. I am he, O my God, who hath embraced Thy love and accepted all the adversities which the world can inflict, who hath offered up himself as a ransom for the sake of Thy loved ones, that they may ascend into the heavens of Thy knowledge and be drawn nearer unto Thee, and may soar in the atmosphere of Thy love and Thy good-pleasure.

Ordain, O my God, for me and for them that which Thou didst decree for such of Thy chosen ones as are wholly devoted unto Thee. Cause them, then, to be numbered among those whose eyes Thou hast cleansed and kept from turning to any one save Thee, and whose eyes Thou hast protected from beholding any face except Thy face.

Thou art, verily, the Almighty, the Most Exalted, the All-Glorious, the Supreme King, the Help in Peril, the All-Pardoner, the Ever-Forgiving.

XXIII

Glorified art Thou, O Lord my God! I implore Thee by the onrushing winds of Thy grace, and by them Who are the Day-Springs of Thy purpose and the Dawning-Places of Thine inspiration, to send down upon me and upon all that have sought Thy face that which beseemeth Thy generosity and bountiful grace, and is worthy of Thy bestowals and favors. Poor and desolate I am, O my Lord! Immerse me in the ocean of Thy wealth; athirst, suffer me to drink from the living waters of Thy loving-kindness.

I beseech Thee, by Thine own Self and by Him Whom Thou hast appointed as the Manifestation of Thine own Being and Thy discriminating Word unto all that are in heaven and on earth, to gather together Thy servants beneath the shade of the Tree of Thy gracious providence. Help them, then, to partake of its fruits, to incline their ears to the rustling of its leaves, and to the sweetness of the voice of the Bird that chanteth upon its branches. Thou art, verily, the

Help in Peril, the Inaccessible, the Almighty, the Most Bountiful.

Steadfastness
trials

XXIV

Praised be Thou, O Lord my God! I implore Thee by Them Who are the Tabernacles of Thy Divine holiness, Who are the Manifestations of Thy transcendent unity and the Day-Springs of Thine inspiration and revelation, to grant that Thy servants may not be kept back from this Divine Law which, at Thy will and according to Thy pleasure, hath branched out from Thy most great Ocean. Do Thou, then, ordain for them that which Thou didst ordain for Thy chosen ones and for the righteous among Thy creatures, whose constancy in Thy Cause the tempests of trials have failed to shake, and whom the tumults of tests have been powerless to hinder from magnifying Thy most exalted Word—the Word through Which the heavens of men's idle fancies and vain imaginations have been split asunder. Thou art, verily, the Almighty, the All-Glorious, the All-Knowing.

Enable, then, Thy servants, O my God, to recognize the Day-Star that hath shone forth above the horizon of Thine irrevocable decree and purpose, and suffer them not to be deprived of the Paradise which Thou, by Thy name, the All-Glorious, hast called into

being in the heavens of Thine exalted omnipotence.
Cause them, moreover, O my God, to hearken to
Thy most sweet voice, that they may all hasten to
recognize Thy unity and acknowledge Thy oneness,
O Thou Who art the Beloved of the hearts of all that
yearn after Thee, and the Object of the adoration of
such as have known Thee!

I beseech Thee, by them that have cut down all
the idols in this Revelation through which the Most
Grievous Convulsion and the Great Terror have appeared, to assist, at all times, Thy servants with the
signs of Thine almighty power and the evidences of
Thy transcendent and all-compelling might. Grant,
then, that their hearts may be made as strong as brass,
that they may remain unmoved by the overpowering
might of such as have transgressed against Him Who
is the Manifestation of Thine Essence and the Day-
Spring of Thine invisible Self, and that they may all
arise to glorify and help Thee, so that through them
the ensigns of Thy triumph may be lifted up in Thy
realm, and the standards of Thy Cause may be unfurled throughout Thy dominions. Thou art He who
from everlasting hath, through the potency of His
will, been all-powerful, and will continue to remain
the same for ever and ever. Thou art, verily, the All-
Glorious, the Most High. No God is there but Thee,
the Most Powerful, the Most Exalted, the Help in
Peril, the Most Great, the One Being, the Incomparable, the All-Glorious, the Unrestrained.

XXV

Glorified art Thou, O Lord my God! I beseech Thee by Thy Chosen Ones, and by the Bearers of Thy Trust, and by Him Whom Thou hast ordained to be the Seal of Thy Prophets and of Thy Messengers, to let Thy remembrance be my companion, and Thy love my aim, and Thy face my goal, and Thy name my lamp, and Thy wish my desire, and Thy pleasure my delight.

I am a sinner, O my Lord, and Thou art the Ever-Forgiving. As soon as I recognized Thee, I hastened to attain the exalted court of Thy loving-kindness. Forgive me, O my Lord, my sins which have hindered me from walking in the ways of Thy good-pleasure, and from attaining the shores of the ocean of Thy oneness.

There is no one, O my Lord, who can deal bountifully with me to whom I can turn my face, and none who can have compassion on me that I may crave his mercy. Cast me not out, I implore Thee, of the presence of Thy grace, neither do Thou withhold from me the outpourings of Thy generosity and bounty. Ordain for me, O my Lord, what Thou hast ordained for them that love Thee, and write down for me what Thou hast written down for Thy chosen ones. My gaze hath, at all times, been fixed on the horizon of Thy gracious providence, and mine eyes bent upon the court of Thy tender mercies. Do with me as beseemeth Thee. No God is there but Thee, the God of power, the God of glory, Whose help is implored by all men.

XXVI

Suffer me, O my God, to draw nigh unto Thee, and to abide within the precincts of Thy court, for remoteness from Thee hath well-nigh consumed me. Cause me to rest under the shadow of the wings of Thy grace, for the flame of my separation from Thee hath melted my heart within me. Draw me nearer unto the river that is life indeed, for my soul burneth with thirst in its ceaseless search after Thee. My sighs, O my God, proclaim the bitterness of mine anguish, and the tears I shed attest my love for Thee.

I beseech Thee, by the praise wherewith Thou praisest Thyself and the glory wherewith Thou glorifiest Thine own Essence, to grant that we may be numbered among them that have recognized Thee and acknowledged Thy sovereignty in Thy days. Help us then to quaff, O my God, from the fingers of mercy the living waters of Thy loving-kindness, that we may utterly forget all else except Thee, and be occupied only with Thy Self. Powerful art Thou to do what Thou willest. No God is there beside Thee, the Mighty, the Help in Peril, the Self-Subsisting.

Glorified be Thy name, O Thou Who art the King of all Kings!

Justice

XXVII

Thou beholdest, O my God, the Day-Star of Thy Word shining above the horizon of Thy prison-city, inasmuch as within its walls He who is the Manifestation of Thy Self and the Day-Spring of the light of Thy unity hath raised His voice and uttered Thy praise. The fragrances of Thy love have thereby been wafted over Thy cities and have encompassed all the dwellers of Thy realm.

Mercy

Since Thou hast revealed Thy grace, O my God, deter not Thy servants from directing their eyes towards it. Consider not, O my God, their estate, and their concerns and their works. Consider the greatness of Thy glory, and the plenteousness of Thy gifts, and the power of Thy might, and the excellence of Thy favors. I swear by Thy glory! Wert Thou to look upon them with the eye of justice, all would deserve Thy wrath and the rod of Thine anger. Hold Thou Thy creatures, O my God, with the hands of Thy grace, and make Thou known unto them what is best for them of all the things that have been created in the kingdom of Thine invention.

We testify, O my God, that Thou art God, and that there is no God besides Thee. From eternity Thou hast existed with none to equal or rival Thee, and wilt abide for ever the same. I beseech Thee, by the eyes which see Thee stablished upon the throne of unity and the seat of oneness, to aid all them that love Thee by Thy Most Great Name, and to lift them up into such heights that they will testify with their own beings and with their tongues that Thou art God alone, the Incomparable, the One, the Ever-Abiding. Thou hast had at no time any peer or partner. Thou, in truth, art the All-Glorious, the Almighty, Whose help is implored by all men.

XXVIII

Praised be Thou, O Lord my God! I bear witness that from eternity Thou wert exalted in Thy transcendent majesty and might, and wilt to eternity abide in Thy surpassing power and glory. None in the kingdoms of earth and heaven can frustrate Thy purpose; none throughout the realms of revelation and of creation can prevail against Thee. At Thy command Thou doest what Thou willest, and by the power of Thy sovereignty Thou rulest as Thou pleasest.

I implore Thee, O Thou Who causest the dawn to appear, by Thy Lamp which Thou didst light with the fire of Thy love before all that are in heaven and on earth, and whose flame Thou feedest with the fuel of Thy wisdom in the kingdom of Thy creation, to make me to be of those who have soared in Thine atmosphere, and surrendered their will to Thy decree.

I am all wretchedness, O my Lord, and Thou art the Most Powerful, the Almighty. Have pity upon me by Thy grace and bountiful favor, and graciously aid me to serve Thee and them that are dear to Thee. Potent art Thou to do as Thou willest. No God is there but Thee, the God of strength, of glory and wisdom.

XXIX

Many a chilled heart, O my God, hath been set ablaze with the fire of Thy Cause, and many a slumberer hath been wakened by the sweetness of Thy voice. How many are the strangers who have sought shelter beneath the shadow of the tree of Thy oneness, and how numerous the thirsty ones who have panted after the fountain of Thy living waters in Thy days!

Blessed is he that hath set himself towards Thee, and hasted to attain the Day-Spring of the lights of Thy face. Blessed is he who with all his affections hath turned to the Dawning-Place of Thy Revelation and the Fountain-Head of Thine inspiration. Blessed is he that hath expended in Thy path what Thou didst bestow upon him through Thy bounty and favor. Blessed is he who, in his sore longing after Thee, hath cast away all else except Thyself. Blessed is he who hath enjoyed intimate communion with Thee, and rid himself of all attachment to any one save Thee.

I beseech Thee, O my Lord, by Him Who is Thy Name, Who, through the power of Thy sovereignty and might, hath risen above the horizon of His prison, to ordain for every one what becometh Thee and beseemeth Thine exaltation.

Thy might, in truth, is equal to all things.

XXX

Lauded be Thy name, O Lord my God! Thou seest me in this day shut up in my prison, and fallen into the hands of Thine adversaries, and beholdest my son (The Purest Branch) lying on the dust before Thy face. He is Thy servant, O my Lord, whom Thou hast caused to be related to Him Who is the Manifestation of Thyself and the Day-Spring of Thy Cause.

At his birth he was afflicted through his separation from Thee, according to what had been ordained for him through Thine irrevocable decree. And when he had quaffed the cup of reunion with Thee, he was cast into prison for having believed in Thee and in Thy

signs. He continued to serve Thy Beauty until he
entered into this Most Great Prison. Thereupon I
offered him up, O my God, as a sacrifice in Thy path.
Thou well knowest what they who love Thee have
endured through this trial that hath caused the kindreds of the earth to wail, and beyond them the Concourse on high to lament.

I beseech Thee, O my Lord, by him and by his
exile and his imprisonment, to send down upon such
as loved him what will quiet their hearts and bless
their works. Potent art Thou to do as Thou willest.
No God is there but Thee, the Almighty, the Most
Powerful.

XXXI

Praised be Thou, O my God! I beseech Thee by
them who have circled round the throne of Thy will,
and soared in the atmosphere of Thy good-pleasure,
and turned with all their affections towards the Horizon of Thy Revelation and the Day-Spring of Thine
inspiration, and the Dawning-Place of Thy names, to
aid Thy servants to observe what Thou hast commanded them in Thy days—commandments through
which the sacredness of Thy Cause will be demonstrated unto Thy servants and the affairs of Thy
creatures and of Thy realm will be set aright.

I testify, O my God, that this is the Day whereon

Thy testimony hath been fulfilled, and Thy clear tokens have been manifested, and Thine utterances have been revealed, and Thy signs have been demonstrated, and the radiance of Thy countenance hath been diffused, and Thy proof hath been perfected, and Thine ascendancy hath been established, and Thy mercy hath overflowed, and the Day-Star of Thy grace hath shone forth with such brilliance that Thou didst manifest Him Who is the Revealer of Thyself and the Treasury of Thy wisdom and the Dawning-Place of Thy majesty and power. Thou didst establish His covenant with every one who hath been created in the kingdoms of earth and heaven and in the realms of revelation and of creation. Thou didst raise Him up to such heights that the wrongs inflicted by the oppressors have been powerless to deter Him from revealing Thy sovereignty, and the ascendancy of the wayward hath failed to prevent Him from demonstrating Thy power and from exalting Thy Cause.

So highly didst Thou exalt Him that He openly delivered unto the kings Thy messages and commandments, and hath never for one moment sought His own protection, but striven to protect Thy servants from whatever might withhold them from approaching the kingdom of Thy nearness, and from setting their faces towards the horizon of Thy good-pleasure.

Thou seest, O my God, how, notwithstanding the swords that are drawn against Him, He calleth the nations unto Thee, and though Himself a prisoner summoneth them to turn in the direction of Thy

gifts and bounties. With every fresh tribulation He
manifested a fuller measure of Thy Cause, and exalted
more highly Thy word.

I testify that through Him the Pen of the Most
High was set in motion, and with His remembrance
the Scriptures in the kingdom of names were em-
bellished. Through Him Thy fragrances were wafted,
and the sweet smell of Thy raiment was shed abroad
amongst all the dwellers of the earth and the inmates
of heaven. Thou seest and knowest full well, O my
God, how He hath been made to dwell within the
most desolate of cities, so that He may build up the
hearts of Thy servants, and hath been willing to
suffer the most grievous abasement, that Thy creatures may be exalted.

I pray Thee, O Thou Who causest the dawn to
appear, by Thy Name through Which Thou hast subjected the winds, and sent down Thy Tablets, that
Thou wilt grant that we may draw near unto what
Thou didst destine for us by Thy favor and bounty,
and to be far removed from whatsoever may be re-
pugnant unto Thee. Give us, then, to drink from
the hands of Thy grace every day and every moment
of our lives of the waters that are life indeed, O Thou
Who art the Most Merciful! Make us, then, to be of
them who helped Thee when fallen into the hands of
those Thine enemies who are numbered with the rebellious among Thy creatures and the wicked amidst
Thy people. Write down, then, for us the recompense ordained for him that hath attained Thy pres-

ence, and gazed on Thy beauty, and supply us with
every good thing ordained in Thy Book for such of
Thy creatures as enjoy near access to Thee.

Brighten our hearts, O my Lord, with the splendor
of Thy knowledge, and illumine our sight with the
light of such eyes as are fixed upon the horizon of
Thy grace and the Day-Spring of Thy glory. Preserve
us, then, by Thy Most Great Name, Which Thou
didst cause to overshadow such nations as lay claim
to what Thou hast forbidden in Thy Book. This,
verily, is what Thou didst announce unto us in Thy
Scriptures and Thy Tablets.

Cause us, then, to be so steadfast in our love
towards Thee that we will turn to none except Thee,
and will be reckoned amongst them that are brought
nigh to Thee, and acknowledge Thee as One Who is
exalted above every comparison and is holy beyond
all likeness, and will lift up our voices amongst Thy
servants and cry aloud that He is the one God, the
Incomparable, the Ever-Abiding, the Most Powerful,
the All-Glorious, the All-Wise.

Strengthen Thou, O my Lord, the hearts of them
that love Thee, that they may not be affrighted by
the hosts of the infidels that are turned back from
Thee, but may follow Thee in whatsoever hath been
revealed by Thee. Aid them, moreover, to remember
and to praise Thee, and to teach Thy Cause with
eloquence and wisdom. Thou art He Who hath called
Himself the Most Merciful. Ordain, then, O my God,
for me and for whosoever hath sought Thee what

beseemeth the excellence of Thy glory and the greatness of Thy majesty. No God is there but Thee, the
Ever-Forgiving, the Most Compassionate.

XXXII

Thou seest Thy dear One, O my God, lying at
the mercy of Thine enemies, and hearest the voice of
His lamentation from the midst of such of Thy creatures as have dealt wickedly in Thy sight. He it is,
O my Lord, through Whose name Thou didst beau-
tify Thy Tablets, and for Whose greater glory Thou
didst send down the Bayán, and at Whose separation
from Thee Thou didst weep continually. Look Thou,
then, upon His loneliness, O my God, and behold
Him fallen into the hands of them that have disbelieved in Thy signs, have turned their backs upon
Thee, and have forgotten the wonders of Thy mercy.

He it is, O my God, about Whom Thou hast said:
"But for Thee the Scriptures would have remained
unrevealed, and the Prophets unsent." And no sooner
had He, by Thy behest, been manifested and spoken
forth Thy praise, than the wicked doers among Thy
creatures compassed Him round, with the swords of
hate drawn against Him, O Thou the Lord of all
names! Thou well knowest what befell Him at the
hands of such as have rent asunder the veil of Thy

grandeur, and cast behind their backs Thy Covenant and Thy Testament, O Thou Who art the Maker of the heavens! He is the One for Whose sake Thou (the Báb) hast yielded Thy life, and hast consented to be touched by the manifold ills of the world that He may manifest Himself, and summoned all mankind in His name. As soon as He came down, however, from the heaven of majesty and power, Thy servants stretched out against Him the hands of cruelty and sedition, and caused Him to be afflicted with such troubles that the scrolls of the world are insufficient to contain a full recital of them.

Thou seest, therefore, O Thou Beloved of the world, Him Who is dear to Thee in the clutches of such as have denied Thee, and beholdest Thy heart's desire under the swords of the ungodly. Methinks He, from His most exalted station, saith unto me: "Would that my soul, O Prisoner, could be a ransom for Thy captivity, and my being, O wronged One, be sacrificed for the adversities Thou didst suffer! Thou art He through Whose captivity the standards of Thine almighty power were hoisted, and the day-star of Thy revelation shone forth above the horizon of tribulation, in such wise that all created things bowed down before the greatness of Thy majesty.

"The more they strove to hinder Thee from remembering Thy God and from extolling His virtues, the more passionately didst Thou glorify Him and the more loudly didst Thou call upon Him. And every time the veils of the perverse came in between

Thee and Thy servants, Thou didst shed the splendors of the light of Thy countenance out of the heaven of Thy grace. Thou art, in very truth, the Self-Subsisting as testified by the tongue of God, the All-Glorious, the one alone Beloved; and Thou art the Desire of the world as attested by what hath flowed down from the Pen of Him Who hath announced unto Thy servants Thy hidden Name, and adorned the entire creation with the ornament of Thy love, the Most Precious, the Most Exalted.

"The eyes of the world were gladdened at the sight of Thy luminous countenance, and yet the peoples have united to put out Thy light, O Thou in Whose hands are the reins of the worlds! All the atoms of the earth have celebrated Thy praise, and all created things have been set ablaze with the drops sprinkled by the ocean of Thy love, and yet the people still seek to quench Thy fire. Nay—and to this Thine own Self beareth me witness—they are all weakness, and Thou, verily, art the All-Powerful; and they are but paupers and Thou, in truth, art the All-Possessing; and they are impotent and Thou art, truly, the Almighty. Naught can ever frustrate Thy purpose, neither can the dissensions of the world harm Thee. Through the breaths of Thine utterance the heaven of understanding hath been adorned, and by the effusions of Thy pen every moldering bone hath been quickened. Grieve not at what hath befallen Thee, neither do Thou lay hold on them for the things they have committed in Thy days. Do Thou be forbearing toward them. Thou art the Ever-Forgiving, the Most Compassionate."

steadfastness

knowledge

[illegible]

XXXIII

Praise be unto Thee, O my God! Thou art He Who by a word of His mouth hath revolutionized the entire creation, and by a stroke of His pen hath divided Thy servants one from another. I bear witness, O my God, that through a word spoken by Thee in this Revelation all created things were made to expire, and through yet another word all such as Thou didst wish were, by Thy grace and bounty, endued with new life.

I render Thee thanks, therefore, and extol Thee, in the name of all them that are dear to Thee, for that Thou hast caused them to be born again, by reason of the living waters which have flowed down out of the mouth of Thy will. Since Thou didst quicken them by Thy bounteousness, O my God, make them steadfastly inclined, through Thy graciousness, towards Thy will; and since Thou didst suffer them to enter into the Tabernacle of Thy Cause, grant by Thy grace that they may not be kept back from Thee.

Unlock, then, to their hearts, O my God, the portals of Thy knowledge, that they may recognize Thee as One Who is far above the reach and ken of the understanding of Thy creatures, and immeasurably exalted above the strivings of Thy people to hint at Thy nature, and may not follow every clamorous impostor that presumeth to speak in Thy name. Enable them, moreover, O my Lord, to cleave so tenaciously to Thy Cause that they may remain unmoved by the perplexing suggestions of them who, prompted by their desires, utter what hath been forbidden unto them in Thy Tablets and Thy Scriptures.

Thou art well aware, O my Lord, that I hear the howling of the wolves which appear in Thy servants' clothing. Keep safe, therefore, Thy loved ones from their mischief, and enable them to cling steadfastly to whatsoever hath been manifested by Thee in this Revelation, which no other Revelation within Thy knowledge hath excelled.

Do Thou destine for them, O my Lord, that which will profit them. Illumine, then, their eyes with the light of Thy knowledge, that they may see Thee visibly supreme over all things, and resplendent amidst Thy creatures, and victorious over all that are in Thy heaven and all that are on Thy earth. Powerful art Thou to do Thy pleasure. No God is there but Thee, the All-Glorious, Whose help is implored by all men.

Praised be Thou, Who art the Lord of all creation.

XXXIV

Praised be Thou, O Lord my God! I implore Thee by Thine Ancient Beauty and Most Great Name, Whom Thou hast sacrificed that all the dwellers of Thine earth and heaven may be born anew, and Whom Thou hast cast into prison that mankind may, as a token of Thy bounty and of Thy sovereign might, be released from the bondage of evil passions and corrupt desires, to number me with those who have so deeply inhaled the fragrance of Thy mercy, and hastened with such speed unto the living waters of Thy grace, that no dart could hinder them from turning unto Thee, nor any spear from setting their faces towards the orient of Thy Revelation.

We testify, O my Lord, that Thou art God and that there is none other God besides Thee. From everlasting Thou wast enthroned on the inaccessible heights of Thy power, and wilt unto everlasting continue to exercise Thy transcendent and unrestrained dominion. The hosts of the world are powerless to frustrate Thy will, nor can all the dwellers of the earth and all the inmates of heaven annul Thy decree. Thou truly art the Almighty, the Most Exalted, the Most Great.

Bless, O my God, those of the followers of the Bayán as have been numbered with the people of Bahá, who have entered within the Crimson Ark in

Thy Name, the Most Exalted, the Most High. Thy might, verily, is equal to all things.

XXXV

I give praise to Thee, O Lord my God! I entreat Thee by Thy Name through which Thou didst cause the dawn to appear, and the winds to blow, and the seas to surge, and the trees to bring forth their fruits, and the earth to be beautified with its rivers, that Thou wilt aid all them that are dear to Thee with both Thy visible and invisible hosts. Render them, moreover, victorious over all those who have so rebelled in Thy land, and dishonored Thy name, and disbelieved in Thy signs, and broken Thy Covenant, and cast behind their backs Thy laws, and have to such an extent risen up against Thee, that they carried into captivity Thy kindred, and flung the Manifestation of Thy Self into prison, and immured Him Who is the Day-Spring of Thine Essence in the most desolate of cities.

Thou, O my Lord, art He whose strength is immense, Whose decree is terrible. Lay hold on Thine adversaries by the power of Thy sovereignty, and assemble Thy loved ones beneath the shadow of the tree of Thy oneness, that they may stand before Thy throne, and catch the accents of Thy voice, and gaze on Thy beauty, and discover the power of Thy might. Thou art, verily, the All-Powerful, the Almighty.

XXXVI

unity

Lauded be Thy name, O my God! I am so carried away by the breezes blowing from Thy presence that I have forgotten my self and all that I possess. This is but a sign of the wonders of Thy grace and bountiful favors vouchsafed unto me. I give praise to Thee, O my God, that Thou hast chosen me out of all Thy creatures, and made me to be the Day-Spring of Thy strength and the Manifestation of Thy might, and empowered me to reveal such of Thy signs and such tokens of Thy majesty and power as none, whether in Thy heaven or on Thy earth, can produce.

I beseech Thee, O my Lord, by Thy most effulgent Name, to acquaint my people with the things Thou didst destine for them. Do Thou, then, preserve them within the stronghold of Thy guardianship and the tabernacle of Thine unerring protection, lest through them may appear what will divide Thy servants. Assemble them, O my Lord, on the shores of this Ocean, every drop of which proclaimeth Thee to be God, besides Whom there is none other God, the All-Glorious, the All-Wise.

Uncover before them, O my Lord, the majesty of
Thy Cause, lest they be led to doubt Thy sovereignty
and the power of Thy might. I swear by Thy glory,
O Thou Who art the Beloved of the worlds! Had they
been aware of Thy power they would of a certainty
have refused to utter what Thou didst not ordain
for them in the heaven of Thy will.

Inspire them, O my Lord, with a sense of their own
powerlessness before Him Who is the Manifestation
of Thy Self, and teach them to recognize the poverty
of their own nature in the face of the manifold tokens
of Thy self-sufficiency and riches, that they may
gather together round Thy Cause, and cling to the
hem of Thy mercy, and cleave to the cord of the
good-pleasure of Thy will.

Thou art the Lord of the worlds, and of all those
who show mercy, art the Most Merciful.

XXXVII

Glory be to Thee, O King of eternity, and the
Maker of nations, and the Fashioner of every moldering bone! I pray Thee, by Thy Name through which
Thou didst call all mankind unto the horizon of Thy
majesty and glory, and didst guide Thy servants to
the court of Thy grace and favors, to number me
with such as have rid themselves from everything ex-

steadfastness

cept Thyself, and have set themselves towards Thee, and have not been kept back by such misfortunes as were decreed by Thee, from turning in the direction of Thy gifts.

guidance

I have laid hold, O my Lord, on the handle of Thy bounty, and clung steadfastly to the hem of the robe of Thy favor. Send down, then, upon me, out of the clouds of Thy generosity, what will purge out from me the remembrance of any one except Thee, and make me able to turn unto Him Who is the Object of the adoration of all mankind, against Whom have been arrayed the stirrers of sedition, who have broken Thy covenant, and disbelieved in Thee and in Thy signs.

Deny me not, O my Lord, the fragrances of Thy raiment in Thy days, and deprive me not of the breathings of Thy Revelation at the appearance of the splendors of the light of Thy face. Powerful art Thou to do what pleaseth Thee. Naught can resist Thy will, nor frustrate what Thou hast purposed by Thy power.

No God is there but Thee, the Almighty, the All-Wise.

XXXVIII

Lauded be Thy name, O Lord my God! I testify that Thou wast a hidden Treasure wrapped within

steadfastness

Thine immemorial Being and an impenetrable Mystery enshrined in Thine own Essence. Wishing to reveal Thyself, Thou didst call into being the Greater and the Lesser Worlds, and didst choose Man above all Thy creatures, and didst make Him a sign of both of these worlds, O Thou Who art our Lord, the Most Compassionate!

Thou didst raise Him up to occupy Thy throne before all the people of Thy creation. Thou didst enable Him to unravel Thy mysteries, and to shine with the lights of Thine inspiration and Thy Revelation, and to manifest Thy names and Thine attributes. Through Him Thou didst adorn the preamble of the book of Thy creation, O Thou Who art the Ruler of the universe Thou hast fashioned!

I bear witness that in His person solidity and fluidity have been joined and combined. Through His immovable constancy in Thy Cause, and His unwavering adherence to whatsoever Thou, in the plenitude of the light of Thy glory, didst unveil to His eyes, throughout the domains of Thy Revelation and creation, the souls of Thy servants were stirred up in their longing for Thy Kingdom, and the dwellers of Thy realms rushed forth to enter into Thy heavenly dominion. Through the restlessness He evinced in Thy path, the feet of all them that are devoted to Thee were steeled and confirmed to manifest Thy Cause amidst Thy creatures, and to demonstrate Thy sovereignty throughout Thy realm.

How great, O my God, is this Thy most excellent

handiwork, and how consummate Thy creation, which hath caused every understanding heart and mind to marvel! And when the set time was fulfilled, and what had been preordained came to pass, Thou didst unloose His tongue to praise Thee, and to lay bare Thy mysteries before all Thy creation, O Thou Who art the Possessor of all names, and the Fashioner of earth and heaven! Through Him all created things were made to glorify Thee, and to celebrate Thy praise, and every soul was directed towards the kingdom of Thy revelation and Thy sovereignty.

At one time, Thou didst raise Him up, O my God, and didst attire Him with the ornament of the name of Him Who conversed with Thee (Moses), and didst through Him uncover all that Thy will had decreed and Thine irrevocable purpose ordained. At another time, Thou didst adorn Him with the name of Him Who was Thy Spirit (Jesus), and didst send Him down out of the heaven of Thy will, for the edification of Thy people, infusing thereby the spirit of life into the hearts of the sincere among Thy servants and the faithful among Thy creatures. Again, Thou didst reveal Him, decked forth by the name of Him Who was Thy Friend (Muḥammad), and caused Him to shine brightly above the horizon of Ḥijáz, as a token of Thy power and an evidence of Thy might. Through Him Thou didst send unto Thy servants what enabled them to scale the heights of Thy unity, and to yearn over the wonders of Thy manifold knowledge and wisdom.

I testify, O Thou Who art the Lord of the whole creation, and the Desire of whosoever hath sought Thee, that, amidst Thy creatures, They resemble the sun which no matter how often it riseth and setteth is still the one and the same sun. Whoso maketh any distinction between any of Them hath truly failed to attain the ultimate purpose, and to reach the highest goal, and hath been deprived of the mysteries of unity and of the lights of sanctity and oneness. I testify, moreover, that Thou hast decreed that none on the face of the earth should equal Them, and none of Thy creatures be able to be compared with any of Them, in order that Thine own singleness and peerlessness might be recognized and established.

Glorified, immeasurably glorified be Thy name, O my God! How can I ever befittingly mention Thee or sufficiently praise Thee, that Thou hast manifested Him by the power of Thy might, and caused Him to shine above the horizon of Thy will, and made Him the Day-Spring of Thy signs, and the Dawning-Place of the revelation of Thy names and Thine attributes? How bewilderingly mysterious, moreover, O my God, is His nature and all that Thou hast infused into Him, through Thy strength and by the power of Thy might! At one time He appeareth as the water which is Life indeed, sent down out of the heaven of Thy grace, and poured forth from the clouds of Thy mercy, that Thy creatures may be endued with new life, and live as long as Thine own Kingdom endureth. Every drop of that water would suffice to quicken the dead, and to set their faces in the direction of Thy favors and Thy gifts, and to rid them of all attachment to aught else except Thee. At another time He revealeth Himself as the Fire which Thou didst kindle in the tree of Thy unity, whose heat melted the hearts of Thine ardent lovers when He Who is the Day-Star of the world shone forth above the horizon of 'Iráq. I testify, O my God, that through Him the veils of human fancy were burnt up, and the hearts of men were set towards the scene of Thy most resplendent glory.

I implore Thee, O Thou Who art the Supreme Ordainer, not to suffer me to be deprived of the breezes which are wafted in Thy days, the days whereon the sweet smell of the raiment of Thy mercy hath been shed abroad. Neither do Thou keep me back from Thy most great Ocean, every drop of which crieth out and saith: "Great is the blessedness that awaiteth him who hath been awakened from his sleep by the breath of God which, from the source of His mercy, hath blown over all such of His creatures as have set themselves towards Him!"

Thou seest, O my Lord, how Thy servants are held captive by their own selves and desires. Redeem them from their bondage, O my God, by the power of Thy sovereignty and might, that they may turn towards Thee when He Who is the Revealer of Thy names and attributes is manifested unto men.

Cast upon this poor and desolate creature, O my Lord, the glance of Thy wealth, and flood his heart with the beams of Thy knowledge, that he may apprehend the verities of the unseen world, and discover the mysteries of Thy heavenly realm, and perceive the signs and tokens of Thy kingdom, and behold the manifold revelations of this earthly life all set forth before the face of Him Who is the Revealer of Thine own Self. Direct, then, his eyes, O my God, towards the horizon of Thy loving-kindness, and make steadfast his heart in its attachment to Thee, and unloose his tongue to praise Thee, and make him able to hold fast the cord of Thy love, and to cling to the hem of Thy bounteousness, and to proclaim Thy name amidst Thy creatures, and to recount Thy virtues throughout Thy realm, in such wise that no obstacle will deter him from turning to Thy name, the All-Bountiful, and no veil shut him out from Thee, in Whose hand is the dominion of utterance and the kingdom of all names and attributes!

Hold Thou the hand of this seeker who hath set his face towards Thee, O my Lord, and draw him out of the depths of his vain imaginations, that the light of certainty may shine brightly above the horizon of his heart in the days whereon the sun of the knowledge of Thy creatures hath been darkened through the shining of the Day-Star of Thy glory; the days whereon the moon of the world's wisdom hath been eclipsed through the appearance of Thy hidden knowledge, and the manifestation of Thy well-guarded secret, and the revelation of Thine enshrined mystery; the days whereon the stars of men's doings have fallen

Will of God

through the rising of the orb of Thy unity and the shedding of the radiance of Thy transcendent oneness.

I beg of Thee, O my God, by Thy most exalted Word which Thou hast ordained as the Divine Elixir unto all who are in Thy realm, the Elixir through whose potency the crude metal of human life hath been transmuted into purest gold, O Thou in Whose hands are both the visible and invisible kingdoms, to ordain that my choice be conformed to Thy choice and my wish to Thy wish, that I may be entirely content with that which Thou didst desire, and be wholly satisfied with what Thou didst destine for me by Thy bounteousness and favor. Potent art Thou to do as Thou willest. Thou, in very truth, art the All-Glorious, the All-Wise.

Happy is the man who hath recognized Thee, and discovered the sweetness of Thy fragrance, and set himself towards Thy kingdom, and tasted of the things that have been perfected therein by Thy grace and favor. Great is the blessedness of him who hath acknowledged Thy most excellent majesty, and whom the veils that have shut out the nations from Thee have not hindered from directing his eyes towards Thee, O Thou Who art the King of eternity and the Quickener of every moldering bone! Blessed, also, is he that hath inhaled Thy sweet savors, and been carried away by Thine utterances in Thy days. Blessed, moreover, be the man that hath turned unto Thee, and woe betide him that hath turned his back upon Thee.

Praised be Thou, the Lord of the worlds!

XXXIX

O Thou Who dealest equitably with all who are in heaven and on earth, and rulest over the kingdom of Thy creation and of Thy Revelation! I testify that every man of equity hath recognized his unfairness in the face of the revelation of the splendors of the Day-Star of Thy Justice, and the ablest of pens hath confessed its impotence before the movement of Thy most exalted Pen.

By Thy life, O Thou the Possessor of all names! The minds of the profoundest thinkers are sore perplexed as they contemplate the ocean of Thy knowledge, and the heaven of Thy wisdom, and the Luminary of Thy grace. How can he who is but a creation of Thy will claim to know what is with Thee, or to conceive Thy nature?

Praise, immeasurable praise be to Thee! I swear by Thy glory! My inner and outer tongue, openly and secretly, testify that Thou hast been exalted above the reach and ken of Thy creatures, above the utterance of Thy servants, above the testimonies of Thy dear ones and Thy chosen ones, and the apprehension of Thy Prophets and of Thy Messengers.

I beseech Thee, O my Lord, by Thy Name which Thou hast made to be the Day-Spring of Thy Revelation and the Dawning-Place of Thine inspiration, to ordain for this wronged One and for them that are dear to Thee what becometh Thy loftiness. Thou, in very truth, art the All-Bountiful, the All-Powerful, the All-Knowing, the All-Wise.

XL

Praise be to Thee, O Lord my God! I implore Thee, by Thy Name which none hath befittingly recognized, and whose import no soul hath fathomed; I beseech Thee, by Him Who is the Fountain-Head of Thy Revelation and the Day-Spring of Thy signs, to make my heart to be a receptacle of Thy love and of remembrance of Thee. Knit it, then, to Thy most great Ocean, that from it may flow out the living waters of Thy wisdom and the crystal streams of Thy glorification and praise.

The limbs of my body testify to Thy unity, and the hair of my head declareth the power of Thy sovereignty and might. I have stood at the door of Thy grace with utter self-effacement and complete abnegation, and clung to the hem of Thy bounty, and fixed mine eyes upon the horizon of Thy gifts.

Do Thou destine for me, O my God, what becometh the greatness of Thy majesty, and assist me, by Thy strengthening grace, so to teach Thy Cause that the dead may speed out of their sepulchers, and rush forth towards Thee, trusting wholly in Thee, and fixing their gaze upon the orient of Thy Cause, and the dawning-place of Thy Revelation.

Thou, verily, art the Most Powerful, the Most High, the All-Knowing, the All-Wise.

XLI *unity*

Thy unity is inscrutable, O my God, to all except them that have recognized Him Who is the Manifestation of Thy singleness and the Day-Spring of Thy oneness. Whoso assigneth a rival unto Him hath assigned a rival unto Thee, and whoso hath set up a peer for Him hath set up a peer for Thyself. No, no, none can withstand Thee in the whole of creation. Thou hast everlastingly been exalted far above all comparison and likeness. Thy oneness hath been demonstrated by the oneness of Him Who is the Dawning-Place of Thy Revelation. Whosoever denieth this, hath denied Thy unity, and disputed with Thee about Thy sovereignty, and contended with Thee in Thy realm, and repudiated Thy commandments.

Assist Thou Thy servants, O my Lord, to recognize Thy unity and to declare Thy oneness, that all may gather together around what Thou didst desire in this Day whereon the sun of Thine essence hath shone forth above the horizon of Thy will, and the moon of Thine own being hath risen from the Day-Spring of Thy behest. Thou art He, O my Lord, from Whose knowledge nothing whatsoever escapeth, and Whom no one can frustrate. Thou doest Thy pleasure, by Thy sovereignty that overshadoweth the worlds.

Thou well knowest, O my God, my Best-Beloved, that naught can quench the thirst I suffer in my separation from Thee except the waters of Thy presence, and that the tumult of my heart can never be stilled save through the living fountain of my reunion with Thee. Send down, then, upon me, O my Lord, out of the heaven of Thy bounty what will draw me nearer unto the chalice of Thy gifts, and make me able to quaff the choice sealed Wine, Whose seal hath been loosed in Thy name, and from Which the sweet savors of Thy days have been shed abroad. Thou, in truth, art the All-Bountiful, Whose grace is infinite.

The whole universe testifieth to Thy generosity. Have mercy, then, upon me by Thy graciousness, and deal bountifully with me through the power of Thy sovereignty, and suffer me to enjoy near access to Thee by Thy manifold favors. Thou, truly, art the Great Giver, the Almighty, the Ever-Forgiving, the Most Bountiful.

XLII

Lauded be Thy name, O my God and the God of all things, my Glory and the Glory of all things, my Desire and the Desire of all things, my Strength and the Strength of all things, my King and the King of all things, my Possessor and the Possessor of all things, my Aim and the Aim of all things, my Mover and the Mover of all things! Suffer me not, I implore Thee, to be kept back from the ocean of Thy tender mercies, nor to be far removed from the shores of nearness to Thee.

Aught else except Thee, O my Lord, profiteth me not, and near access to any one save Thyself availeth me nothing. I entreat Thee by the plenteousness of Thy riches, whereby Thou didst dispense with all else except Thyself, to number me with such as have set their faces towards Thee, and arisen to serve Thee.

Forgive, then, O my Lord, Thy servants and Thy handmaidens. Thou, truly, art the Ever-Forgiving, the Most Compassionate.

XLIII

O God, Who art the Author of all Manifestations, the Source of all Sources, the Fountain-Head of all

Attachment

Revelations, and the Well-Spring of all Lights! I testify that by Thy Name the heaven of understanding hath been adorned, and the ocean of utterance hath surged, and the dispensations of Thy providence have been promulgated unto the followers of all religions.

I beseech Thee so to enrich me as to dispense with all save Thee, and be made independent of any one except Thyself. Rain down, then, upon me out of the clouds of Thy bounty that which shall profit me in every world of Thy worlds. Assist me, then, through Thy strengthening grace, so to serve Thy Cause amidst Thy servants that I may show forth what will cause me to be remembered as long as Thine own kingdom endureth and Thy dominion will last.

This is Thy servant, O my Lord, who with his whole being hath turned unto the horizon of Thy bounty, and the ocean of Thy grace, and the heaven of Thy gifts. Do with me then as becometh Thy majesty, and Thy glory, and Thy bounteousness, and Thy grace.

Thou, in truth, art the God of strength and power, Who art meet to answer them that pray Thee. There is no God save Thee, the All-Knowing, the All-Wise.

God answers prayer.

XLIV

Lauded be Thy name, O Thou Who art my God and throbbest within my heart! Thou art well aware and dost witness that whatsoever shameth them that are dear to Thee must shame also Him Who is the Manifestation of Thyself and the Day-Spring of Thy Revelation. Nay, He is put to greater shame than they when they are led to confess the good things which have escaped them in Thy days.

These are Thy servants, O my Lord, who for love of Thee have abandoned their homes, and sustained the tribulations decreed by Thee in Thy path. I swear by Thy glory! Every time any one of them testifieth before Thee to his evil doings, shame covereth my face, for they are Thy servants who have tasted of the cup of woe in Thy Cause, who have quaffed from the chalice of adversity when the light of Thy countenance was lifted upon them, and who were so vexed by trials that peace was utterly denied them within the precincts of Thy court.

The power of Thy might beareth me witness! My heart hath melted by reason of my love for them that are dear to Thee, and my soul is laden with anguish for the sorrows which have afflicted them at the revelation of Thy Cause and the appearance of the billowing oceans of Thy grace and favors. The sighs they uttered, O my Lord, have caused my sighs to

Station of Believers

guidance

ascend towards Thee, and the burning of their hearts hath consumed mine own heart within me.

I beseech Thee, O Thou Who art the Lord of all being and the Enlightener of all things visible and invisible, to grant that every one of them may become an ensign of Thy guidance among Thy servants, and a revelation of the splendors of the Day-Star of Thy loving-kindness amidst Thy creatures. Thou hast, O my God, chosen them to love Thee, and to stand before the throne of Thy majesty. No other station hath excelled the station to which Thou hast called them. How many the nights, O my God, when sleep failed to overtake them because of their remembrance of Thee, and how numerous the days which they spent in lamentation over the things that have befallen Thee at the hands of Thine enemies! I entreat Thee, O Thou Who art the Ruler of rulers, and the Uplifter of the downtrodden, to aid them so to assist Thy Cause and exalt Thy word that through them Thy praise may be shed abroad amidst Thy creatures, and Thy virtues recounted throughout Thy realm. Thou art, verily, the Almighty, the Most Exalted, the Ever-Forgiving, the Most Generous.

Praised be Thou, O Lord my God! This is Thy servant whom Thou hast in the kingdom of Thy names called by Thine own name, and whom Thou hast reared under the wings of Thy grace and favors. Thou seest him, therefore, hastening in the direction of Thy gifts, and rushing forth towards Thee seeking after Thy bounty. Attire him, O my God, with the

mantle of Thy favor and the robe of Thy munifi-
cence and generosity, that all created things may perceive from him the sweet smell of the raiment of
Thy love. Adorn, then, his head with the crown of
Thy remembrance, in such wise that his fame may be
noised abroad among Thy servants as one who loveth
Thee and cleaveth steadfastly to Thy Cause. Assist
him, moreover, at all times and under all conditions
to help Thee and to remember Thee, and to extol Thy
virtues amidst Thy creatures.

I swear by Thy glory, O my God! Every time I
muse on Thy glory and Thy sovereignty I find myself
as the most guilty among them that have transgressed
against Thee in Thy realm, and every time I contemplate the heights in which none except Thee can
abide, I discover that I am the most sinful of all the
creatures that dwell in Thy land. Had it not been for
Thy name, the Concealer, and for Thy name, the
Ever-Forgiving, and for the sweet savors of Thy
name, the Most Merciful, all Thy chosen ones had
been reckoned amongst the perverse and the wicked.

I render Thee thanks that Thy mercy hath overtaken them and Thy grace and bountiful favors compassed them on every side.

And now, having confessed the things Thou didst
cause to flow down from my Pen, I implore Thee,
by Thy name which Thou hast raised up above every
other name, and hast caused to overshadow all that
are in heaven and all that are on earth, to cast not
away him that hath turned towards Thee, and to

deny him not the wonders of Thy grace and the hidden evidences of Thy mercy. Let the hands of Thine omnipotence kindle in his heart a lamp that will enable him to shine brightly in Thy days, and to cry out with such vehemence in Thy name that no timidity will deter him from soaring in the atmosphere of Thy love, and from ascending to the horizon of rapture and longing for Thee, and that the pursuits of Thy creatures will not withhold him from magnifying Thy word, that Thou mayest behold him sanctified as Thou wishest and as beseemeth Thy majesty and glory.

Exalted though this station may be, O my God, and however excellent this position—for who else except Thyself hath the power to show forth what may be deemed worthy of Thine exaltation and befit Thy greatness—yet Thou art He Who is the All-Bountiful, the Most Compassionate. All the atoms of the earth testify that Thou art the Ever-Forgiving, the Benevolent, the Great Giver, the All-Glorious, the All-Wise. Look, then, upon him, O my God, with the eyes of Thy loving-kindness, and cast upon him the glance of Thy generosity. Enrapture him, moreover, with the sweet melodies of Him Who is the Fountain-Head of Thy Revelation, in such wise that he may wholly surrender his will to Thy pleasure, and fix his hopes upon the things Thou didst ordain in Thy Tablets. Strengthen, then, his heart by Thy name, the Almighty, the Faithful, that he may draw forth the hand of power, and with it help Thy Cause when the light of Thy beauty is manifested and the Day-Star of Thy majesty is risen.

Since Thou hast called him by Thy name, O my Lord, single him out among Thy servants for Thy service. Thou well knowest, O my Lord, that in revealing myself I have sought only to reveal Thy Cause, and have turned to no one except for the sake of Thy Revelation and for the purpose of manifesting Thy loving-kindness. I beseech Thee, by Thy treasured Name Who, at this very moment, is speaking, to send down upon him and upon them that love Thee that which is enshrined in the heaven of Thy favor and bounties, that they may be filled with vehement longing towards Thee, and exult in Thy Covenant, O Thou Who art the Lord of Lords! Ordain, then, for him and for them that which becometh Thy name, the All-Bountiful.

Thou art, in truth, the Almighty, the Most Exalted, the Most Powerful, the All-Glorious, the Most Great.

XLV

My God, my Fire and my Light! The days which Thou hast named the Ayyám-i-Há (the Days of Há, Intercalary days) in Thy Book have begun, O Thou Who art the King of names, and the fast which Thy most exalted Pen hath enjoined unto all who are in the kingdom of Thy creation to observe is approaching. I entreat Thee, O my Lord, by these days and by all such as have during that period clung to the cord of Thy commandments, and laid hold on the handle of Thy precepts, to grant that unto every soul may be assigned a place within the precincts of Thy court, and a seat at the revelation of the splendors of the light of Thy countenance.

These, O my Lord, are Thy servants whom no corrupt inclination hath kept back from what Thou didst send down in Thy Book. They have bowed themselves before Thy Cause, and received Thy Book with such resolve as is born of Thee, and observed what Thou hadst prescribed unto them, and chosen to follow that which had been sent down by Thee.

Thou seest, O my Lord, how they have recognized and confessed whatsoever Thou hast revealed in Thy Scriptures. Give them to drink, O my Lord, from the hands of Thy graciousness the waters of Thine eternity. Write down, then, for them the recompense ordained for him that hath immersed himself in the ocean of Thy presence, and attained unto the choice wine of Thy meeting.

I implore Thee, O Thou the King of kings and the Pitier of the downtrodden, to ordain for them the good of this world and of the world to come. Write down for them, moreover, what none of Thy creatures hath discovered and number them with those who have circled round Thee, and who move about Thy throne in every world of Thy worlds.

Thou, truly, art the Almighty, the All-Knowing, the All-Informed.

XLVI

Praised be Thou, O my God, that Thou hast ordained Naw-Rúz as a festival unto those who have observed the fast for love of Thee and abstained from all that is abhorrent unto Thee. Grant, O my Lord, that the fire of Thy love and the heat produced by the fast enjoined by Thee may inflame them in Thy Cause, and make them to be occupied with Thy praise and with remembrance of Thee.

Since Thou hast adorned them, O my Lord, with the ornament of the fast prescribed by Thee, do Thou adorn them also with the ornament of Thine acceptance, through Thy grace and bountiful favor. For the doings of men are all dependent upon Thy good-pleasure, and are conditioned by Thy behest. Shouldst Thou regard him who hath broken the fast as one who hath observed it, such a man would be reckoned among them who from eternity had been keeping the fast. And shouldst Thou decree that he who hath observed the fast hath broken it, that person would be numbered with such as have caused the Robe of Thy Revelation to be stained with dust, and been far removed from the crystal waters of this living Fountain.

Thou art He through Whom the ensign "Praiseworthy art Thou in Thy works" hath been lifted up, and the standard "Obeyed art Thou in Thy behest" hath been unfurled. Make known this Thy station, O my God, unto Thy servants, that they may be made aware that the excellence of all things is dependent upon Thy bidding and Thy word, and the virtue of every act is conditioned by Thy leave and the good-pleasure of Thy will, and may recognize that the reins of men's doings are within the grasp of Thine acceptance and Thy commandment. Make this known unto them, that nothing whatsoever may shut them out from Thy Beauty, in these days whereon the Christ exclaimeth: "All dominion is Thine, O Thou the Begetter of the Spirit (Jesus);" and Thy Friend (Muḥammad) crieth out: "Glory be to Thee, O Thou the Best-Beloved, for that Thou hast uncovered Thy Beauty, and written down for Thy chosen ones what will cause them to attain unto the seat of the revelation of Thy Most Great Name, through which all the peoples have lamented except such as have detached themselves from all else except Thee, and set themselves towards Him Who is the Revealer of Thyself and the Manifestation of Thine attributes."

He Who is Thy Branch and all Thy company, O my Lord, have broken this day their fast, after having observed it within the precincts of Thy court, and in their eagerness to please Thee. Do Thou ordain for Him, and for them, and for all such as have entered Thy presence in those days all the good Thou didst destine in Thy Book. Supply them, then, with that which will profit them, in both this life and in the life beyond.

Thou, in truth, art the All-Knowing, the All-Wise.

XLVII

O Thou the Lord of the visible and the invisible, and the Enlightener of all creation! I beseech Thee, by Thy sovereignty which is hid from the eyes of men, to reveal in all directions the signs of Thy manifold blessings and the tokens of Thy loving-kindness, that I may arise with exultation and rapture and extol Thy wondrous virtues, O Thou the Most Merciful, and stir up by Thy name all created things, and so kindle the fire of Thy glorification amidst Thy creatures, that all the world may be filled with the brightness of the light of Thy glory, and all existence be inflamed with the fire of Thy Cause.

Roll not up, O my Lord, what hath been spread out in Thy name, and extinguish not the lamp which Thine own fire hath lit. Withhold not, O my Lord, the water that is life indeed from running down— the water from whose murmuring the wondrous

melodies which extol and glorify Thee can be heard.
Deny not, moreover, Thy servants the sweet fra-
grance of the breath which hath been wafted through
Thy love.

Thou seest, O Thou Who art my All-Glorious
Beloved, the restless waves that surge within the ocean
of my heart, in my love and yearning towards Thee.
I implore Thee, by the signs of Thy majesty and the
evidences of Thy sovereignty, to subdue Thy servants
by this Name Which Thou hast made to be the King
of all names in the kingdom of Thy creation. Potent
art Thou to rule as Thou pleasest. No God is there
but Thee, the All-Glorious, the All-Bountiful.

Do Thou ordain, moreover, for every one who
hath turned towards Thee what will make him steadfast in Thy Cause, in such wise that neither the vain
imaginations of the infidels among Thy creatures, nor
the idle talk of the froward amidst Thy servants will
have the power to shut him out from Thee. Thou,
verily, art the Help in Peril, the Almighty, the Most
Powerful.

XLVIII

Unto Thee be praise, O Lord my God! I beseech
Thee by Thy Most Great Name Who hath been shut
up in the prison-town of 'Akká, and Who—as Thou
beholdest, O my God—hath fallen into the hands of

His enemies, and is threatened by the swords of the wicked doers, to make me steadfast in His Cause, and to direct mine eyes continually towards His court, in such wise that nothing whatsoever will have the power to turn me back from Him.

I testify, O my Lord, that He hath surrendered His life in Thy path, and hath wished for Himself nothing but tribulation in the love He beareth to Thee. He hath endured all manner of vexations that He may manifest Thy sovereignty unto Thy servants, and exalt Thy word amidst Thy creatures. As the adversities deepened, and the troubles sent down by Thee compassed Him on every side, He became so impassioned by His thought of Thee, that the hosts of all them that had disbelieved in Thee and repudiated Thy signs ceased to affright Him.

I implore Thee, O my Lord, by Him and by whatsoever pertaineth unto Him, to set my affections upon Him even as He hath set His own affections upon Thyself. I testify that His love is Thy love, and His self Thy self, and His beauty Thy beauty, and His Cause Thy Cause.

Deny me not, O my Lord, what is with Thee, and suffer me not to be forgetful of what Thou didst desire in Thy days. Thou art, verily, the Almighty, the Most Exalted, the All-Glorious, the All-Wise.

For Believers

XLIX

Lauded be Thy name, O Lord my God! I entreat Thee by Thy Name through which the Hour hath struck, and the Resurrection came to pass, and fear and trembling seized all that are in heaven and all that are on earth, to rain down, out of the heaven of Thy mercy and the clouds of Thy tender compassion, what will gladden the hearts of Thy servants, who have turned towards Thee and helped Thy Cause.

Keep safe Thy servants and Thy handmaidens, O my Lord, from the darts of idle fancy and vain imaginings, and give them from the hands of Thy grace a draught of the soft-flowing waters of Thy knowledge.

Thou, truly, art the Almighty, the Most Exalted, the Ever-Forgiving, the Most Generous.

L

Glory be to Thee, O my God! Thou hearest Thine ardent lovers lamenting in their separation from Thee, and such as have recognized Thee wailing because of their remoteness from Thy presence. Open Thou outwardly to their faces, O my Lord, the gates of Thy grace, that they may enter them by Thy leave and in conformity with Thy will, and may stand before the throne of Thy majesty, and catch the accents of Thy voice, and be illumined with the splendors of the light of Thy face.

Potent art Thou to do what pleaseth Thee. None can withstand the power of Thy sovereign might. From everlasting Thou wert alone, with none to equal Thee, and wilt unto everlasting remain far above all thought and every description of Thee. Have mercy, then, upon Thy servants by Thy grace and bounty, and suffer them not to be kept back from the shores of the ocean of Thy nearness. If Thou abandonest them, who is there to befriend them; and if Thou puttest them far from Thee, who is he that can favor them? They have none other Lord beside Thee, none to adore except Thyself. Deal Thou generously with them by Thy bountiful grace.

Thou, in truth, art the Ever-Forgiving, the Most Compassionate.

LI

Thou dost witness, O my God, how He Who is Thy splendor calleth Thee to remembrance, notwithstanding the manifold troubles that have touched Him, troubles which none except Thee can number. Thou beholdest how, in His prison-house, He re-

counteth Thy wondrous praises with which Thou
didst inspire Him. Such is His fervor that His enemies are powerless to deter Him from mentioning
Thee, O Thou Who art the Possessor of all names!

Praised be Thou that Thou hast so strengthened
Him with Thy strength, and endowed Him by Thine
almighty power with such potency, that aught save
Thee is in His estimation but a handful of dust. The
lights of unfading splendor have so enveloped Him
that all else but Thee is in His eyes but a shadow.

And when Thine irresistible summons reached me, I
arose, fortified by Thy strength, and called all that
are in Thy heaven and all that are on Thy earth to
turn in the direction of Thy favors and the horizon
of Thy bounties. Some caviled at me, and determined to hurt me and slay me. Others drank to the
full of the wine of Thy grace, and hastened towards
the habitation of Thy throne.

I beseech Thee, O Thou Who art the Creator of
earth and heaven and the Source of all things, to
attract Thy servants through the fragrances of the
Robe of Thine Inspiration and Thy Revelation, and
to help them attain the Tabernacle of Thy behest
and power. From eternity Thou wert by Thy transcendent might supreme over all things, and Thou
wilt be exalted unto eternity in Thy Godhead and
surpassing sovereignty.

Let Thy mercy, then, be upon Thy servants and
Thy creatures. Thou art, in truth, the Almighty, the
Inaccessible, the All-Glorious, the Unconditioned.

LII

Lauded be Thy name, O my God! I entreat Thee by the fragrances of the Raiment of Thy grace which at Thy bidding and in conformity with Thy desire were diffused throughout the entire creation, and by the Day-Star of Thy will that hath shone brightly, through the power of Thy might and of Thy sovereignty, above the horizon of Thy mercy, to blot out from my heart all idle fancies and vain imaginings, that with all my affections I may turn unto Thee, O Thou Lord of all mankind!

I am Thy servant and the son of Thy servant, O my God! I have laid hold on the handle of Thy grace, and clung to the cord of Thy tender mercy. Ordain for me the good things that are with Thee, and nourish me from the Table Thou didst send down out of the clouds of Thy bounty and the heaven of Thy favor.

Thou, in very truth, art the Lord of the worlds, and the God of all that are in heaven and all that are on earth.

LIII

I know not, O my God, what the Fire is which Thou didst kindle in Thy land. Earth can never cloud its splendor, nor water quench its flame. All the peoples of the world are powerless to resist its force. Great is the blessedness of him that hath drawn nigh unto it, and heard its roaring.

Some, O my God, Thou didst, through Thy strengthening grace, enable to approach it, while others Thou didst keep back by reason of what their hands have wrought in Thy days. Whoso hath hasted towards it and attained unto it hath, in his eagerness to gaze on Thy beauty, yielded his life in Thy path, and ascended unto Thee, wholly detached from aught else except Thyself.

I beseech Thee, O my Lord, by this Fire which blazeth and rageth in the world of creation, to rend asunder the veils that have hindered me from appearing before the throne of Thy majesty, and from standing at the door of Thy gate. Do Thou ordain for me, O my Lord, every good thing Thou didst send down in Thy Book, and suffer me not to be far removed from the shelter of Thy mercy.

Powerful art Thou to do what pleaseth Thee. Thou art, verily, the All-Powerful, the Most Generous.

LIV

Lauded be Thy name, O my God! Aid Thou by Thy strengthening grace Thy servants and Thy handmaidens to recount Thy virtues and to be steadfast in their love towards Thee. How many the leaves which the tempests of trials have caused to fall, and how many, too, are those which, clinging tenaciously to the tree of Thy Cause, have remained unshaken by the tests that have assailed them, O Thou Who art our Lord, the Most Merciful!

I render Thee thanks that Thou hast made known unto me such servants as have utterly abolished, by the power of Thy might and of Thy sovereignty, the idols of their corrupt desires, and were not kept back by the things which are possessed by Thy creatures from turning in the direction of Thy grace. These have so vehemently rent the veils asunder that the dwellers of the cities of self have wept, and fear and trembling seized the people of envy and wickedness who, adorning their heads and their bodies with the emblems of knowledge, have proudly rejected Thee and turned away from Thy beauty.

I implore Thee, O my Lord, by Thy surpassing majesty and Thine Ancient Name, to enable Thy loved ones to assist Thee. Direct, then, continually their faces towards Thy face, and write down for them what will cause all hearts to exult and all eyes to be gladdened.

Thou, truly, art the Help in peril, the Self-Sub-sisting.

LV

O God! The trials Thou sendest are a salve to the sores of all them who are devoted to Thy will; the remembrance of Thee is a healing medicine to the hearts of such as have drawn nigh unto Thy court; nearness to Thee is the true life of them who are Thy lovers; Thy presence is the ardent desire of such as yearn to behold Thy face; remoteness from Thee is a torment to those that have acknowledged Thy one-ness, and separation from Thee is death unto them that have recognized Thy truth!

I beseech Thee by the sighs which they whose souls pant after Thee have uttered in their remoteness from Thy court, and by the cries of such of Thy lovers as bemoan their separation from Thee, to nourish me with the wine of Thy knowledge and the living waters of Thy love and pleasure. Behold Thy hand-maiden, O my Lord, who hath forgotten all else ex-cept Thee, and who hath delighted herself with Thy love, and lamented over the things that have befallen Thee at the hands of the wicked doers among Thy creatures. Do Thou ordain for her that which Thou didst ordain for such of Thy handmaidens as circle round the throne of Thy majesty, and gaze, at eventide and at dawn, on Thy beauty.

Thou art, verily, the Lord of the Judgment Day.

LVI

Glory be to Thee, O Lord my God! These are the days whereon Thou hast bidden all men to observe the fast, that through it they may purify their souls and rid themselves of all attachment to any one but Thee, and that out of their hearts may ascend that which will be worthy of the court of Thy majesty and may well beseem the seat of the revelation of Thy oneness. Grant, O my Lord, that this fast may become a river of life-giving waters and may yield the virtue wherewith Thou hast endowed it. Cleanse Thou by its means the hearts of Thy servants whom the evils of the world have failed to hinder from turning towards Thine all-glorious Name, and who have remained unmoved by the noise and tumult of such as have repudiated Thy most resplendent signs which have accompanied the advent of Thy Manifestation Whom Thou hast invested with Thy sovereignty, Thy power, Thy majesty and glory. These are the servants who, as soon as Thy call reached them, hastened in the direction of Thy mercy and were not kept back from Thee by the changes and chances of this world or by any human limitations.

I am he, O my God, who testifieth to Thy unity, who acknowledgeth Thy oneness, who boweth humbly before the revelations of Thy majesty, and who recognizeth with downcast countenance the splendors of the light of Thy transcendent glory. I have believed in Thee after Thou didst enable me to know Thy Self, Whom Thou hast revealed to men's eyes through the power of Thy sovereignty and might. Unto Him I have turned, wholly detached from all things, and cleaving steadfastly unto the cord of Thy gifts and favors. I have embraced His truth, and the truth of all the wondrous laws and precepts that have been sent down unto Him. I have fasted for love of Thee and in pursuance of Thine injunction, and have broken my fast with Thy praise on my tongue and in conformity with Thy pleasure. Suffer me not, O my Lord, to be reckoned among them who have fasted in the daytime, who in the night-season have prostrated themselves before Thy face, and who have repudiated Thy truth, disbelieved in Thy signs, gainsaid Thy testimony, and perverted Thine utterances.

Open Thou, O my Lord, mine eyes and the eyes of all them that have sought Thee, that we may recognize Thee with Thine own eyes. This is Thy bidding given us in the Book sent down by Thee unto Him Whom Thou hast chosen by Thy behest, Whom Thou hast singled out for Thy favor above all Thy creatures, Whom Thou hast been pleased to invest with Thy sovereignty, and Whom Thou hast specially favored and entrusted with Thy Message unto Thy people. Praised be Thou, therefore, O my God, inasmuch as Thou hast graciously enabled us to recognize Him and to acknowledge whatsoever hath been sent down unto Him, and conferred upon us the honor of attaining the presence of the One Whom Thou didst promise in Thy Book and in Thy Tablets.

Thou seest me then, O my God, with my face turned towards Thee, cleaving steadfastly to the cord of Thy gracious providence and generosity, and clinging to the hem of Thy tender mercies and bountiful favors. Destroy not, I implore Thee, my hopes of attaining unto that which Thou didst ordain for Thy servants who have turned towards the precincts of Thy court and the sanctuary of Thy presence, and have observed the fast for love of Thee. I confess, O my God, that whatever proceedeth from me is wholly unworthy of Thy sovereignty and falleth short of Thy majesty. And yet I beseech Thee by Thy Name through which Thou hast revealed Thy Self, in the glory of Thy most excellent titles, unto all created things, in this Revelation whereby Thou hast, through Thy most resplendent Name, manifested Thy beauty, to give me to drink of the wine of Thy mercy and of the pure beverage of Thy favor, which have streamed forth from the right hand of Thy will, that I may so fix my gaze upon Thee and be so detached from all else but Thee, that the world and all that hath been created therein may appear before me as a fleeting day which Thou hast not deigned to create.

I moreover entreat Thee, O my God, to rain down, from the heaven of Thy will and the clouds of Thy mercy, that which will cleanse us from the noisome savors of our transgressions, O Thou Who hast called Thyself the God of Mercy! Thou art, verily, the Most Powerful, the All-Glorious, the Beneficent.

Cast not away, O my Lord, him that hath turned towards Thee, nor suffer him who hath drawn nigh unto Thee to be removed far from Thy court. Dash not the hopes of the suppliant who hath longingly stretched out his hands to seek Thy grace and favors, and deprive not Thy sincere servants of the wonders of Thy tender mercies and loving-kindness. Forgiving and Most Bountiful art Thou, O my Lord! Power hast Thou to do what Thou pleasest. All else but Thee are impotent before the revelations of Thy might, are as lost in the face of the evidences of Thy wealth, are as nothing when compared with the manifestations of Thy transcendent sovereignty, and are destitute of all strength when face to face with the signs and tokens of Thy power. What refuge is there beside Thee, O my Lord, to which I can flee, and where is there a haven to which I can hasten? Nay, the power of Thy might beareth me witness! No protector is there but Thee; no place to flee to except Thee, no refuge to seek save Thee. Cause me to taste, O my Lord, the divine sweetness of Thy remembrance and praise. I swear by Thy might! Whosoever tasteth of its sweetness will rid himself of all attachment to the world and all that is therein, and will set his face towards Thee, cleansed from the remembrance of any one except Thee.

Inspire then my soul, O my God, with Thy wondrous remembrance, that I may glorify Thy name. Number me not with them who read Thy words and fail to find Thy hidden gift which, as decreed by Thee, is contained therein, and which quickeneth the souls of Thy creatures and the hearts of Thy servants. Cause me, O my Lord, to be reckoned among them who have been so stirred up by the sweet savors that have been wafted in Thy days that they have laid down their lives for Thee and hastened to the scene of their death in their longing to gaze on Thy beauty and in their yearning to attain Thy presence. And were any one to say unto them on their way, "Whither go ye?" they would say, "Unto God, the All-Possessing, the Help in Peril, the Self-Subsisting!"

The transgressions committed by such as have turned away from Thee and have borne themselves haughtily towards Thee have not availed to hinder them from loving Thee, and from setting their faces towards Thee, and from turning in the direction of Thy mercy. These are they who are blessed by the Concourse on high, who are glorified by the denizens of the everlasting Cities, and beyond them by those on whose foreheads Thy most exalted pen hath written: "These! The people of Bahá. Through them have been shed the splendors of the light of guidance." Thus hath it been ordained, at Thy behest and by Thy will, in the Tablet of Thine irrevocable decree.

Proclaim, therefore, O my God, their greatness and the greatness of those who while living or after death have circled round them. Supply them with that which Thou hast ordained for the righteous among Thy creatures. Potent art Thou to do all things. There is no God but Thee, the All-Powerful, the Help in Peril, the Almighty, the Most Bountiful.

Do not bring our fasts to an end with this fast, O my Lord, nor the covenants Thou hast made with this covenant. Do Thou accept all that we have done for love of Thee, and for the sake of Thy pleasure, and all that we have left undone as a result of our subjection to our evil and corrupt desires. Enable us, then, to cleave steadfastly to Thy love and Thy good-pleasure, and preserve us from the mischief of such as have denied Thee and repudiated Thy most resplendent signs. Thou art, in truth, the Lord of this world and of the next. No God is there beside Thee, the Exalted, the Most High.

Magnify Thou, O Lord my God, Him Who is the Primal Point, the Divine Mystery, the Unseen Essence, the Day-Spring of Divinity, and the Manifestation of Thy Lordship, through Whom all the knowledge of the past and all the knowledge of the future were made plain, through Whom the pearls of Thy hidden wisdom were uncovered, and the mystery

of Thy treasured name disclosed, Whom Thou hast
appointed as the Announcer of the One through
Whose name the letter B and the letter E have been
joined and united, through Whom Thy majesty, Thy
sovereignty and Thy might were made known,
through Whom Thy words have been sent down, and
Thy laws set forth with clearness, and Thy signs
spread abroad, and Thy Word established, through
Whom the hearts of Thy chosen ones were laid bare,
and all that were in the heavens and all that were on
the earth were gathered together, Whom Thou hast
called 'Alí-Muḥammad in the kingdom of Thy
names, and the Spirit of Spirits in the Tablets of
Thine irrevocable decree, Whom Thou hast invested
with Thine own title, unto Whose name all other
names have, at Thy bidding and through the power
of Thy might, been made to return, and in Whom
Thou hast caused all Thine attributes and titles to
attain their final consummation. To Him also belong such names as lay hid within Thy stainless tabernacles, in Thine invisible world and Thy sanctified
cities.

Magnify Thou, moreover, such as have believed in
Him and in His signs and have turned towards Him,
from among those that have acknowledged Thy
unity in His Latter Manifestation—a Manifestation
whereof He hath made mention in His Tablets, and
in His Books, and in His Scriptures, and in all the
wondrous verses and gem-like utterances that have
descended upon Him. It is this same Manifestation

Whose covenant Thou hast bidden Him establish ere He had established His own covenant. He it is Whose praise the Bayán hath celebrated. In it His excellence hath been extolled, and His truth established, and His sovereignty proclaimed, and His Cause perfected. Blessed is the man that hath turned unto Him, and fulfilled the things He hath commanded, O Thou Who art the Lord of the worlds and the Desire of all them that have known Thee!

Praised be Thou, O my God, inasmuch as Thou hast aided us to recognize and love Him. I, therefore, beseech Thee by Him and by Them Who are the Day-Springs of Thy Divinity, and the Manifestations of Thy Lordship, and the Treasuries of Thy Revelation, and the Depositories of Thine inspiration, to enable us to serve and obey Him, and to empower us to become the helpers of His Cause and the dispersers of His adversaries. Powerful art Thou to do all that pleaseth Thee. No God is there beside Thee, the Almighty, the All-Glorious, the One Whose help is sought by all men!

LVII

God testifieth to the unity of His Godhood and to the singleness of His own Being. On the throne of eternity, from the inaccessible heights of His station, His tongue proclaimeth that there is none other God but Him. He Himself, independently of all else, hath ever been a witness unto His own oneness, the revealer of His own nature, the glorifier of His own essence. He, verily, is the All-Powerful, the Almighty, the Beauteous.

He is supreme over His servants, and standeth over His creatures. In His hand is the source of authority and truth. He maketh men alive by His signs, and causeth them to die through His wrath. He shall not be asked of His doings and His might is equal unto all things. He is the Potent, the All-Subduing. He holdeth within His grasp the empire of all things, and on His right hand is fixed the Kingdom of His Revelation. His power, verily, embraceth the whole of creation. Victory and overlordship are His; all might and dominion are His; all glory and greatness are His. He, of a truth, is the All-Glorious, the Most Powerful, the Unconditioned.

LVIII

Praise be to Thee, to Whom the tongues of all created things have, from eternity, called, and yet failed to attain the heaven of Thine eternal holiness and grandeur. The eyes of all beings have been opened to behold the beauty of Thy radiant countenance, yet none hath succeeded in gazing on the brightness of the light of Thy face. The hands of them that are nigh unto Thee have, ever since the foundation of Thy glorious sovereignty and the establishment of Thy holy dominion, been raised suppliantly towards Thee, yet no one hath been able to touch the hem of the robe that clotheth Thy Divine and sovereign Essence. And yet none can deny that Thou hast ever been, through the wonders of Thy generosity and bounty, supreme over all things, art powerful to do all things, and art nearer unto all things than they are unto themselves.

Far be it, then, from Thy glory that anyone should gaze on Thy wondrous beauty with any eye save Thine own eye, or hear the melodies proclaiming Thine almighty sovereignty with any ear except Thine own ear. Too high art Thou exalted for the eye of any creature to behold Thy beauty, or for the understanding of any heart to scale the heights of Thine immeasurable knowledge. For should the birds of the hearts of them that are nigh unto Thee be ever enabled to soar as long as Thine own overpowering sovereignty can endure, or to ascend as long as the empire of Thy Divine holiness can last, they shall, in no wise, be able to transcend the limitations which a contingent world hath imposed upon them, nor pass beyond its confines. How, then, can he whose very creation is restricted by such limitations, attain unto Him Who is the Lord of the Kingdom of all created things, or ascend into the heaven of Him Who ruleth the realms of loftiness and grandeur?

Glorified, immeasurably glorified art Thou, my Best-Beloved! Inasmuch as Thou hast ordained that the utmost limit to which they who lift their hearts to Thee can rise is the confession of their powerlessness to enter the realms of Thy holy and transcendent unity, and that the highest station which they who aspire to know Thee can reach is the acknowledgment of their impotence to attain the retreats of Thy sublime knowledge I, therefore, beseech Thee, by this very powerlessness which is beloved of Thee, and which Thou hast decreed as the goal of them that have reached and attained Thy court, and by the splendors of Thy countenance that have encompassed all things, and by the energies of Thy Will whereby the entire creation hath been generated, not to deprive them that have set their hopes in Thee of the wonders of Thy mercy, nor to withhold from such as have sought Thee the treasures of Thy grace. Ignite, then, within their hearts the torch of Thy love, that its flame may consume all else except their wondrous remembrance of Thee, and that no trace may be left in those hearts except the gem-like evidences of Thy most holy sovereignty, so that from the land wherein they dwell no voice may be heard except the voice that extolleth Thy mercifulness and might, that on the earth on which they walk no light may shine except the light of Thy beauty, and that within every soul naught may be discovered except the revelation of Thy countenance and the tokens of Thy glory, that haply Thy servants may show forth only that which shall please

Thee and shall conform wholly unto Thy most potent will.

Glory be to Thee, O my God! The power of Thy might beareth me witness! I can have no doubt that should the holy breaths of Thy loving-kindness and the breeze of Thy bountiful favor cease, for less than the twinkling of an eye, to breathe over all created things, the entire creation would perish, and all that are in heaven and on earth would be reduced to utter nothingness. Magnified, therefore, be the marvelous evidences of Thy transcendent power! Magnified be the potency of Thine exalted might! Magnified be the majesty of Thine all-encompassing greatness, and the energizing influence of Thy will! Such is Thy greatness that wert Thou to concentrate the eyes of all men in the eye of one of Thy servants, and to compress all their hearts within his heart, and wert Thou to enable him to behold within himself all the things Thou hast created through Thy power and fashioned through Thy might, and were he to ponder, throughout eternity, over the realms of Thy creation and the range of Thy handiwork, he would unfailingly discover that there is no created thing but is overshadowed by Thine all-conquering power, and is vitalized through Thine all-embracing sovereignty.

Behold me, then, O my God, fallen prostrate upon the dust before Thee, confessing my powerlessness and Thine omnipotence, my poverty and Thy wealth, mine evanescence and Thine eternity, mine utter abasement and Thine infinite glory. I recognize that there is none other God but Thee, that Thou hast no peer nor partner, none to equal or rival Thee. In Thine unapproachable loftiness Thou hast, from eternity, been exalted above the praise of any one but Thee, and shalt continue for ever, in Thy transcendent singleness and glory, to be sanctified from the glorification of any one except Thine own Self.

I swear by Thy might, O my Beloved! To make mention of any created thing beseemeth not Thy most exalted Self, and to bestow any praise upon any one of Thy creatures would be wholly unworthy of Thy great glory. Nay, such a mention would be but blasphemy uttered within the court of Thy holiness, and such praise would amount to no less than a transgression in the face of the evidences of Thy Divine sovereignty. For the mere mention of any one of Thy creatures would in itself imply an assertion of their existence before the court of Thy singleness and unity. Such an assertion would be naught but open blasphemy, an act of impiety, the essence of profanity and a wanton crime.

Wherefore, I bear witness with my soul, my spirit, my entire being, that should They Who are the Day-Springs of Thy most holy unity and the Manifestations of Thy transcendent oneness be able to soar so long as Thine own sovereignty endureth and Thine all-compelling authority can last, they will fail in the end to attain unto even the precincts of the court wherein Thou didst reveal the effulgence of but one of Thy most mighty Names. Glorified, glorified be, therefore, Thy wondrous majesty. Glorified, glorified be Thine unattainable loftiness. Glorified, glorified be the preëminence of Thy kingship and the sublimity of Thine authority and power.

The highest faculties which the learned have possessed, and whatsoever truths they, in their search after the gems of Thy knowledge, have discovered; the brightest realities with which the wise have been endowed, and whatever secrets they, in their attempts to fathom the mysteries of Thy wisdom, have unraveled, have all been created through the generative power of the Spirit that was breathed into the Pen which Thy hands have fashioned. How, then, can the thing which Thy Pen hath created be capable of comprehending those treasures of Thy Faith with which, as decreed by Thee, that Pen hath been invested? How can it ever know of the Fingers that grasp Thy Pen, and of Thy merciful favors with which it hath been endowed? How can it, already unable to reach this station, be made aware of the existence of Thy Hand that controlleth the Fingers of Thy might? How can it attain unto the comprehension of the nature of Thy Will that animateth the movement of Thy Hand?

Glorified, glorified be Thou, O my God! How can I ever hope to ascend into the heaven of Thy most holy will, or gain admittance into the tabernacle of Thy Divine knowledge, knowing as I do that the minds of the wise and learned are impotent to fathom the secrets of Thy handiwork—a handiwork which is itself but a creation of Thy will?

Praise be to Thee, O Lord, my God, my Master, my Possessor, my King. Now that I have confessed unto Thee my powerlessness and the powerlessness of all created things, and have acknowledged my poverty and the poverty of the entire creation, I call unto Thee with my tongue and the tongues of all that are in heaven and on earth, and beseech Thee with my heart and the hearts of all that have entered beneath the shadow of Thy names and Thine attributes, not to shut us from the doors of Thy loving-kindness and grace, nor to suffer the breeze of Thy bountiful care and favor to cease from being wafted over our souls, nor to permit that our hearts be occupied with any one except Thee, or our minds to be busied with any remembrance save remembrance of Thy Self.

By the glory of Thy might, O my God! Wert Thou to set me king over Thy realms, and to establish me upon the throne of Thy sovereignty, and to deliver, through Thy power, the reins of the entire creation into my hands, and wert Thou to cause me, though it be for less than a moment, to be occupied with these things and be oblivious of the wondrous memories associated with Thy most mighty, most perfect, and most exalted Name, my soul would still remain unsatisfied, and the pangs of my heart unstilled. Nay, I would, in that very state, recognize myself as the poorest of the poor, and the most wretched of the wretched.

Magnified be Thy name, O my God! Now that Thou hast caused me to apprehend this truth, I beseech Thee by Thy Name which no scroll can bear, which no heart can imagine and no tongue can utter —a Name which will remain concealed so long as Thine own Essence is hidden, and will be glorified so long as Thine own Being is extolled—to unfurl, ere the present year draw to a close, the ensigns of Thine undisputed ascendancy and triumph, that the whole creation may be enriched by Thy wealth, and may be exalted through the ennobling influence of Thy transcendent sovereignty, and that all may arise and promote Thy Cause.

Thou art, verily, the Almighty, the All-Highest, the All-Glorious, the All-Subduing, the All-Possessing.

LIX

All praise, O my God, be to Thee Who art the Source of all glory and majesty, of greatness and honor, of sovereignty and dominion, of loftiness and grace, of awe and power. Whomsoever Thou willest Thou causest to draw nigh unto the Most Great Ocean, and on whomsoever Thou desirest Thou conferrest the honor of recognizing Thy Most Ancient Name. Of all who are in heaven and on earth, none can withstand the operation of Thy sovereign Will.

From all eternity Thou didst rule the entire creation, and Thou wilt continue for evermore to exercise Thy dominion over all created things. There is none other God but Thee, the Almighty, the Most Exalted, the All-Powerful, the All-Wise.

Illumine, O Lord, the faces of Thy servants, that they may behold Thee; and cleanse their hearts that they may turn unto the court of Thy heavenly favors, and recognize Him Who is the Manifestation of Thy Self and the Day-Spring of Thine Essence. Verily, Thou art the Lord of all worlds. There is no God but Thee, the Unconstrained, the All-Subduing.

LX

Glorified be Thou, O my God! Behold Thou my head ready to fall before the sword of Thy Will, my neck prepared to bear the chains of Thy Desire, my heart yearning to be made a target for the darts of Thy Decree, mine eyes expectant to gaze on the tokens and signs of Thy wondrous Mercy. For whatsoever may befall me from Thee is the cherished desire of them who thirst to meet Thee, and the supreme aspiration of such as have drawn nigh unto Thy court.

By the glory of Thy might, O Thou my Well-Beloved! To have sacrificed my life for the Manifestations of Thy Self, to have offered up my soul in the path of the Revealers of Thy wondrous Beauty, is to have sacrificed my spirit for Thy Spirit, my being for Thy Being, my glory for Thy glory. It is as if I had offered up all these things for Thy sake, and for the sake of Thy loved ones.

Though my body be pained by the trials that befall me from Thee, though it be afflicted by the revelations of Thy Decree, yet my soul rejoiceth at having partaken of the waters of Thy Beauty, and at having attained the shores of the ocean of Thine eternity. Doth it beseem a lover to flee from his beloved, or to desert the object of his heart's desire? Nay, we all believe in Thee, and eagerly hope to enter Thy presence.

LXI

Lauded be Thy name, O Lord my God! Thou dost witness that Thy will hath prevailed over all created things, and Thy mercy hath surpassed all who are in heaven and on earth. And when Thou didst purpose to unveil Thy sovereignty, and to glorify Thy word, and to reveal Thy bounteousness and mercy, Thou didst raise up one of Thy servants, and didst choose Him above all Thy creatures, and didst single Him out for Thy purpose, and didst clothe Him with the robe of Thy guidance, and didst immerse Him beneath the seas of Thy majesty and grandeur, and didst sanctify Him from all that beseemeth not the greatness of Thy glory and the power of Thy might, and didst bid Him to cry out before all that are in heaven and on earth, and summon the multitudes to the Manifestation of Thy Self and the Revealer of Thy signs.

No sooner had He proclaimed Thy Cause, and risen up to carry out the things prescribed unto Him in the Tablets of Thy decree, than the Great Terror fell upon Thy creatures. Some turned towards Thee, and detached themselves from all except Thee, and sanctified their souls from the world and all that is therein, and were so enravished by the sweetness of Thy voice that they forsook all Thou hadst created in the kingdom of Thy creation. Others recognized Thee and then hesitated, others allowed the world to come in between them and Thee and to withhold them from recognizing Thee. Others disdained Thee, and turned back from Thee, and wished to prevent Thee from achieving Thy purpose. And yet behold how all of them are calling upon Thee, and are expecting the things they were promised in Thy Tablets. And when the Promised One came unto them, they recognized Him not, and disbelieved in Thy signs, and repudiated Thy clear tokens, and strayed so grievously from Thy path that they slew Thy servants, through the brightness of whose faces the countenances of the Concourse on high have been illumined.

I beseech Thee, O Thou Who art the Lord of all names, to guard Thy loved ones against Thine enemies, and to strengthen them in their love for Thee and in fulfilling Thy pleasure. Do Thou protect them, that their footsteps may slip not, that their hearts may not be shut out as by a veil from Thee, and that their eyes may be restrained from beholding anything that is not of Thee. Cause them to be so enraptured by the sweetness of Thy divine melodies that they will rid themselves of all attachment to any one except Thee, and will turn wholly towards Thee, and extol Thee under all conditions, saying: "Praised be Thou, O Lord our God, inasmuch as Thou hast enabled us to recognize Thy most exalted and all-glorious Self. We will, by Thy mercy, cleave to Thee, and will detach ourselves from any one but Thee. We have realized that Thou art the Beloved of the worlds and the Creator of earth and heaven!"

Glorified be God, the Lord of all creation!

LXII

Lauded and glorified art Thou, O Lord my God! Thou art He Who from everlasting hath been clothed with majesty, with authority and power, and will continue unto everlasting to be arrayed with honor, with strength and glory. The learned, one and all, stand aghast before the signs and tokens of Thy handiwork, while the wise find themselves, without exception, impotent to unravel the mystery of Them Who are the Manifestations of Thy might and power. Every man of insight hath confessed his powerlessness to scale the heights of Thy knowledge, and every man of learning hath acknowledged his failure to fathom the nature of Thine Essence.

Having barred the way that leadeth unto Thee, Thou hast, by virtue of Thine authority and through the potency of Thy will, called into being Them Who are the Manifestations of Thy Self, and hast entrusted Them with Thy message unto Thy people, and caused Them to become the Day-Springs of Thine inspiration, the Exponents of Thy Revelation, the Treasuries of Thy Knowledge and the Repositories of Thy Faith, that all men may, through Them, turn their faces towards Thee, and may draw nigh unto the kingdom of Thy Revelation and the heaven of Thy grace.

I beseech Thee, therefore, by Thyself and by Them, to send down, from the right hand of the throne of Thy grace, upon all that dwell on earth, that which shall wash them from the stain of their trespasses against Thee, and cause them to become wholly devoted to Thy Self, O Thou in Whose hand is the source of all gifts, that they may all arise to serve Thy Cause, and may detach themselves entirely from all except Thee. Thou art the Almighty, the All-Glorious, the Unrestrained.

O my God, my Master, my Best-Beloved! I am

Thy servant and the son of Thy servant. I have held fast the cord of Thy grace, and clung to the hem of the garment of Thy loving providence. I entreat Thee, by Thy Most Great Name, Whom Thou hast appointed as the unerring Balance among the nations, and Thine infallible Proof unto all men, not to forsake me, nor to abandon me to my corrupt desires. Do Thou preserve me beneath the shadow of Thy Supreme Sinlessness, and enable me to magnify Thine own Self amidst the concourse of Thy creatures. Withhold not from me the Divine fragrance of Thy days, and deprive me not of the sweet savors wafting from the Day-Spring of Thy Revelation. Bestow on me the good of this world and of the next, through the power of Thy grace that hath encompassed all created things and Thy mercy that hath surpassed the entire creation. Thou art He Who holdeth in His grasp the kingdom of all things. Thou doest what Thou willest through Thy decree, and choosest, through the power of Thy might, whatsoever Thou desirest. None can resist Thy will; naught can exhaust the impelling force of Thy command. There is no God but Thee, the Almighty, the All-Glorious, the Most Bountiful.

strength and courage

LXIII

Thou beholdest, O my God, Thy servant who dwelleth in this prison-house, wholly detached from any one but Thee, his eyes turned in the direction of the Day-Spring of Thy mercy, his heart longing for the wondrous manifestations of Thy grace. Thou, O my Lord, hast reckoned up the ills that have afflicted him in Thy path. Thou seest him compassed about with such of Thy creatures as have transgressed and rebelled against Thee, who have come in between him and Thy loved ones, who have fixed his abode in this land and wronged Thee, and who have hindered Thy servants from turning towards Thee.

For all these things I offer thanksgiving unto Thee, O my Lord! I implore Thee to assist me and them that love me to magnify Thy Word, and to endow us with such strength that the ills of this world and its tribulations will be powerless to hinder us from remembering Thee and from extolling Thy virtues. Powerful art Thou to do all things; resplendent art Thou above all things.

Every conqueror is but a serf whom Thy hand hath subjected, and the richest of the rich is as destitute before the immensity of Thy wealth. The noblest of nobles is humbled when faced with the manifestations of Thy glory, and the mightiest of potentates is a mere abject one when confronted with the compelling evidences of Thine authority.

Tear asunder, O my God, the veil of vain imaginings that hath obscured the vision of Thy people, that all may haste towards Thee, may tread the path of Thy pleasure, and walk in the ways of Thy Faith. We are, O my God, Thy servants and Thy bondsmen. Thou art sufficient unto us so that we can dispense with the world and all that is therein. We are wholly satisfied with all that hath befallen us in Thy path, and exclaim: "Praised be Thou, in Whose hand are the realms of revelation and of creation, and all the kingdoms of earth and heaven!"

LXIV

Praise be to Thee, O Lord my God, my Master! Thou hearest the sighing of those who, though they long to behold Thy face, are yet separated from Thee and far distant from Thy court. Thou testifiest to the lamentations which those who have recognized Thee pour forth because of their exile from Thee and their yearning to meet Thee. I beseech Thee by those hearts which contain naught except the treasures of Thy remembrance and praise, and which show forth only the testimonies of Thy greatness and the evidences of Thy might, to bestow on Thy servants who desire Thee power to approach the seat of the revelation of the splendor of Thy glory and to assist them whose hopes are set on Thee to enter into the tabernacle of Thy transcendent favor and mercy.

Naked am I, O my God! Clothe me with the robe of Thy tender mercies. I am sore athirst; give me to drink of the oceans of Thy bountiful favor. I am a stranger; draw me nearer unto the source of Thy gifts. I am sick; sprinkle upon me the healing waters of Thy grace. I am a captive; rid me of my bondage, by the power of Thy might and through the force of Thy will, that I may soar on the wings of detachment towards the loftiest summits of Thy creation. Thou, verily, doest what Thou choosest. There is no God but Thee, the Help in Peril, the All-Glorious, the Unconstrained.

LXV

Glorified art Thou, O my God! Thou knowest that my sole aim in revealing Thy Cause hath been to reveal Thee and not my self, and to manifest Thy glory rather than my glory. In Thy path, and to attain Thy pleasure, I have scorned rest, joy, delight. At all times and under all conditions my gaze hath been fixed on Thy precepts, and mine eyes bent upon the things Thou hast bidden me observe in Thy Tablets. I have wakened every morning to the light of

Thy praise and Thy remembrance, and reached every evening inhaling the fragrances of Thy mercy.

And when the entire creation was stirred up, and the whole earth was convulsed, and the sweet savors of Thy name, the All-Praised, had almost ceased to breathe over Thy realms, and the winds of Thy mercy had well-nigh been stilled throughout Thy dominions, Thou didst, through the power of Thy might, raise me up among Thy servants, and bid me to show forth Thy sovereignty amidst Thy people. Thereupon I arose before all Thy creatures, strengthened by Thy help and Thy power, and summoned all the multitudes unto Thee, and announced unto all Thy servants Thy favors and Thy gifts, and invited them to turn towards this Ocean, every drop of the waters of which crieth out, proclaiming unto all that are in heaven and on earth that He is, in truth, the Fountain of all life, and the Quickener of the entire creation, and the Object of the adoration of all worlds, and the Best-Beloved of every understanding heart, and the Desire of all them that are nigh unto Thee.

Though the fierce winds of the hatred of the wicked doers blew and beat on this Lamp, He was, at no time, in His love for Thy beauty, hindered from shedding the fragrance of His light. As the transgressions committed against Thee waxed greater and greater, my eagerness to reveal Thy Cause correspondingly increased, and as the tribulations deepened—and to this Thy glory beareth me witness—

a fuller measure of Thy sovereignty and of Thy power was vouchsafed by me unto Thy creatures.

And finally, I was cast by the transgressors into the prison-city of 'Akká, and my kindred were made captives in Baghdád. The power of Thy might beareth me witness, O my God! Every trouble that hath touched me in Thy path hath added to my joy and increased my gladness. I swear by Thee, O Thou Who art the King of Kings! None of the kings of the earth hath power to hinder me from remembering Thee or from extolling Thy virtues. Were they to be leagued—as they have been leagued—against me, and to brandish their sharpest swords and most afflictive spears against me, I would not hesitate to magnify Thy name before all them that are in Thy heaven and on Thy earth. Nay rather, I would cry out and say: "This, O my Beloved, is my face which I have offered up for Thy face, and this is my spirit which I have sacrificed for Thy spirit, and this is my blood that seetheth in my veins, in its longing to be shed for love of Thee and in Thy path."

Though—as Thou beholdest me, O my God—I be dwelling in a place within whose walls no voice can be heard except the sound of the echo, though all the gates of ease and comfort be shut against us, and thick darkness appear to have compassed us on every side, yet my soul hath been so inflamed by its love for Thee, that nothing whatsoever can either quench the fire of its love or abate the consuming flame of its desire. Lifting up its voice, it crieth aloud amidst

Thy servants, and calleth them, at all times and under all conditions, unto Thee.

I beseech Thee, by Thy Most Great Name, to open the eyes of Thy servants, that they may behold Thee shining above the horizon of Thy majesty and glory, and that they may not be hindered by the croaking of the raven from hearkening to the voice of the Dove of Thy sublime oneness, nor be prevented by the corrupt waters from partaking of the pure wine of Thy bounty and the everlasting streams of Thy gifts.

Gather them, then, together around this Divine Law, the covenant of which Thou hast established with all Thy Prophets and Thy Messengers, and Whose ordinances Thou hast written down in Thy Tablets and Thy Scriptures. Raise them up, moreover, to such heights as will enable them to perceive Thy Call.

Potent art Thou to do what pleaseth Thee. Thou art, verily, the Inaccessible, the All-Glorious.

LXVI

Glorified art Thou, O Lord my God! Thou seest me dwelling in this prison-house that lieth behind the seas and the mountains, and knowest full well what I have endured for love of Thee and for the sake of

Thy Cause. Thou art He, O my God, Who hath raised me up at Thy behest, and bidden me to occupy Thy seat, and to summon all men to the court of Thy mercy. It is Thou Who hast commanded me to tell out the things Thou didst destine for them in the Tablet of Thy decree and didst inscribe with the pen of Thy Revelation, and Who hast enjoined on me the duty of kindling the fire of Thy love in the hearts of Thy servants, and of drawing all the peoples of the earth nearer to the habitation of Thy throne.

And when, as bidden by Thee, I arose and called out, by Thy leave, all Thy creatures, the wayward among Thy servants opposed me. Some turned away from me, others disowned my claim, a few hesitated, while others were sore perplexed, notwithstanding that Thy testimony was set forth before the followers of all religions, and Thy proof demonstrated unto all the peoples of the earth, and the signs of Thy might so powerfully manifested as to encompass the entire creation.

I was, moreover, opposed by mine own kindred, although, as Thou knowest, they were dear to me and I had desired for them that which I had desired for mine own self. These are the ones who, when learning that I had been cast into prison, perpetrated against me what no man else on earth had perpetrated.

I entreat Thee, therefore, O my God, by Thy name by which Thou hast separated between truth and denial, to purify their hearts of all evil suggestions, and to enable them to draw nigh unto Him

Who is the Day-Spring of Thy names and Thine attributes.

Thou knowest, O my God, that I have severed every tie that bindeth me to any of Thy creatures except that most exalted tie that uniteth me with whosoever cleaveth unto Thee, in this the day of the revelation of Thy most august Self, that hath appeared in Thy name, the All-Glorious. Thou knowest that I have dissolved every bond that knitteth me to any one of my kindred except such as have enjoyed near access to Thy most effulgent face.

I have no will but Thy will, O my Lord, and cherish no desire except Thy desire. From my pen floweth only the summons which Thine own exalted pen hath voiced, and my tongue uttereth naught save what the Most Great Spirit hath itself proclaimed in the kingdom of Thine eternity. I am stirred by nothing else except the winds of Thy will, and breathe no word except the words which, by Thy leave and Thine inspiration, I am led to pronounce.

Praise be to Thee, O Thou Who art the Well-Beloved of all that have known Thee, and the Desire of the hearts of such as are devoted to Thee, inasmuch as Thou hast made me a target for the ills that I suffer in my love for Thee, and the object of the assaults launched against me in Thy path. Thy glory beareth me witness! I can, on no account, feel impatient of the adversities that I have borne in my love for Thee. From the very day Thou didst reveal Thyself unto me, I have accepted for myself every manner of tribulation. Every moment of my life my head crieth out to Thee and saith: "Would, O my Lord, that I could be raised on the spear-point in Thy path!" while my blood entreateth Thee saying: "Dye the earth with me, O my God, for the sake of Thy love and Thy pleasure!" Thou knowest that I have, at no time, sought to guard my body against any affliction, nay rather I have continually anticipated the things Thou didst ordain for me in the Tablet of Thy decree.

Behold, then, O my God, my loneliness among Thy servants and my remoteness from Thy friends and Thy chosen ones. I beseech Thee, by the showers of the clouds of Thy mercy, whereby Thou hast caused the blossoms of Thy praise and utterance and the flowers of Thy wisdom and testimony to spring forth in the hearts of all them that have recognized Thy oneness, to supply Thy servants and my kindred with the fruits of the tree of Thy unity, in these days when Thou hast been established upon the throne of Thy mercy. Hinder them not, O my Lord, from attaining unto the things Thou dost possess, and write down for them that which will aid them to scale the heights of Thy grace and favor. Give them, moreover, to drink of the living waters of Thy knowledge, and ordain for them the good of this world and of the world to come.

Thou art, verily, the Lord of Bahá, and the Beloved of his heart, and the Object of his desire, and the Inspirer of his tongue, and the Source of his soul. No

Prayer for unity of the Believers

good of Worlds

Prayer for Knowledge

God is there but Thee, the Inaccessible, the Most High. Thou art, verily, the Almighty, the Most Exalted, the Ever-Forgiving, the Most Merciful.

LXVII

Glorified art Thou, O Lord my God! I yield Thee thanks for having enabled me to recognize the Manifestation of Thyself, and for having severed me from Thine enemies, and laid bare before mine eyes their misdeeds and wicked works in Thy days, and for having rid me of all attachment to them, and caused me to turn wholly towards Thy grace and bountiful favors. I give Thee thanks, also, for having sent down upon me from the clouds of Thy will that which hath so sanctified me from the hints of the infidels and the allusions of the misbelievers that I have fixed my heart firmly on Thee, and fled from such as have denied the light of Thy countenance. Again I thank Thee for having empowered me to be steadfast in Thy love, and to speak forth Thy praise and to extol Thy virtues, and for having given me to drink of the cup of Thy mercy that hath surpassed all things visible and invisible.

Thou art the Almighty, the Most Exalted, the All-Glorious, the All-Loving.

LXVIII

for Believers

Praised be Thou, O my God! Thou seest me shut up
in this Prison, and art well aware that I have entered
it solely for Thy sake and for the sake of the glorification of Thy word and the proclamation of Thy
Cause. I cry out to Thee, this very moment, O Thou
Who art the Lord of all worlds, beseeching Thee, by
Thine undoubted Name, to attract the hearts of Thy
servants unto the Day-Spring of Thy most excellent
titles and the Dawning-Place of Thy most resplendent signs.

But for the troubles that touch me in Thy path,
O my God, how else could my heart rejoice in Thy
days; and were it not for the blood which is shed for
love of Thee, what else could tinge the faces of Thy
chosen ones before the eyes of Thy creatures? I swear
by Thy might! The ornament that adorneth the
countenance of Thy dear ones is the blood which, in
their love for Thee, floweth out of their foreheads
over their faces.

Thou beholdest, O my God, how every bone in my
body soundeth like a pipe with the music of Thine
inspiration, revealing the signs of Thy oneness and the
clear tokens of Thy unity. I entreat Thee, O my God,
by Thy Name which irradiateth all things, to raise up
such servants as shall incline their ears to the voice
of the melodies that hath ascended from the right
hand of the throne of Thy glory. Make them, then,

to quaff from the hand of Thy grace the wine of
Thy mercy, that it may assure their hearts, and cause
them to turn away from the left hand of idle fancies
and vain imaginings to the right hand of confidence
and certitude.

Now that Thou hast guided them unto the door of
Thy grace, O my Lord, cast them not away, by Thy
bounty; and now that Thou hast summoned them
unto the horizon of Thy Cause, keep them not back
from Thee, by Thy graciousness and favor. Powerful
art Thou to do as Thou pleasest. No God is there but
Thee, the Omniscient, the All-Informed.

LXIX

Glorified art Thou, O Lord my God! My tongue,
both the tongue of my body and the tongue of my
heart, my limbs and members, every pulsating vein
within me, every hair of my head, all proclaim that
Thou art God, and that there is none other God
beside Thee. From everlasting Thou hast been immeasurably exalted above all similitudes and comparisons, and sanctified from whatsoever pertaineth to
the creation Thou hast created and fashioned. From
eternity Thou hast been alone, with none to share
the majesty of Thy singleness, and hast remained far

above the changes and chances to which all Thy creatures are subjected.

And when Thou didst purpose to demonstrate the power of Thy sovereign might, and to glorify Thy word, and to guide the steps of Thy people, Thou didst raise up from among Thy creatures One of Thy servants, Whom Thou didst send forth with the signs of Thy sovereignty, and Whom Thou didst endue with the clear tokens of Thy oneness, that He might fulfill Thy testimony unto all created things, and perfect Thy proof before all men.

As soon as He revealed Himself, as bidden by Thee, and called Thy servants to turn in the direction of Thy gifts, and to set their faces towards the horizon of Thy knowledge, the signs of dissension appeared amongst them. Some responded to Thy call and, without the least hesitation, obeyed Thy summons. Others turned their backs to Thee, and followed the desires of a corrupt inclination.

I implore Thee, O my God, by Thy Most Great Name, to enrapture the nations through the potency of the Word which Thou didst ordain to be the king of all words, the Word whereby the goodly pearls of Thy hidden wisdom were uncovered, and the gemlike mysteries which were wrapped up within Thee were unraveled. Deprive them not, by Thy grace and bounty, of the things Thou didst desire for them, and suffer them not to be far removed from the shores of the ocean of Thy presence.

Every existence, whether seen or unseen, O my

Lord, testifieth that Thy mercy hath surpassed all created things, and Thy loving-kindness embraced the entire creation. Look upon them, I entreat Thee, with the eyes of Thy mercy. Thou art the Ever-Forgiving, the Most Compassionate. Do with them as beseemeth Thy glory, and Thy majesty, and Thy greatness, and Thy bounteousness and Thy grace. Deal not with them according to the limitations imposed upon them, or the manifold vicissitudes of their earthly life.

Thou knowest, O my Lord, that I am but one of Thy servants. I have tasted of the sweetness of Thy speech, and acknowledged Thy unity and Thy singleness, and set my face towards the Source of Thy most excellent names and the Day-Spring of Thy transcendent attributes, and wished to be enabled by Thee to immerse myself beneath the ocean of Thy oneness and to be submerged by the mighty waters of Thy unity.

Assist me, by Thy strengthening grace, O my Lord, to do what Thou didst will, and withhold not from me the things Thou dost possess. So enravish me with the wonders of Thine utterances that the noise and distraction of this world may be powerless to deter me from turning unto Thee, and may fail to shake my constancy in Thy Cause, or to distract my gaze from the horizon of Thy grace. Aid me, then, O my God, to do what pleaseth Thee, and to carry out Thy will. Write down for me, moreover, the good of this world and of the world which is to come, and ordain for me a seat of truth in Thy presence. Potent art Thou to do what Thou willest, and to rule as Thou pleasest. No God is there but Thee, the Inaccessible, the All-Glorious, the Most Great.

All-praise to Thee, O Lord of the worlds and the Object of the adoration of the entire creation!

LXX

Faded now is all that erstwhile flourished in the Paradise of Thy transcendent oneness, O my God! Where are the rain-giving clouds of Thy mercy? Shorn are the branches of the Tree of Thy unity of the vesture of Thy majesty and wisdom; where is the spring-time of Thy gifts and bounties? Motionless lies the Ark of Thy Cause on the sea of Thy creation; where are the winds of Thy grace and favors? Encompassed on every side is Thy Lamp by the tempests of discord blowing from every land; where is the globe of Thy graciousness and protection?

Thou seest, O my God, how the eyes of these poor creatures are bent upon the horizon of Thy riches, how the hearts of these helpless ones are set in the direction of Thy might. I beseech Thee, O Thou Who art the sole Desire of them that have recognized Thee, and the Object of the adoration of the entire creation, not to suffer them, now that Thou hast attracted them by Thy most exalted Word, to be far removed from the Tabernacle which Thou hast reared up by Thy name, the All-Glorious.

They are sore pressed with cares, O my Lord, and are encompassed about by the wicked. Send down, therefore, from the heaven of Thy behest Thine invisible hosts, that, holding aloft the ensigns of Thy victory, they may help them in Thy land, and may shield them against Thine adversaries.

I entreat Thee, O my God, by Thy name through which the clouds have rained down their rain, and the streams have flowed, and the fire of Thy love hath been kindled throughout Thy dominion, to assist Thy servant who hath turned towards Thee, and hath spoken forth Thy praise, and determined to help Thee. Fortify, then, his heart, O my God, in Thy love and in Thy Faith. Better is this for him than all that hath been created on Thine earth, for the world and whatsoever is therein must perish, and what pertaineth unto Thee must endure as long as Thy most excellent names endure. By Thy Glory! Were the world to last as long as Thine own kingdom will last, to set their affections upon it would still be unseemly for such as have quaffed, from the hands of Thy mercy, the wine of Thy presence; how much more when they recognize its fleetingness and are persuaded of its transience. The chances that overtake it, and the changes to which all things pertaining unto it are continually subjected, attest its impermanence.

Whosoever hath recognized Thee will turn to none

save Thee, and will seek from Thee naught else except Thyself. Thou art the sole Desire of the heart of him whose thoughts are fixed on Thee, and the highest Aspiration of whosoever is wholly devoted unto Thee.

No God is there beside Thee, the Almighty, the Help in Peril, the All-Glorious, the Most Powerful.

LXXI

Magnified be Thy name, O my God, for that Thou hast manifested the Day which is the King of Days, the Day which Thou didst announce unto Thy chosen Ones and Thy Prophets in Thy most excellent Tablets, the Day whereon Thou didst shed the splendor of the glory of all Thy names upon all created things. Great is his blessedness whosoever hath set himself towards Thee, and entered Thy presence, and caught the accents of Thy voice.

I beseech Thee, O my Lord, by the name of Him round Whom circleth in adoration the kingdom of Thy names, that Thou wilt graciously assist them that are dear to Thee to glorify Thy word among Thy servants, and to shed abroad Thy praise amidst Thy creatures, so that the ecstasies of Thy revelation may fill the souls of all the dwellers of Thine earth.

Since Thou hast guided them, O my Lord, unto the living waters of Thy grace, grant, by Thy bounty,

detachment

that they may not be kept back from Thee; and since Thou hast summoned them to the habitation of Thy throne, drive them not out from Thy presence, through Thy loving-kindness. Send down upon them what shall wholly detach them from aught else except Thee, and make them able to soar in the atmosphere of Thy nearness, in such wise that neither the ascendancy of the oppressor nor the suggestions of them that have disbelieved in Thy most august and most mighty Self shall be capable of keeping them back from Thee.

LXXII

Lauded be Thy name, O Thou in Whose hands is the kingdom of all names, and in the grasp of Whose might are all that are in heaven and all that are on earth! I entreat Thee, by Him Who is Thy Most Effulgent Name Whom Thou hast made a target for the darts of Thy decree in Thy path, O Thou the King of eternity, to rend asunder the veils that have shut off Thy creatures from the horizon of Thy glory, that haply they may turn their faces in the direction of Thy mercy, and draw nigh unto the Day-Spring of Thy loving-kindness.

Leave not Thy servants to themselves, O my Lord! Draw them through the influence of Thine utterances unto the Dawning-Place of Thine inspiration, and to the Fountain of Thy Revelation, and to the Treasury of Thy wisdom. Thou art He to Whose strength and power all things have testified, Whose Purpose nothing whatsoever of all that hath been created in Thy heaven and on Thy earth hath been able to frustrate.

Render, then, victorious, O my God, Thy servants who have set their faces towards Thee, and directed their steps to the seat of Thy grace. Send down, then, upon them what will keep them safe from the danger of turning to any one but Thee, and from fixing their eyes upon aught else except Thyself.

Potent art Thou to do what Thou willest, and to rule as Thou pleasest. There is no God but Thee, the God of glory and wisdom.

Protection

LXXIII

Glorified art Thou, O Lord my God! I beseech Thee by Thy Name, the Restrainer, to withhold from us the maleficence of Thine adversaries who have disbelieved in Thy testimony, and caviled at Thy beauty. Overpower by Thy Name, the All-Subduing, such as have wronged Thy Previous Manifestation Who hath now appeared invested with Thy title, the All-Glorious. Lay hold, by Thy name, the Chastiser, on them that have treated Thy Cause with scorn, have jested at Thy most mighty utterances, and were hin-

*Mohammed
Bahaullah*

dered from attaining this most exalted station. Enable Thy loved ones, by Thy Name, the Victorious, to prevail against Thine enemies and the infidels among Thy creatures. Rend asunder, by Thy Name, the Cleaver, the veil that hideth the doings of them that have besmirched Thine honor and undermined Thy Faith among Thy people. Bind, by Thy Name, the Restorer, the broken hearts of them that love Thee, and graciously bless them in their affairs. Teach them, by Thy Name, the All-Knowing, the wonders of Thy wisdom, that they may cleave steadfastly to Thy Faith and walk in the ways of Thy pleasure. Keep them safe, by Thy Name, the Withholder, from the tyranny of the oppressor and the wickedness of the evil-doers and the malice of the stirrers of mischief. Shield them, by Thy Name, the Preserver, within the stronghold of Thy might and power, that haply they may be protected from the darts of doubt that are hurled by such as have rebelled against Thee. Sanctify for Thy servants, by Thy Name which Thou hast blessed above all other names, which Thou hast singled out for Thy favor, and by which Thou didst reveal Thy beauty, these days of which the Pen of Thy decree hath distinctly written, and which, according to Thy will and wisdom, have been preordained in Thine irrevocable Tablet. Subject to Thy rule, by Thy Name, the Conqueror, the people of Thy realm, that all may turn towards Thy face and forsake their all for love of Thee and for the sake of Thy pleasure.

Abase Thou, O my Lord, Thine enemies, and lay hold on them with Thy power and might, and let them be stricken by the blast of Thy wrath. Make them taste, O my God, of Thine awful majesty and vengeance, for they have repudiated the truth of the One in Whom they had believed, Who came unto them with Thy signs and Thy clear tokens and the evidences of Thy power and the manifold revelations of Thy might. Gather, then, together Thy loved ones beneath the shadow of the Tree of Thy oneness, and of the Manifestation of the effulgent light of Thy unity.

Thou art, verily, the One Whose power is immense, Whose vengeance is terrible. No God is there beside Thee, the Almighty, the Most Powerful.

LXXIV

Magnified be Thy name, O Lord my God, inasmuch as Thou hast inclined mine ear to Thy voice, and called me to Thyself, and opened mine eyes to gaze on Thy beauty, and illumined my heart with Thy knowledge, and sanctified my breast from the doubts of the infidels in Thy days. I am the one, O my God, who lay fast asleep on his couch, when lo, the messengers of Thy manifold mercies were sent down upon me by Thee, and the gentle winds of Thy

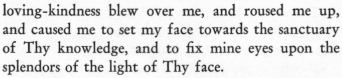

loving-kindness blew over me, and roused me up, and caused me to set my face towards the sanctuary of Thy knowledge, and to fix mine eyes upon the splendors of the light of Thy face.

I am but a poor creature, O my Lord! Behold me clinging to the hem of Thy riches. I have fled from darkness and from waywardness unto the brightness of the light of Thy countenance. Were I—and to this Thy glory beareth me witness—to render thanksgiving unto Thee, through the whole continuance of Thy kingdom and the duration of the heaven of Thine omnipotence, I would still have failed to repay Thy manifold bestowals.

I implore Thee, O my Lord, by Thy name, the Ever-Abiding, and by Thy name which Thou didst ordain to be the most great Instrument binding Thee to Thy servants, to grant that I may flee for shelter to Thy door, and speak forth Thy praise. Write down, then, for me, in every world of Thine, that which will enable me to enter beneath Thy shadow and within the borders of Thy court.

Thou art, verily, the Almighty, the Most Bountiful, the Most Exalted, the Ever-Forgiving, the Most Generous.

LXXV

All-praise be to Thee, O Lord, my God! I know not how to sing Thy praise, how to describe Thy glory, how to call upon Thy Name. If I call upon Thee by Thy Name, the All-Possessing, I am compelled to recognize that He Who holdeth in His hand the immediate destinies of all created things is but a vassal dependent upon Thee, and is the creation of but a word proceeding from Thy mouth. And if I proclaim Thee by the name of Him Who is the All-Compelling, I readily discover that He is but a suppliant fallen upon the dust, awe-stricken by Thy dreadful might, Thy sovereignty and power. And if I attempt to describe Thee by glorifying the oneness of Thy Being, I soon realize that such a conception is but a notion which mine own fancy hath woven, and that Thou hast ever been immeasurably exalted above the vain imaginations which the hearts of men have devised.

The glory of Thy might beareth me witness! Whoso claimeth to have known Thee hath, by virtue of such a claim, testified to his own ignorance; and whoso believeth himself to have attained unto Thee, all the atoms of the earth would attest his powerlessness and proclaim his failure. Thou hast, however, by virtue of Thy mercy that hath surpassed the kingdoms of earth and heaven, deigned to accept from Thy servants the laud and honor they pay to Thine own exalted Self, and hast bidden them celebrate Thy glory, that the ensigns of Thy guidance may be unfurled in Thy cities and the tokens of Thy mercy be spread abroad among Thy nations, and that each and all may be enabled to attain unto that which Thou hast destined for them by Thy decree, and ordained unto them through Thine irrevocable will and purpose.

Having testified, therefore, unto mine own impotence and the impotence of Thy servants, I beseech Thee, by the brightness of the light of Thy beauty, not to refuse Thy creatures attainment to the shores of Thy most holy ocean. Draw them, then, O my God, through the Divine sweetness of Thy melodies, towards the throne of Thy glory and the seat of Thine eternal holiness. Thou art, verily, the Most Powerful, the Supreme Ruler, the Great Giver, the Most Exalted, the Ever-Desired.

Grant, then, O my God, that Thy servant who hath turned towards Thee, hath fixed his gaze upon Thee, and clung to the cord of Thy mercifulness and favor, may be enabled to partake of the living waters of Thy mercy and grace. Cause him, then, to ascend unto the heights to which he aspireth, and withhold him not from that which Thou dost possess. Thou art, verily, the Ever-Forgiving, the Most Bountiful.

LXXVI

Praised be Thou, O Lord my God! Every time I attempt to make mention of Thee, I am hindered by the sublimity of Thy station and the overpowering greatness of Thy might. For were I to praise Thee throughout the length of Thy dominion and the duration of Thy sovereignty, I would find that my praise of Thee can befit only such as are like unto me, who are themselves Thy creatures, and who have been generated through the power of Thy decree and been fashioned through the potency of Thy will. And at whatever time my pen ascribeth glory to any one of Thy names, methinks I can hear the voice of its lamentation in its remoteness from Thee, and can recognize its cry because of its separation from Thy Self. I testify that everything other than Thee is but Thy creation and is held in the hollow of Thy hand. To have accepted any act or praise from Thy creatures is but an evidence of the wonders of Thy grace and bountiful favors, and a manifestation of Thy generosity and providence.

I entreat Thee, O my Lord, by Thy Most Great Name whereby Thou didst separate light from fire, and truth from denial, to send down upon me and upon such of my loved ones as are in my company the good of this world and of the next. Supply us, then, with Thy wondrous gifts that are hid from the eyes of men. Thou art, verily, the Fashioner of all creation. No God is there but Thee, the Almighty, the All-Glorious, the Most High.

LXXVII

O Thou, at Whose dreadful majesty all things have trembled, in Whose grasp are the affairs of all men, towards Whose grace and mercy are set the faces of all Thy creatures! I entreat Thee, by Thy Name which Thou hast ordained to be the spirit of all names that are in the kingdom of names, to shield us from the whisperings of those who have turned away from Thee, and have repudiated the truth of Thy most august and most exalted Self, in this Revelation that hath caused the kingdom of Thy names to tremble.

I am one of Thy handmaidens, O my Lord! I have turned my face towards the sanctuary of Thy gracious favors and the adored tabernacle of Thy glory. Purify me of all that is not of Thee, and strengthen me to love Thee and to fulfill Thy pleasure, that I may delight myself in the contemplation of Thy beauty, and be rid of all attachment to any of Thy creatures, and may, at every moment, proclaim: "Magnified be God, the Lord of the worlds!"

Let my food, O my Lord, be Thy beauty, and my drink the light of Thy presence, and my hope Thy

pleasure, and my work Thy praise, and my companion Thy remembrance, and my aid Thy sovereignty, and my dwelling-place Thy habitation, and my home the seat which Thou hast exalted above the limitations of them that are shut out as by a veil from Thee.

Thou art, in truth, the God of power, of strength and glory.

LXXVIII

Praised be Thou, O Lord my God! Every time I am reminded of Thee and muse on Thy virtues, I am seized with such ecstasies and am so enravished by Thee that I find myself unable to make mention of Thy name and to extol Thee. I am carried back to such heights that I recognize my self to be the same as the remembrance of Thee in Thy realm, and the essence of Thy praise among Thy servants. As long as that self endureth, so long will Thy praise continue to be shed abroad among Thy creatures and Thy remembrance glorified by Thy people.

Every man endued with insight among Thy servants is persuaded that my self liveth eternally and can never perish, inasmuch as remembrance of Thee is eternal and will endure so long as Thine own Self endureth, and Thy praise is everlasting and will last as long as Thine own sovereignty will last. By its means

Thou art glorified by such of Thy chosen ones as call upon Thee and by the sincere among Thy servants. Nay, the praise wherewith any one, in the entire creation, praiseth Thee proceedeth from this exalted self and returneth unto it, even as the sun which, while it shineth, sheddeth its splendor upon whatsoever may be exposed to its rays. From this sun is generated, and unto it must return, the light which is shed over all things.

Exalted, immeasurably exalted art Thou above any attempt to measure the greatness of Thy Cause, above any comparison that one may seek to make, above the efforts of the human tongue to utter its import! From everlasting Thou hast existed, alone with no one else beside Thee, and wilt, to everlasting, continue to remain the same, in the sublimity of Thine essence and the inaccessible heights of Thy glory.

And when Thou didst purpose to make Thyself known unto men, Thou didst successively reveal the Manifestations of Thy Cause, and ordained each to be a sign of Thy Revelation among Thy people, and the Day-Spring of Thine invisible Self amidst Thy creatures, until the time when, as decreed by Thee, all Thy previous Revelations culminated in Him Whom Thou hast appointed as the Lord of all who are in the heaven of revelation and the kingdom of creation, Him Whom Thou hast established as the Sovereign Lord of all who are in the heavens and all who are on the earth. He it was Whom Thou hast determined to be the Herald of Thy Most Great

Revelation and the Announcer of Thy Most Ancient Splendor. In this Thou hadst no other purpose except to try them who have manifested Thy most excellent titles unto all who are in heaven and on earth. He it was Whom Thou hast commanded to establish His covenant with all created things.

And when Thy promise came to pass and the set time was fulfilled, He Who is the Possessor of all Names and Attributes was made manifest unto men. Thereupon all that were in the heavens and all that were on the earth were terror-stricken save those whom Thou didst keep under Thy protection and preserve within the shelter of Thy power and gracious providence. There befell Him, at the hands of such of Thy creatures as have transgressed against Thee, that which the tongue of no one of Thy servants can recount.

Look down, then, upon Him, O my God, with the eye of Thy tender mercy, and send down upon Him and upon those that love Him all the good Thou didst ordain in the heaven of Thy will and the Tablet of Thy decree. Aid them, then, with Thy succor, for Thou art, verily, the Almighty, the Most Exalted, the All-Glorious, the All-Compelling.

LXXIX

All glory be to Thee, O Lord my God! I bear witness for Thee to that whereto Thou Thyself didst bear witness for Thine own Self, ere the day Thou hadst created the creation or made mention thereof, that Thou art God, and that there is none other God beside Thee. From eternity Thou hast, in Thy transcendent oneness, been immeasurably exalted above Thy servants' conception of Thy unity, and wilt to eternity remain, in Thine unapproachable singleness, far above the praise of Thy creatures. No words that any one beside Thee may utter can ever beseem Thee, and no man's description except Thine own description can befit Thy nature. All who adore Thy unity have been sore perplexed to fathom the mystery of Thy oneness, and all have confessed their powerlessness to attain unto the comprehension of Thine essence and to scale the pinnacle of Thy knowledge. The mighty have all acknowledged their weakness, and the learned recognized their ignorance. They that are possessed of influence are as nothing when compared with the revelations of Thy stupendous sovereignty, and they who are exalted sink into oblivion when brought before the manifestations of Thy great glory. The radiance of the brightest luminaries is eclipsed by the effulgent splendors of Thy face, and the tongues of the most eloquent of speakers falter under the unrestrained effusions of Thy holy utterance, and

steadfastness

the foundations of the mightiest structures tremble
before the onrushing force of Thy compelling power.

Who is there, O my God, that can be deemed
worthy to be remembered when Thou art remembered, and where is he to be found who can be regarded as capable of hinting at Thy nature or worthy
of mention in the court of Thy transcendent oneness?
From everlasting Thou hast been alone with no one
else beside Thee, and to everlasting Thou wilt continue to be one and the same. No God is there beside
Thee, the God of power, of glory and wisdom.

Glorified be Thy name, O Lord my God! I beseech Thee by Him Who is Thine exalted and supreme
Remembrance, Whom Thou hast sent down unto all
Thy creatures and invested with Thy name, the All-
Glorious, Whose will Thou hast ordained to be Thine
own will, Whose self Thou hast decreed to be the
revealer of Thine own Self, and His essence the Day-
Spring of Thy wisdom, and His heart the treasury of
Thine inspiration, and His breast the dawning-place
of Thy most excellent attributes and most exalted
titles, and His tongue the fountain-head of the waters
of Thy praise and the well-spring of the soft-flowing
streams of Thy wisdom, to send down upon us that
which will enable us to dispense with all else except
Thee, and will cause us to direct our steps towards
the sanctuary of Thy pleasure and to aspire after the
things Thou didst ordain for us according to Thine
irrevocable decree. Empower us, then, O my God,
to forsake ourselves and cleave steadfastly to Him

Who is the Manifestation of Thy Self, the Most Exalted, the Most High. Supply us also with that which is best for us, and write us down with such of Thy servants as have repudiated the Idol (Mírzá Yaḥyá), and firmly believed in Thee, and been so established on the throne of certitude that the whisperings of the Evil One have been powerless to hinder them from turning their faces towards Thy name, the All-Merciful.

Powerful art Thou to do what Thou pleasest and to ordain what Thou willest. No God is there but Thee, the All-Possessing, the All-Highest, the Almighty, the All-Bountiful, the All-Knowing, the All-Wise.

LXXX

O Thou Whose remembrance is the delight of the souls of all them that yearn after Thee, Whose name is the exultation of the hearts of all who are wholly devoted to Thy will, Whose praise is cherished by such as have drawn nigh unto Thy court, Whose face is the ardent desire of all them that have recognized Thy truth, Whose trial is the healer of the sicknesses of them who have embraced Thy Cause, Whose calamity is the highest aspiration of such as are rid of all attachment to any one but Thyself!

Glorified, immeasurably glorified art Thou, in

Whose hands is the empire of whatsoever is in the heavens and whatsoever is on earth, Thou, Who through but one word of Thy mouth, caused all things to expire and dissolve asunder, and Who, by yet another word, caused whatever had been separated to be combined and reunited! Magnified be Thy name, O Thou Who hast power over all that are in the heavens and all that are on earth, Whose dominion embraceth whatsoever is in the heaven of Thy Revelation and the kingdom of Thy creation. None can equal Thee in Thy created realms; none can compare with Thee in the universe Thou hast fashioned. The mind of no one hath comprehended Thee, and the aspiration of no soul hath reached Thee. I swear by Thy might! Were any one to soar, on whatever wings, as long as Thine own Being endureth, throughout the immensity of Thy knowledge, he would still be powerless to transgress the bounds which the contingent world hath set for him. How can, then, such a man aspire to wing his flight into the atmosphere of Thy most exalted presence?

He, indeed, is endued with understanding who acknowledgeth his powerlessness and confesseth his sinfulness, for should any created thing lay claim to any existence, when confronted with the infinite wonders of Thy Revelation, so blasphemous a pretension would be more heinous than any other crime in all the domains of Thine invention and creation. Who is there, O my Lord, that, when Thou revealest the first glimmerings of the signs of Thy transcendent sovereignty and might, hath the power to claim for himself any existence whatever? Existence itself is as nothing when brought face to face with the mighty and manifold wonders of Thine incomparable Self.

Far, immeasurably far, art Thou exalted above all things, O Thou Who art the King of Kings! I entreat Thee by Thy Self and by Them Who are the Manifestations of Thy Cause and the Day-Springs of Thine authority to write down for us that which Thou hast written down for Thy chosen ones. Withhold not from us that which Thou didst ordain for Thy loved ones, who, as soon as Thy call reached them, hastened unto Thee, and when the splendors of the light of Thy countenance were shed upon them, instantly prostrated themselves in adoration before Thy face.

We are Thy servants, O my Lord, and in the grasp of Thy power. If Thou chastisest us with the chastisement inflicted upon the former and the latter generations, Thy verdict would be assuredly just and Thine act praiseworthy. Powerful art Thou to do what pleaseth Thee. None other God is there beside Thee, the Almighty, the All-Glorious, the Help in Peril, the Self-Subsisting.

LXXXI

Unto Thee be praise, O Thou Who inclinest Thine ear to the sighing of them that have rid themselves of all attachment to any one but Thee, and Who hearest the voice of the lamentation of those who are wholly devoted to Thy Self! Thou beholdest all that hath befallen them at the hands of such of Thy creatures as have transgressed and rebelled against Thee. Thy might beareth me witness, O Thou Who art the King of the realms of justice and the Ruler of the cities of mercy! The tribulations they have been made to suffer are such as no pen, in the entire creation, can reckon. Should any one attempt to make mention of them, he would find himself powerless to describe them.

As these tribulations, however, were sustained in Thy path and for love of Thee, they who were afflicted by them render thanks, under all conditions, unto Thee, and say: "O Thou Who art the Delight of our hearts and the Object of our adoration! Were the clouds of Thy decree to rain down upon us the darts of affliction, we would, in our love for Thee, refuse to be impatient. We would yield Thee praise and thanksgiving, for we have recognized and are persuaded that Thou hast ordained only that which will be best for us. If our bodies be, at times, weighed down by our troubles, yet our souls rejoice with exceeding gladness. We swear by Thy might, O Thou

Who art the Desire of our hearts and the Exultation
of our souls! Every trouble that toucheth us in our
love for Thee is an evidence of Thy tender mercy,
every fiery ordeal a sign of the brightness of Thy
light, every woeful tribulation a cooling draught,
every toil a blissful repose, every anguish a fountain
of gladness."

Whosoever, O my Lord, is impatient in the tribulations befalling him in Thy path, hath not drunk
of the cup of Thy love nor tasted of the sweetness
of Thy remembrance. I implore Thee, by Him Who
is the King of all names and their Sovereign, Who is
the Revealer of all attributes and their Creator, and
by them who have soared aloft and drawn nigh unto
Thee and winged their flight into the atmosphere of
Thy presence, and have endured the galling of chains
for Thy sake, to grant that all Thy people may be
graciously aided to recognize Him Who is the Manifestation of Thine own Self, Who, because He summoned mankind unto Thee, hath been exiled and
cast into prison.

The tenderness of Thy mercy, O my Lord, sur-
passeth the fury of Thy wrath, and Thy loving-kindness exceedeth Thy hot displeasure, and Thy grace
excelleth Thy justice. Hold Thou, through Thy wondrous favors and mercies, the hands of Thy creatures,
and suffer them not to be separated from the grace
which Thou hast ordained as the means whereby they
can recognize Thee. The glory of Thy might beareth
me witness! Were such a thing to happen, every

soul would be sore shaken, every man endued with understanding would be bewildered, and every possessor of knowledge would be dumbfounded, except those who have been succored through the hands of Thy Cause, and have been made the recipients of the revelations of Thy grace and of the tokens of Thy favors.

I swear by Thy might, O my God! Wert Thou to regard Thy servants according to their deserts in Thy days, they would assuredly merit naught except Thy chastisement and torment. Thou art, however, the One Who is of great bounteousness, Whose grace is immense. Look not down upon them, O my God, with the glance of Thy justice, but rather with the eyes of Thy tender compassions and mercies. Do, then, with them according to what beseemeth Thy generosity and bountiful favor. Potent art Thou to do whatsoever may please Thee. Incomparable art Thou. No God is there beside Thee, the Lord of the throne on high and of earth below, the Ruler of this world and of the world to come. Thou art the God of Bounty, the Ever-Forgiving, the Great Giver, the Most Generous.

Do Thou bless, O Lord my God, the One through Whom the mysteries of Thine omnipotence have been disclosed, through Whom the revelations of Thy divinity have been glorified, through Whom the goodly pearls of Thy knowledge and wisdom have been uncovered, through Whom Thy signs and tokens have been noised abroad, through Whom Thy word hath been set forth with clearness, through Whom the light of Thy countenance hath shone forth and the power of Thy sovereignty been established. Bless Thou all those also who, wholly for Thy sake, have turned towards Thee. Send down, moreover, upon Him and them such of Thy wondrous mercies as may well beseem Thy highness. Thou art, verily, the Almighty, the Help in Peril, the All-Glorious, the Self-Subsisting.

LXXXII

Praised be Thou, O Lord my God! Thou art He Who hath created all things through a word uttered by Thy behest, and fashioned the entire creation through the power of Thy sovereignty and might. The mightiest of men are abased before the revelations of Thy glory, and they who are endued with strength tremble when faced with the evidences of Thy might. Every man of insight is bereft of vision when confronted with the effulgence of the glory of Thy face, and he who is possessed of riches is poor and desolate when beholding the plenteousness of Thy wealth.

I implore Thee by Thine All-Glorious Name, wherewith Thou didst adorn all the denizens of the kingdom of Thy revelation and the inmates of the heaven of Thy will, to grant that my soul may be attracted by the sweetness of the melody of the Bird of Heaven that chanteth amidst the branches of the tree of Thy decree that Thou art God, that there is none other God beside Thee.

Cleanse me with the waters of Thy mercy, O my Lord, and make me wholly Thine, and cause me to approach the Tabernacle of Thy Cause and the adored Sanctuary of Thy Presence. Ordain, then, for me all the things Thou didst ordain for the chosen ones among Thy handmaidens, and rain down upon me that which will illuminate my face and enlighten my heart.

Thou hast power to do what Thou willest, and Thou ordainest what Thou pleasest.

LXXXIII

Praised be Thou, O Lord my God! Thou seest my poverty and my misery, my troubles and my needs, my utter helplessness and my extreme lowliness, my lamentations and my bitter wailing, the anguish of my soul and the afflictions which beset me. The power of Thy might beareth me witness! Such is the depth of mine abasement that Thy servants who have strayed far from Thy path deride me. Thou knowest that I am recognized as the bearer of Thy name among Thy creatures. Thou knowest that my station is but an image of Thy station, that my virtues recount

Thy virtues, that within mine inmost being naught can be found except the revelations of Thy signs, and that my very essence is but a reflection of the evidences of Thy unity.

All these things Thou hast noised abroad among Thy creatures, in such wise that none can recognize me, except as one who beareth Thy name. I swear by Thy glory! My lamentations are not for the things which have befallen me in Thy path, but are due to my recognition that by reason of mine abasement the hearts of them that love Thee have been sore shaken, and the souls of Thine adversaries have been so filled with joy that they rejoice over those who have detached themselves from all except Thee and have hastened towards the river of Thy remembrance and praise. So great is their waywardness that when meeting Thy loved ones, they shake their heads in derision of Thy Cause and say: "Where is your Lord Whom ye mention in the daytime and in the night season? Where is He to be found Whom ye call your Sovereign, to Whom ye summon all men to turn?" Their pride and haughtiness waxed greater and greater until they denied the power of Thy might and rejected Thy sovereignty and dominion.

Thy glory beareth me witness! I delight in mine own afflictions and in the afflictions which they who love me suffer in Thy path. Neither I nor they, however, are able to bear such affronts and reproaches as are uttered by Thine enemies against Thy Self, the Unrestrained. How long shalt Thou remain seated,

O my God, on the throne of Thy forbearance and patience? Speak Thou Thy word of wrath, O Thou Whom no eyes can see! Well-beloved is Thy mercy unto the sincere among Thy servants, and well-beseeming Thy chastisement of the infidels among Thine enemies. Send down upon them, therefore, O my Lord, that which will unmistakably reveal unto them the fury of Thy wrath and the ascendancy of Thy power, and will enable them to recognize the weight of Thy might and the greatness of Thy strength. If Thou refusest, O my God, to aid them that love Thee, assist Thou, then, Thine own Self and Him Who is Thy Remembrance.

I entreat Thee by Thy name, that hath caused the ocean of Thy wrath to surge, to chastise them who have repudiated Thy truth and disowned Thine utterances. Abase them, then, by Thy might and power, and exalt such as have, wholly for Thy sake, set their faces towards Thee, that through them the ensigns of Thy glorification may be unfurled among all nations, and Thy tokens be spread abroad among all peoples, and that all may testify that Thou art God, that there is none other God beside Thee, the God of power, of majesty and glory.

LXXXIV

Magnified art Thou, O Lord my God! I ask Thee by Thy Name which Thou hast set up above all other names, through which the veil of heaven hath been split asunder and the Day-Star of Thy beauty hath risen above the horizon, shining with the brightness of Thy Name, the Exalted, the Most High, to succor me with Thy wondrous help and to preserve me in the shelter of Thy care and protection.

I am one of Thy handmaidens, O my Lord! Unto Thee have I turned, and in Thee have I placed my trust. Grant that I may be so confirmed in my love for Thee, and in fulfilling that which is well-pleasing unto Thee, that neither the defection of the infidels among Thy people, nor the clamor of the hypocrites among Thy creatures, may avail to keep me back from Thee.

Purge Thou mine ear, O my Lord, that I may hearken unto the verses sent down unto Thee, and illuminate my heart with the light of Thy knowledge, and loose my tongue that it may make mention of Thee and sing Thy praise. By Thy might, O my God! My soul is wedded to none beside Thee, and my heart seeketh none except Thine own Self.

No God is there beside Thee, the All-Glorious, the Great Giver, the Forgiving, the Compassionate.

LXXXV

These are, O my God, the days whereon Thou didst enjoin Thy servants to observe the fast. With it Thou didst adorn the preamble of the Book of Thy Laws revealed unto Thy creatures, and didst deck forth the Repositories of Thy commandments in the sight of all who are in Thy heaven and all who are on Thy earth. Thou hast endowed every hour of these days with a special virtue, inscrutable to all except Thee, Whose knowledge embraceth all created things. Thou hast, also, assigned unto every soul a portion of this virtue in accordance with the Tablet of Thy decree and the Scriptures of Thine irrevocable judgment. Every leaf of these Books and Scriptures Thou hast, moreover, allotted to each one of the peoples and kindreds of the earth.

For Thine ardent lovers Thou hast, according to Thy decree, reserved, at each daybreak, the cup of Thy remembrance, O Thou Who art the Ruler of rulers! These are they who have been so inebriated with the wine of Thy manifold wisdom that they forsake their couches in their longing to celebrate Thy praise and extol Thy virtues, and flee from sleep in their eagerness to approach Thy presence and partake of Thy bounty. Their eyes have, at all times, been bent upon the Day-Spring of Thy loving-kindness, and their faces set towards the Fountain-Head of Thine inspiration. Rain down, then, upon us and

upon them from the clouds of Thy mercy what beseemeth the heaven of Thy bounteousness and grace.

Lauded be Thy name, O my God! This is the hour
when Thou hast unlocked the doors of Thy bounty
before the faces of Thy creatures, and opened wide the
portals of Thy tender mercy unto all the dwellers of
Thine earth. I beseech Thee, by all them whose blood
was shed in Thy path, who, in their yearning over
Thee, rid themselves from all attachment to any of
Thy creatures, and who were so carried away by the
sweet savors of Thine inspiration that every single
member of their bodies intoned Thy praise and
vibrated to Thy remembrance, not to withhold from
us the things Thou hast irrevocably ordained in this
Revelation—a Revelation the potency of which hath
caused every tree to cry out what the Burning Bush
had aforetime proclaimed unto Moses, Who conversed
with Thee, a Revelation that hath enabled every least
pebble to resound again with Thy praise, as the stones
glorified Thee in the days of Muḥammad, Thy Friend.

These are the ones, O my God, whom Thou hast
graciously enabled to have fellowship with Thee and
to commune with Him Who is the Revealer of Thyself. The winds of Thy will have scattered them
abroad until Thou didst gather them together beneath
Thy shadow, and didst cause them to enter into the
precincts of Thy court. Now that Thou hast made
them to abide under the shade of the canopy of Thy
mercy, do Thou assist them to attain what must befit
so august a station. Suffer them not, O my Lord, to

be numbered with them who, though enjoying near access to Thee, have been kept back from recognizing Thy face, and who, though meeting with Thee, are deprived of Thy presence.

These are Thy servants, O my Lord, who have entered with Thee in this, the Most Great Prison, who have kept the fast within its walls according to what Thou hadst commanded them in the Tablets of Thy decree and the Books of Thy behest. Send down, therefore, upon them what will thoroughly purge them of all Thou abhorrest, that they may be wholly devoted to Thee, and may detach themselves entirely from all except Thyself.

Rain down, then, upon us, O my God, that which beseemeth Thy grace and befitteth Thy bounty. Enable us, then, O my God, to live in remembrance of Thee and to die in love of Thee, and supply us with the gift of Thy presence in Thy worlds here-after—worlds which are inscrutable to all except Thee. Thou art our Lord and the Lord of all worlds, and the God of all that are in heaven and all that are on earth.

Thou beholdest, O my God, what hath befallen Thy dear ones in Thy days. Thy glory beareth me witness! The voice of the lamentation of Thy chosen ones hath been lifted up throughout Thy realm. Some were ensnared by the infidels in Thy land, and were hindered by them from having near access to Thee and from attaining the court of Thy glory. Others were able to approach Thee, but were kept back from beholding Thy face. Still others were permitted, in their eagerness to look upon Thee, to enter the precincts of Thy court, but they allowed the veils of the imaginations of Thy creatures and the wrongs inflicted by the oppressors among Thy people to come in between them and Thee.

This is the hour, O my Lord, which Thou hast caused to excel every other hour, and hast related it to the choicest among Thy creatures. I beseech Thee, O my God, by Thy Self and by them, to ordain in the course of this year what shall exalt Thy loved ones. Do Thou, moreover, decree within this year what will enable the Day-Star of Thy power to shine brightly above the horizon of Thy glory, and to illuminate, by Thy sovereign might, the whole world.

Render Thy Cause victorious, O my Lord, and abase Thou Thine enemies. Write down, then, for us the good of this life and of the life to come. Thou art the Truth, Who knoweth the secret things. No God is there but Thee, the Ever-Forgiving, the All-Bountiful.

LXXXVI

Glorified art Thou, O Lord my God! I yield Thee thanks for that Thou hast made me the target of divers tribulations and the mark of manifold trials,

steadfastness

in order that Thy servants may be endued with new life and all Thy creatures may be quickened.

I swear by Thy glory, O Thou the Best Beloved of the worlds and the Desire of all such as have recognized Thee! The one reason I wish to live is that I may reveal Thy Cause, and I seek the continuance of life only that I may be touched by adversity in Thy path.

I implore Thee, O Thou by Whose summons the hearts of all them who were nigh unto Thee have soared into the atmosphere of Thy presence, to send down upon Thy loved ones what will enable them to dispense with all else except Thee. Endue them, then, with such constancy that they will arise to proclaim Thy Cause, and will call on Thy name, before all that are in Thy heaven and on Thy earth, in such wise that the Pharaohic cruelties inflicted by the oppressors among Thy servants will not succeed in keeping them back from Thee.

detachment

Thou art, verily, the God of power, the God of glory, the God of strength and wisdom.

LXXXVII

Magnified be Thy name, O Lord my God! Behold Thou mine eye expectant to gaze on the wonders of Thy mercy, and mine ear longing to hearken unto

Thy sweet melodies, and my heart yearning for the living waters of Thy knowledge. Thou seest Thy handmaiden, O my God, standing before the habitation of Thy mercy, and calling upon Thee by Thy name which Thou hast chosen above all other names and set up over all that are in heaven and on earth. Send down upon her the breaths of Thy mercy, that she may be carried away wholly from herself, and be drawn entirely towards the seat which, resplendent with the glory of Thy face, sheddeth afar the radiance of Thy sovereignty, and is established as Thy throne. Potent art Thou to do what Thou willest. No God is there beside Thee, the All-Glorious, the Most Bountiful.

Cast not out, I entreat Thee, O my Lord, them that have sought Thee, and turn not away such as have directed their steps towards Thee, and deprive not of Thy grace all that love Thee. Thou art He, O my Lord, Who hath called Himself the God of Mercy, the Most Compassionate. Have mercy, then, upon Thy handmaiden who hath sought Thy shelter, and set her face towards Thee.

Thou art, verily, the Ever-Forgiving, the Most Merciful.

LXXXVIII

Lauded be Thy name, O my God! I testify that no thought of Thee, howsoever wondrous, can ever ascend into the heaven of Thy knowledge, and no praise of Thee, no matter how transcendent, can soar up to the atmosphere of Thy wisdom. From eternity Thou hast been removed far above the reach and the ken of the comprehension of Thy servants, and immeasurably exalted above the strivings of Thy bond-slaves to express Thy mystery. What power can the shadowy creature claim to possess when face to face with Him Who is the Uncreated?

I bear witness that the highest thoughts of all such as adore Thy unity, and the profoundest contemplations of all them that have recognized Thee, are but the product of what hath been generated through the movement of the Pen of Thy behest, and hath been begotten by Thy will. I swear by Thy glory, O Thou Who art the Beloved of my soul and the Fountain of my life! I am persuaded of my powerlessness to describe and extol Thee in a manner that becometh the greatness of Thy glory and the excellence of Thy majesty. Aware as I am of this, I beseech Thee, by Thy mercy that hath surpassed all created things, and Thy grace that hath embraced the entire creation, to accept from Thy servants what they are capable of showing forth in Thy path. Aid them, then, by

Thy strengthening grace, to exalt Thy word and to blazon Thy praise.

Powerful art Thou to do what pleaseth Thee. Thou, truly, art the All-Glorious, the All-Wise.

LXXXIX

I know not, O my God, what the Fire is with which Thou didst light the Lamp of Thy Cause, or what the Glass wherewith Thou didst preserve it from Thine enemies. By Thy might! I marvel at the wonders of Thy Revelation, and at the tokens of Thy glory. I recognize, O Thou Who art my heart's Desire, that were fire to be touched by water it would instantly be extinguished, whereas the Fire which Thou didst kindle can never go out, though all the seas of the earth be poured upon it. Should water at any time touch it, the hands of Thy power would, as decreed in Thy Tablets, transmute that water into a fuel that would feed its flame.

I, likewise, recognize, O my God, that every lamp, when exposed to the fury of the winds, must cease from burning. As to Thy Lamp, however, O Beloved of the worlds, I cannot think what power except Thy power could have kept it safe for so many years from the tempests that have continually been directed upon it by the rebellious among Thy creatures.

I swear by Thy glory, O my God! Thy Lamp which Thou didst light within the tabernacle of man crieth out to Thee and saith: "O Thou the one alone Beloved! How long wilt Thou forsake me? Lift me up to Thee, I pray Thee. Though this wish of mine be the wish of a human creature, yet Thou knowest that my true wish is to sacrifice myself in Thy path. Thou art He Who hath made my desire to be the same as Thy desire, and my will the same as Thy will. Do Thou preserve Thy loved ones, I beseech Thee, in the shelter of Thy shadowing mercy which transcendeth all things, that haply the sufferings they bear may not deter them from turning in the direction of Thy name, the All-Glorious, the Most Bountiful."

XC

Glorified art Thou, O my God! Thou knowest that in my love for Thee I have not sought any rest, that in proclaiming Thy Cause I have denied myself every manner of tranquillity, and that in the observance of whatever Thou hast prescribed in Thy Tablets I have not delayed to do Thy bidding. I have, for this reason, suffered what no man among all the inhabitants of Thy realm hath suffered.

Thy glory beareth me witness! Nothing whatsoever can withhold me from remembering Thee, though all the tribulations of the earth were to assault me from every direction. All the limbs and members of my body proclaim their readiness to be torn asunder in Thy path and for the sake of Thy pleasure, and they yearn to be scattered in the dust before Thee. O would that they who serve Thee could taste what I have tasted of the sweetness of Thy love!

I implore Thee to supply whosoever hath sought Thee with the living waters of Thy bounty, that they may rid him of all attachment to any one but Thee. Thou art, verily, the Omniscient, the All-Glorious, the Almighty.

XCI

Lauded be Thy name, O Lord my God! How great is Thy might and Thy sovereignty; how vast Thy strength and Thy dominion! Thou hast called into being Him Who speaketh in Thy name before all who are in Thy heaven and on Thy earth, and hast bidden Him cry out amongst Thy creatures.

No sooner had a word gone forth from His lips, however, than the divines among Thy people turned back from Him, and the learned among Thy servants caviled at His signs. Thereby the fire of oppression was kindled in Thy land, until the kings themselves rose up to put out Thy light, O Thou Who art the King of kings!

Hostility waxed so intense that my kindred and my loved ones were made captives in Thy land, and they that are dear to Thee were hindered from gazing on Thy beauty and from turning in the direction of Thy mercy. This hostility failed to cause the fire that burned within them to subside. The enemy finally carried away as captive Him Who is the Manifestation of Thy beauty and the Revealer of Thy signs, and confined Him in the fortress-town of 'Akká, and sought to hinder Him from remembering Thee and from magnifying Thy name. Thy servant, however, could not be restrained from carrying out what Thou hadst bidden Him fulfill. Above the horizon of tribulation He hath lifted up His voice and He crieth out, summoning all the inmates of heaven and all the inhabitants of the earth to the immensity of Thy mercy and the court of Thy grace. Day and night He sendeth down the signs of Thine omnipotent power and revealeth the clear tokens of Thy majesty, so that the souls of Thy creatures may be drawn towards Thee, that they may forsake themselves and turn unto Thee, and may flee from their misery and seek the tabernacle of Thy riches, and may haste away from their wretchedness into the court of Thy majesty and glory.

This is the Lamp which the light of Thine own Essence hath lit, and whose radiance the winds of discord can never extinguish. This is the Ocean that moveth by the power of Thy sovereign might, and whose waves the influence of the infidels that have disbelieved in the Judgment Day can never still. This is the Sun that shineth in the heaven of Thy will and the splendor of which the veils of the workers of iniquity and the doubts of the evil doers can never cloud.

I yield Thee thanks, O my God, for that Thou hast offered me up as a sacrifice in Thy path, and made me a target for the arrows of afflictions as a token of Thy love for Thy servants, and singled me out for all manner of tribulation for the regeneration of Thy people.

How sweet to my taste is the savor of woes sent by Thee, and how dear to my heart the dispositions of Thy providence! Perish the soul that fleeth from the threats of kings in its attempt to save itself in Thy days! I swear by Thy glory! Whoso hath quaffed the living waters of Thy favors can fear no trouble in Thy path, neither can he be deterred by any tribulation from remembering Thee or from celebrating Thy praise.

I beseech Thee, O Thou Who art my Governor and the Possessor of all names, to protect them that have branched out from me (Afnán), whom Thou hast caused to be related to Thyself, and to whom Thou hast, in this Revelation, shown Thy special favor, and whom Thou hast summoned to draw nigh unto Thee and to turn towards the horizon of Thy Revelation. Withhold not from them, O my Lord, the outpourings of Thy mercy or the effulgence of the Day-Star of Thy grace. Enable them to distinguish themselves amongst Thy people, that they may exalt Thy word and promote Thy Cause. Aid them, O my God, to do Thy will and pleasure.

No God is there but Thee, the All-Powerful, the Most Exalted, the Most High.

Station of Believers

trials

XCII

Glory to Thee, O my God! But for the tribulations which are sustained in Thy path, how could Thy true lovers be recognized; and were it not for the trials which are borne for love of Thee, how could the station of such as yearn for Thee be revealed? Thy might beareth me witness! The companions of all who adore Thee are the tears they shed, and the comforters of such as seek Thee are the groans they utter, and the food of them who haste to meet Thee is the fragments of their broken hearts.

Spiritual Sustenance

How sweet to my taste is the bitterness of death suffered in Thy path, and how precious in my estimation are the shafts of Thine enemies when encountered for the sake of the exaltation of Thy word! Let me quaff in Thy Cause, O my God, whatsoever Thou didst desire, and send down upon me in Thy love all Thou didst ordain. By Thy glory! I wish only what Thou wishest, and cherish what Thou cherishest. In

Thee have I, at all times, placed my whole trust and confidence.

Raise up, I implore Thee, O my God, as helpers to this Revelation such as shall be counted worthy of Thy name and of Thy sovereignty, that they may remember me among Thy creatures, and hoist the ensigns of Thy victory in Thy land.

Potent art Thou to do what pleaseth Thee. No God is there but Thee, the Help in Peril, the Self-Subsisting.

XCIII

Glory to Thee, O my God! One of Thy handmaidens, who hath believed in Thee and in Thy signs, hath entered beneath the shadow of the tree of Thy oneness. Give her to quaff, O my God, by Thy Name, the Manifest and the Hidden, of Thy choice sealed Wine that it may take her away from her own self, and make her to be entirely devoted to Thy remembrance, and wholly detached from any one beside Thee.

Now that Thou hast revealed unto her the knowledge of Thee, O my Lord, deny her not, by Thy bounty, Thy grace; and now that Thou hast called her unto Thyself, drive her not away from Thee, through Thy favor. Supply her, then, with that which excelleth all that can be found on Thine earth.

Thou art, verily, the Most Bountiful, Whose grace is immense.

Wert Thou to bestow on one of Thy creatures what would equal the kingdoms of earth and heaven, it would still not diminish by even as much as an atom the immensity of Thy dominion. Far greater art Thou than the Great One men are wont to call Thee, for such a title is but one of Thy names all of which were created by a mere indication of Thy will.

There is no God but Thee, the God of power, the God of glory, the God of knowledge and wisdom.

XCIV

The hearts that yearn after Thee, O my God, are burnt up with the fire of their longing for Thee, and the eyes of them that love Thee weep sore by reason of their crushing separation from Thy court, and the voice of the lamentation of such as have set their hopes on Thee hath gone forth throughout Thy dominions.

Thou hast Thyself, O my God, protected them, by Thy sovereign might, from both extremities. But for the burning of their souls and the sighing of their hearts, they would be drowned in the midst of their tears, and but for the flood of their tears they would be burnt up by the fire of their hearts and the heat of their souls. Methinks, they are like the angels which Thou hast created of snow and of fire. Wilt Thou, despite such vehement longing, O my God, debar them from Thy presence, or drive them away, notwithstanding such fervor, from the door of Thy mercy? All hope is ready to be extinguished in the hearts of Thy chosen ones, O my God! Where are the breezes of Thy grace? They are hemmed in on all sides by their enemies; where are the ensigns of Thy triumph which Thou didst promise in Thy Tablets?

Thy glory is my witness! At each daybreak they who love Thee wake to find the cup of woe set before their faces, because they have believed in Thee and acknowledged Thy signs. Though I firmly believe that Thou hast a greater compassion on them than they have on their own selves, though I recognize that Thou hast afflicted them for no other purpose except to proclaim Thy Cause, and to enable them to ascend into the heaven of Thine eternity and the precincts of Thy court, yet Thou knowest full well the frailty of some of them, and art aware of their impatience in their sufferings.

Help them through Thy strengthening grace, I beseech Thee, O my God, to suffer patiently in their love for Thee, and unveil to their eyes what Thou hast decreed for them behind the Tabernacle of Thine unfailing protection, so that they may rush forward to meet what is preordained for them in Thy path, and may vie in hasting after tribulation in their love *protection from dangers*

towards Thee. And if not, do Thou, then, reveal the standards of Thine ascendancy, and make them to be victorious over Thine adversaries, that Thy sovereignty may be manifested unto all the dwellers of Thy realm, and the power of Thy might demonstrated amidst Thy creatures. Powerful art Thou to do what Thou willest. No God is there but Thee, the Omniscient, the All-Wise.

Make steadfast Thou, O my God, Thy servant who hath believed in Thee to help Thy Cause, and keep him safe from all dangers in the stronghold of Thy care and Thy protection, both in this life and in the life which is to come. Thou, verily, rulest as Thou pleasest. No God is there save Thee, the Ever-Forgiving, the Most Generous.

assistance to promote the Faith   *victory over enemies*   *illumination*

XCV

Glorified art Thou, O Lord my God! Rain down, I beseech Thee, from the clouds of Thine overflowing grace, that which shall cleanse the hearts of Thy servants from whatever may prevent their beholding Thy face, or may prevent them from turning unto Thee, that they may all recognize Him Who is their Fashioner and Creator. Help them, then, O God, to reach forth, through the power of Thy sovereign might, towards such a station that they can readily distin-

guish every foul smell from the fragrance of the
raiment of Him Who is the Bearer of Thy most lofty
and exalted name, that they may turn with all their
affections toward Thee, and may enjoy such intimate
communion with Thee that if all that is in heaven
and on earth were given them they would regard it
as unworthy of their notice, and would refuse to
cease from remembering Thee and from extolling
Thy virtues. '

Shield, I pray Thee, O my Beloved, my heart's Desire, Thy servant who hath sought Thy face, from the
darts of them that have denied Thee and from the
shafts of such as have repudiated Thy Truth. Cause
him, then, to be wholly devoted to Thee, to declare
Thy name, and to fix his gaze upon the sanctuary of
Thy Revelation. Thou art, in truth, He Who, at no
time, hath turned away those who have set their hopes
in Thee from the door of Thy mercy, nor prevented
such as have sought Thee from attaining the court of
Thy grace. No God is there but Thee, the Most Powerful, the All-Highest, the Help in Peril, the All-
Glorious, the All-Compelling, the Unconditioned.

XCVI

Magnified, O Lord my God, be Thy Name, whereby the trees of the garden of Thy Revelation have

been clad with verdure, and been made to yield the fruits of holiness during this Springtime when the sweet savors of Thy favors and blessings have been wafted over all things, and caused them to bring forth whatsoever had been preordained for them in the Kingdom of Thine irrevocable decree and the Heaven of Thine immutable purpose. I beseech Thee by this very Name not to suffer me to be far from the court of Thy holiness, nor debarred from the exalted sanctuary of Thy unity and oneness.

Ignite, then, O my God, within my breast the fire of Thy love, that its flame may burn up all else except my remembrance of Thee, that every trace of corrupt desire may be entirely mortified within me, and that naught may remain except the glorification of Thy transcendent and all-glorious Being. This is my highest aspiration, mine ardent desire, O Thou Who rulest all things, and in Whose hand is the kingdom of the entire creation. Thou, verily, doest what Thou choosest. No God is there beside Thee, the Almighty, the All-Glorious, the Ever-Forgiving.

XCVII

Praise be to Thee, O Lord my God! I implore Thee by Thy Name that hath caused to surge within every drop the oceans of Thy loving-kindness and mercy, and to shine within every atom the luminaries of Thy bountiful blessings and favors,—I implore Thee to adorn every soul with the ornament of Thy love, that none may remain on Thine earth who hath not turned towards Thee, or hath failed to detach himself from all except Thy Self.

Thou hast, verily, O my God, suffered Him Who is the Manifestation of Thine own Self to be afflicted with all manner of adversity in order that Thy servants may ascend unto the pinnacle of Thy gracious favor, and attain unto that which Thou hast, through Thy providence and tender mercies, ordained for them in the Tablets of Thine irrevocable decree. The glory of Thy might beareth me witness! Were they, every moment of their lives, to offer up themselves as a sacrifice in Thy path, they would still have done but little in comparison with the manifold bestowals vouchsafed unto them by Thee.

Grant, therefore, I beseech Thee, that their hearts may be inclined towards Thee, and that their faces may be turned in the direction of Thy good-pleasure. Powerful art Thou to do what Thou willest. No God is there but Thee, the Inaccessible, the All-Glorious, the Ever-Forgiving.

Deign, then, to accept, O my God, from Thy servant the things which he hath shown forth in his love for Thee. Fortify him, then, that he may cling to Thy most exalted Word, and to unloose his tongue to celebrate Thy praise, and cause him to be gathered unto such of Thy people as are nigh unto Thee. Thou art He within Whose grasp is the empire of all things. There is no God but Thee, the Almighty, the Help in Peril, the All-Glorious, the Unconstrained.

XCVIII

Magnified be Thy name, O Thou in Whose grasp are the reins of the souls of all them that have recognized Thee, and in Whose right hand are the destinies of all that are in heaven and all that are on earth! Thou doest, through the power of Thy might, what Thou willest, and ordainest, by an act of Thy volition, what Thou pleasest. The will of the most resolute of men is as nothing when compared with the compelling evidences of Thy will, and the determination of the most inflexible among Thy creatures is dissipated before the manifold revelations of Thy purpose.

Thou art He Who, through a word of Thy mouth, hath so enravished the hearts of Thy chosen ones that they have, in their love for Thee, detached themselves from all except Thyself, and laid down their lives and sacrificed their souls in Thy path, and borne, for Thy sake, what none of Thy creatures hath borne.

I am one of Thy handmaidens, O my Lord! I have turned my face towards the habitation of Thy mercy, and have sought the wonders of Thy manifold favors, inasmuch as all the members of my body proclaim Thee to be the All-Bounteous, He Whose grace is immense.

O Thou Whose face is the object of my adoration, Whose beauty is my sanctuary, Whose court is my goal, Whose remembrance is my wish, Whose affection is my solace, Whose love is my begetter, Whose praise is my companion, Whose nearness is my hope, Whose presence is my greatest longing and supreme aspiration! Disappoint me not, I entreat Thee, by withholding from me the things Thou didst ordain for the chosen ones among Thy handmaidens, and supply me with the good of this world and of the world to come.

Thou art, verily, the Lord of creation. No God is there beside Thee, the Ever-Forgiving, the Most Bountiful.

XCIX

Glorified art Thou, O Lord my God! I pray Thee, by Him Who is the Day-Spring of Thy signs and the Manifestation of Thy names, and the Treasury of Thine inspiration, and the Repository of Thy wisdom, to send upon Thy loved ones that which will enable them to cleave steadfastly to Thy Cause, and to recognize Thy unity, and to acknowledge Thy oneness, and to bear witness to Thy divinity. Raise them up, O my God, to such heights that they will recognize in all things the tokens of the power of Him Who is the Manifestation of Thy most august and all-glorious Self.

Thou art He, O my Lord, Who doeth what He willeth, and ordaineth what He pleaseth. Every possessor of power is forlorn before the revelations of Thy might, and every fountain of honor becomes abject when confronted by the manifold evidences of Thy great glory.

I beseech Thee, by Thyself and by whatsoever is of Thee, to grant that I may help Thy Cause and speak of Thy praise, and set my heart on the sanctuary of Thy glory, and detach myself from all that pertaineth not unto Thee. No God is there beside Thee, the God of power, the God of glory and wisdom.

C

Praised be Thou, O Lord my God! Thou beholdest my perplexity, and the depth of mine anguish, and the agony of my soul, and the afflictions which beset me. By Thy glory! My heart crieth to Thee by reason of the things that have befallen my loved ones in Thy path, and mine eyes run down with tears for them who, in these days, have ascended unto Thee, who have cast the world behind their backs, and set their faces towards the shores of Thy transcendent mercy.

Clothe them, O my God, with the robe of Thy favor and the raiment of Thy loving providence, which Thou hast reserved for Thine own Self and woven with the hands of Thy manifold bounties and gifts. Give them, then, to drink, from the hands of Thy loving-kindness, of the cups of Thy measureless mercy. Cause them, moreover, O my Best-Beloved, to abide within the precincts of Thy court and around Thy most effulgent Tabernacle. Powerful art Thou to do what pleaseth Thee.

And now I implore Thee, by the eternity of Thy Self, to enable me to be patient in these tribulations which have caused the Concourse on high to wail and the denizens of the everlasting Paradise to weep, and through which all faces have been covered with the tawny dust provoked by the anguish that hath seized such of Thy servants as have turned towards Thy Name, the Most Exalted, the Most High. No God is there but Thee, the Almighty, the Inaccessible, the Ever-Forgiving, the Most Compassionate.

All Thy servants, O my God, are occupied with their own selves, so great have been the troubles which, as decreed by Thee, have encompassed them on every side. My tongue, however, is busied in extolling Thy chosen ones, and my heart in remembering them that are dear to Thee and are wholly subject to Thy will.

mercy

forgiveness

Look not on my state, O my God, nor my failure to serve Thee, nay rather regard the oceans of Thy mercy and favors, and the things that beseem Thy glory and Thy forgiveness and befit Thy loving-kindness and bounties. Thou art, verily, the Ever-Forgiving, the Most Generous.

CI

trials

Praise be to Thee, O Lord my God! Thou beholdest what the tongue of no one except Thee can utter, and bearest witness unto things which no mouth can recount. The floods of afflictions are let loose, and the winds of Thy judgment have blown, and from the clouds rain down the darts of tests, and the heavens of Thy decree pour forth the arrows of trial.

Thou seest, O my Lord, how Thy servants, who have believed on Thee and acknowledged Thy signs, have fallen into the clutches of Thine enemies, how the doors of ease and comfort have been shut against them, how they languish in the Fortress wherein neither pleasantness nor hope can be found. They have suffered in Thy path what no man before them hath suffered. To this bear witness they who abide around Thy throne, and the dwellers of the earth, and the Concourse on high.

These, O my God, are Thy servants who, for love

of Thy beauty, have forsaken their homes, and been so stirred up by the gentle winds of their desire for Thee that they have sundered every tie in Thy path. Such of Thy servants as dwell in Thy land and have transgressed against Thee have assailed them, and banished them from Thy cities, and made them captives, and delivered them into the hands of workers of iniquity among Thy people and the perverse amidst the wicked doers in Thy realm. And finally, they were made to abide in this place with which no other place, however loathsome, in all Thy dominion, can compare. They were seized with such trials that the clouds weep over them and the thunder groaneth by reason of the manifold tribulations that have afflicted them in their love for Thee and for the sake of Thy pleasure.

Thou knowest full well, O my God, that there is no one on Thine earth who can claim to be related to Thee except these, some of whom have suffered martyrdom for Thy sake, while the rest have been permitted to survive. Though for such as are like unto us, O my God, it beseemeth not to claim to be related to Thee, inasmuch as our misdeeds and our waywardness have hindered us from reaching the depths of the ocean of Thy oneness, and from immersing ourselves beneath the waters of Thy transcendent mercy, yet our tongues, O my God, bear witness, and our hearts testify, and our limbs confess that Thy mercy hath enveloped all created things and Thy compassion surpassed all that are in heaven and all that are on earth.

I beseech Thee, by Thy Most Great Name, through
which all created things were rent asunder and the
whole creation was shaken, to send down from the
clouds of Thy mercy that which will purge them
from every ordeal and from whatever is hateful to
Thee. Raise them up, then, to such heights that no
amount of tribulation will keep them back from Thy
wondrous remembrance, nor any trouble hinder them
from turning toward the court of Thy transcendent
oneness.

By Thy might, O Well-Beloved of Bahá and His
heart's Desire! I myself cry out, under all conditions,
unto Thee saying: "Would I had, ere this day, drawn
nigh unto Thee!" When I hear, however, the sighs of
such of Thy people as are wholly devoted to Thee,
and those of Thy servants as enjoy near access to
Thy court, who have taken no other friend than
Thee, and sought no refuge except Thee, and have
chosen for themselves, in Thy path, what no man
hath chosen in the days of the Manifestations of Thy
transcendent unity and the Day-Springs of Thy most
holy sovereignty, then my heart is saddened and
my soul is vexed, and I cry to Thee, imploring Thee
to protect them, by Thy power that hath encompassed the entire creation both visible and invisible,
from whatsoever may be abhorrent to Thee. This is
not for their own sakes, but that Thy name may,
through them, abide amongst Thy servants, and
Thy remembrance may continue to endure in Thy
dominions.

Thou knowest, O my God, that all Thy servants have turned back from Thee and risen up against Thee. Thou knowest that Thou hast no one to obey Thee except them and such as have believed in Thy Revelation, through which the foundations of the entire universe have been shaken, and the souls of all men have trembled, and all that lay asleep were quickened. Thou art, O my God, the God of bounty, Whose grace is immense.

Send down, then, upon them that which will assure their hearts, and quiet their souls, and renew their spirits, and refresh their bodies. Thou art, verily, their Lord and the Lord of the worlds.

Praised be God, the Lord of all creation!

CII

Glory to Thee, O Thou Who art the Lord of all worlds, and the Beloved of all such as have recognized Thee! Thou seest me sitting under a sword hanging on a thread, and art well aware that in such a state I have not fallen short of my duty towards Thy Cause, nor failed to shed abroad Thy praise, and declare Thy virtues, and deliver all Thou hadst prescribed unto me in Thy Tablets. Though the sword be ready to fall on my head, I call Thy loved ones with such a calling that the hearts are carried away towards the horizon of Thy majesty and grandeur.

Purge out thoroughly their ears, O my Lord, that they may hearken unto the sweet melodies that have ascended from the right hand of the throne of Thy glory. I swear by Thy might! Were any one to attune his ears to their harmony he would soar up to the kingdom of Thy revelation, wherein every created thing proclaimeth that Thou art God, and that there is none other God save Thee, the Omnipotent, the Help in Peril, the Self-Subsisting. Cleanse Thou, O my God, the eyes of Thy servants, and so transport them by the sweetness of Thine utterances that calamities will be powerless to hinder them from turning unto Thee, and from directing their eyes towards the horizon of Thy Revelation.

Darkness hath encompassed every land, O my God, and caused most of Thy servants to tremble. I beseech Thee, by Thy Most Great Name, to raise in every city a new creation that shall turn towards Thee, and shall remember Thee amidst Thy servants, and shall unfurl by virtue of their utterances and wisdom the ensigns of Thy victory, and shall detach themselves from all created things.

Potent art Thou to do Thy pleasure. No God is there but Thee, the Most Powerful, He Whose help is implored by all men.

CIII

Glory be to Thee, Thou in Whose hand are the heaven of omnipotence and the kingdom of creation. Thou doest, by Thy sovereignty, what Thou willest, and ordainest, through the power of Thy might, what Thou pleasest. From eternity Thou hast been exalted above the praise of all created things, and wilt to eternity remain far above the glorification of any one of Thy creatures. Existence itself testifieth to its non-existence when face to face with the manifold revelations of Thy transcendent oneness, and every created thing confesseth, by its very nature, its nothingness when compared with the sacred splendors of the light of Thy unity. Thou hast, in Thyself, been independent of any one besides Thee and rich enough, in Thine own essence, to dispense with any one except Thy Self. Every description by which they who adore Thy unity describe Thee, and every praise wherewith they who are devoted unto Thee praise Thee, are but the traces of the pen which the fingers of Thy strength and power have set in motion—fingers whose movement is controlled by the arm of Thy decree—the arm itself animated by the potency of Thy might.

Thy glory beareth me witness! How can I, aware as I am of this truth, hope to befittingly make mention of Thee and celebrate Thy praise? Howsoever I describe Thee, whichever of Thy virtues I recount,

I cannot but blush and feel ashamed of what my tongue hath uttered or my pen written.

The quintessence of knowledge, O my Lord, proclaimeth its powerlessness to know Thee, and perplexity, in its very soul, confesseth its bewilderment in the face of the revelations of Thy sovereign might, and remembrance, in its inmost spirit, acknowledgeth its forgetfulness and effacement before the manifestations of Thy signs and the evidences of Thy praise. What, then, can this poor creature hope to achieve, and to what cord must this wretched soul cling?

I beseech Thee, O Thou Who art the Lord of the worlds, and the Beloved of such as have recognized Thee, and the Desire of all that are in heaven and on earth, by Thy Name through which the cry of every suppliant hath ascended into the heaven of Thy transcendent holiness, through which every seeker hath soared to the sublimities of Thy unity and grandeur, through which the imperfect have been perfected, and the abased exalted, and the tongue of every stammerer unloosed, and the sick made whole, and whatever was unworthy of Thy highness and beseemed not Thy greatness and Thy sovereignty made acceptable unto Thee,—I beseech Thee to aid us by Thine invisible hosts and by a company of the angels of Thy Cause. Do Thou, then, accept the works we have performed for love of Thee, and for the sake of Thy pleasure. Cast us not away, O my God, from the door of Thy mercy, and break not our hopes in the wonders of Thy grace and favors.

Our limbs, our members, O my Lord, bear witness to Thy unity and oneness. Send down upon us Thy strength and power, that we may become steadfast in Thy Faith and may aid Thee among Thy servants. Illumine our eyes, O my Lord, with the effulgence of Thy beauty, and enlighten our hearts with the splendors of Thy knowledge and wisdom. Write us up, then, with those who have fulfilled their pledge to Thy Covenant in Thy days, and who, through their love for Thee, have detached themselves from the world and all that is therein.

Powerful art Thou to do what Thou pleasest. No God is there beside Thee, the All-Powerful, the Omniscient, the Supreme Ruler, the Help in Peril, the Self-Subsisting.

CIV

O Thou Whose nearness is my wish, Whose presence is my hope, Whose remembrance is my desire, Whose court of glory is my goal, Whose abode is my aim, Whose name is my healing, Whose love is the radiance of my heart, Whose service is my highest aspiration! I beseech Thee by Thy Name, through which Thou hast enabled them that have recognized Thee to soar to the sublimest heights of the knowledge of Thee and empowered such as devoutly worship Thee to ascend into the precincts of the court of Thy holy favors, to aid me to turn my face towards Thy face, to fix mine eyes upon Thee, and to speak of Thy glory.

I am the one, O my Lord, who hath forgotten all else but Thee, and turned towards the Day-Spring of Thy grace, who hath forsaken all save Thyself in the hope of drawing nigh unto Thy court. Behold me, then, with mine eyes lifted up towards the Seat that shineth with the splendors of the light of Thy Face. Send down, then, upon me, O my Beloved, that which will enable me to be steadfast in Thy Cause, so that the doubts of the infidels may not hinder me from turning towards Thee.

Thou art, verily, the God of Power, the Help in Peril, the All-Glorious, the Almighty.

CV

Praised be Thou, O Lord my God! Thou art He the excellence of Whose glory hath exalted them who are the sources of authority and honor, the potency of Whose might hath empowered them who are the fountain-heads of energy and strength, the dominion of Whose will hath elevated the Exponents of Thy Cause above all that are in heaven and on earth, and the life-giving effusions of Whose Pen have quickened the souls of the denizens of the kingdom of creation.

I am he, O my Lord, who, wholly for Thy sake, hath turned his face unto Thee, and who, while acknowledging Thy power and Thy sovereignty, hath directed his steps towards Thy dearly-loved Sanctuary, and Thine adored and hallowed Court. In this state I have reached the City (Baghdád) wherein, in the full glory of Thy names, Thou didst reveal Thy Self unto all created things. In it I have communed with Thy loved ones, and from the House within its walls I have inhaled the breaths of Thy holiness and perceived the fragrances of Thy fellowship.

Cast me not from Thy presence, O my Lord, neither do Thou drive me away from the shores of Thy love and Thy good-pleasure. For the poor can find no refuge unless he knocketh at the door of Thy wealth, and the outcast can find no peace until he be admitted to the court of Thy favor.

Magnified be Thy name, O my Lord, for Thou hast enabled me to recognize the Manifestation of Thine own Self, and hast caused me to be assured of the truth of the verses which have descended upon Thee. Empower me, I implore Thee, to cling steadfastly unto whatsoever Thou hast bidden me observe. Help me to guard the pearls of Thy love which, by Thy decree, Thou hast enshrined within my heart. Send down, moreover, every moment of my life, O my God, that which will preserve me from any one but Thee, and will set my feet firm in Thy Cause.

Thou art, verily, the God of glory, the God of power, the God of knowledge and wisdom. No God is there beside Thee, the Great Giver, the All-Bountiful, the Almighty, the Ever-Forgiving.

Praised be God, the All-Glorious, the All-Compelling.

CVI

Glorified art Thou, O Lord my God! I give Thee thanks inasmuch as Thou hast called me into being in Thy days, and infused into me Thy love and Thy knowledge. I beseech Thee, by Thy name whereby the goodly pearls of Thy wisdom and Thine utterance were brought forth out of the treasuries of the hearts of such of Thy servants as are nigh unto Thee, and through which the Day-Star of Thy name, the Compassionate, hath shed its radiance upon all that are in Thy heaven and on Thy earth, to supply me, by Thy grace and bounty, with Thy wondrous and hidden bounties.

These are the earliest days of my life, O my God, which Thou hast linked with Thine own days. Now that Thou hast conferred upon me so great an honor, withhold not from me the things Thou hast ordained for Thy chosen ones.

I am, O my God, but a tiny seed which Thou hast sown in the soil of Thy love, and caused to spring forth by the hand of Thy bounty. This seed craveth, therefore, in its inmost being, for the waters of Thy mercy and the living fountain of Thy grace. Send down upon it, from the heaven of Thy loving-kindness, that which will enable it to flourish beneath Thy shadow and within the borders of Thy court. Thou art He Who watereth the hearts of all that have recognized Thee from Thy plenteous stream and the fountain of Thy living waters.

Praised be God, the Lord of the worlds.

CVII

I beseech Thee, O my Lord, by that Remembrance of Thee through which all things have been raised to life, and through which all faces have been made to shine, not to frustrate the hopes I have set on the things Thou dost possess. Cause me, then, by Thy mercy, to enter beneath Thy shadow that shadoweth all things.

Be Thou, O my Lord, my sole Desire, my Goal, mine only Hope, my constant Aim, my Habitation and my Sanctuary. Let the object of mine ardent quest be Thy most resplendent, Thine adorable, and ever-blessed Beauty. I implore Thee, O my Lord, by

whatsoever is of Thee, to send, from the right hand
of Thy might, that which will exalt Thy loved ones
and abase Thine enemies.

No God is there beside Thee, Thou alone art my
Beloved in this world and in the world which is to
come. Thou alone art the Desire of all them that have
recognized Thee.

Praised be God, the Lord of the worlds.

CVIII

Praised be Thou, O my God, that Thou hast been
true to what the Pen of Thy Revelation hath inscribed upon the Tablets sent down by Thee unto
Them Whom Thou hast chosen above all Thy creatures, and through Whom Thou hast unlocked the
doors of Thy mercy, and shed abroad the radiance
of the light of Thy guidance. Glory to Thee that
Thou hast laid bare what had from eternity been
wrapped up within the Tabernacle of Thy majesty,
Thine omnipotence and glory, and through which
Thou hadst decked forth the heaven of Thy Revelation and adorned the pages of the book of Thy
testimony.

And when the Pledge was fulfilled and the Promised One appeared, He was rejected by such of Thy
servants as profess to have believed in Him in Whom

Thy Godhead was manifested, Whom Thou didst ordain to be the Herald of this Revelation, and through Whose advent the eyes of the inmates of the sanctuary of Thy unity were cheered.

I know, O my Lord, neither their reasoning with which they have acknowledged Thee and believed in Thy signs, nor their argument whereby they have repudiated Thy sovereignty. Every time I call them to Thee and say: "O people! Consider the utterances of the Lord your God which are in your possession and those that have been sent down from the heaven of His will and power," they cavil at Thee, and turn their backs to Thee, though—as Thou art aware—each of the words that have gone out of the mouth of Thy will sheddeth the fragrance of the breaths of Thy mercy.

Some have chosen to cleave to him who is counted unworthy to converse with any of Thy servants that watch at Thy door (Mírzá Yaḥyá), how much more to enter into the court in which the Tongue of Thy majesty speaketh. Cleanse Thou their hearts and their eyes, O my Lord, that they may see with their eyes and understand with their hearts, that haply they may be attracted by Thine utterances to the Day-Spring of Thine inspiration, and draw nigh unto the soft-flowing stream of Thy knowledge.

Thou art He, O my Lord, Who hath, in every line of Thy Book, entered into covenant with them for me, and made it so sure that none of Thy creatures can any longer evade it. Thou didst say—and Thy word is the truth: "One single letter from Him excelleth all that hath been sent down in the Bayán."

Thou dost consider, therefore, O my God, how they have transgressed against Thy Cause, and beholdest what their hands have wrought in Thy days. They have so grievously wronged me that the Lote-Tree of Thy Revelation moaneth, and the inmates of the Tabernacle of Thy majesty and the dwellers of the cities of Thy names lament. I know not, O my God, for what reason they have risen up to oppress me, and by what proof they have turned aside from Him Who is the Day-Spring of Thy signs. I beseech Thee, O Thou Who art the Lord of all names and the Creator of the heavens, to aid them to act equitably in Thy Cause, that haply they may discover the sweet smell of the robe of Thy mercy, and set their faces towards the horizon that shineth with the brightness of the light of Thy face. Weak are they, O my Lord, and Thou art the Lord of strength and power. They are but paupers, and Thou art the All-Possessing, the Most Generous.

Thou art well aware, O my God, that throughout my life I have sought no advantage for myself. I have offered up my spirit and my whole being for the exaltation of Thy word amidst Thy creatures and the glorification of Thy name among Thy servants. Thou didst send me with such a Testimony that They Who are the Exponents of Thy Revelation and the Day-Springs of Thine inspiration were stirred up with vehement longing. Through it, Thy

proof was established, and Thy bounty fulfilled, and
Thy Cause perfected, and Thine utterances released,
and Thy clear tokens uncovered.

Thou knowest, O my God, that I have wished only
what Thou hast wished, and desire what Thou dost
desire. Were I to speak forth before Thy servants the
things wherewith Thou didst, through Thy bounty,
inspire me and which Thou didst command me to
utter amidst Thy creatures, the oppressors among
Thy people would cavil at me. And were I to hold
my peace and cease to celebrate the wonders of Thy
praise, all the limbs of my body would be stirred up
to extol Thee. I know not what the water is with
which Thou didst create me, or what the fire Thou
didst kindle within me. I swear by Thy glory! I shall
not cease to mention Thee, though all that are in
Thy heaven and on Thy earth rise up against me.
Thee will I magnify, in all circumstances, with a
heart wholly rid of all attachment to the world and
all that is therein.

Praised be Thou, the Well-Beloved of the hearts of
all such as have recognized Thee.

CIX

Lauded be Thy name, O Lord my God! Thou beholdest how my gaze is fixed toward Thy tender

mercies, and how mine eyes are bent upon the horizon of Thy grace, and Thy loving-kindness, and how my hands are stretched out unto the heaven of Thy bestowals. Thy might beareth me witness! Every limb of my body crieth out to Thee and saith: "O Thou Who art the Well-Beloved of the worlds, and the Lord of all that are in heaven and on earth, and the one Desire of the hearts which are devoted to Thee! I implore Thee, by Thine Ocean unto which Thou didst summon all the inmates of heaven and all the dwellers of the earth, to help Thy servants who have been kept back from turning unto it and from approaching its shores. Make them, then, O my God, to be detached from all else but Thee, and enable them to speak forth Thy praise and extol Thy virtues. Supply them, moreover, O my God, with the choice Wine of Thy mercy, that it may cause them to be forgetful of any one except Thee, and to arise to serve Thy Cause, and to be steadfast in their love for Thee. Thou art, verily, the Lord of their lives and the Object of their adoration. If they be driven away by Thee, who will then look upon them; and if they be removed far from Thee, who is there that can help them to approach Thy Presence? I swear by Thy might! No refuge is there to flee to except Thee, and no shelter to seek except Thy shelter, and no protection except Thy protection. Woe betide him who hath taken as Lord any one beside Thee, and blessed are the ones who have rid themselves of all attachment to all the dwellers of Thine earth, and

clung to the hem of Thy bounteousness. These! the
people of Bahá, before all that are in heaven and all
that are on earth. No God is there but Thee, the
Omniscient, the All-Wise."

Praise be to God, the Lord of all worlds.

CX

I know not, O my God, whether I should speak
forth the wonders of Thy praise among Thy servants,
and lay bare before them the secrets of Thy mercy
and the mysteries of Thy Cause, or keep them
wrapped up within the receptacle of my heart.
Though the lover be loth to share with any one the
intimate conversation of his beloved, yet at whatever
time Thine inescapable commandment to declare
Thy Cause reacheth me, I will unhesitatingly obey
it. I would proclaim Thee, undeterred by the darts
of affliction that may rain down upon me from the
clouds of Thy decree.

I swear by Thy might! Neither the hosts of the
earth nor those of heaven can keep me back from
revealing the things I am commanded to manifest.
I have no will before Thy will, and can cherish no
desire in the face of Thy desire. By Thy grace I am,
at all times, ready to serve Thee and am rid of all
attachment to any one except Thee.

What I desire, however, O my God, is that Thou shouldst bid me unveil the things which lie hid in Thy knowledge, so that they who are wholly devoted to Thee may, in their longing for Thee, soar up into the atmosphere of Thy oneness, and the infidels may be seized with trembling and may return to the nethermost fire, the abode ordained for them by Thee through the power of Thy sovereign might.

Thou dost consider, O my Lord, how Thy dear ones are sore pressed by Thine enemies, and hearest from all sides their sighing by reason of what hath befallen them in Thy path. Thou knowest, O my Lord, that their one desire was to seek Thy face, and that the sole Object of their adoration was Thee. They who wronged them had no other purpose except to turn them away from Thee, and to extinguish the fire which Thou hadst kindled with the hands of Thine almighty power.

Unseal the lips of Thy will, O my Lord, and let a word proceed therefrom that shall subject unto itself the world and all that is therein. How long shalt Thou behold these things and tarry, O my God? Darkness hath enveloped the whole earth, and Thy tokens are ready to be blotted out throughout Thy realm.

Forgive me, O my God, for what I have spoken, for Thou art the One that knoweth all things, and in Thee are wrapped up the secrets that are hid from all else except Thyself. When Thy promise shall come to pass, Thou wilt manifest what Thou wilt, and subdue as Thou pleasest. We should wish only what Thou hast wished for us. In Thee is the knowledge of all things, and with Thee is the issue of all things. Thou art, verily, the Truth, the Knower of things unseen.

Forgive me, then, my sins and the sins of them that love me, and supply them with the good of this world and of the next.

Thou art, verily, the Ever-Forgiving, the Most Compassionate.

CXI

Praised be Thou, O my God! Thou beholdest both the helplessness of Thy dear ones and the ascendancy of Thy foes, both the wretchedness of Thy chosen ones and the glory of them who gainsaid Thy Cause and repudiated Thy signs. The latter deny Thy tokens, and fail to repay Thee for the temporal benefits Thou didst bestow upon them, while the former yield Thee thanks for what hath befallen them in their eagerness to partake of the everlasting gifts Thou dost possess.

How sweet is the thought of Thee in times of adversity and trial, and how delightful to glorify Thee when compassed about with the fierce winds of Thy decree! Thou knowest full well, O my God, that I endure patiently whatsoever toucheth me in Thy path. Nay, I perceive that all the members and limbs of my body long for tribulation, that I may manifest Thy Cause, O Thou Who art the Lord of all names! The waters of Thy love have preserved me in the kingdom of Thy creation, and the fire of my remembrance of Thee hath set me ablaze before all that are in heaven and on earth. Great is my blessedness, and great the blessedness of this fire whose flame crieth out: "No God is there save Thee, Who art the Object of my heart's adoration, and the Source and Center of my soul!"

Thy glory beareth me witness! Were all that are in the heavens and all that are on earth to unite and seek to hinder me from remembering Thee and from celebrating Thy praise, they would assuredly have no power over me, and would fail in their purpose. And were the infidels to slay me, my blood would, at Thy command, lift up its voice and proclaim: "There is no God but Thee, O Thou Who art all my heart's Desire!" And were my flesh to be boiled in the cauldron of hate, the smell which it would send forth would rise towards Thee and cry out: "Where art Thou, O Lord of the worlds, Thou One Desire of them that have known Thee!" And were I to be cast into fire, my ashes would—I swear by Thy glory—declare: "The Youth hath, verily, attained that for which he had besought his Lord, the All-Glorious, the Omniscient."

How, then, can such a man be fearful of the combination of the kings to injure him in Thy Cause? No, no, I swear by Thyself, O Thou Who art the King of kings! Such is my love for Thee that I can fear no one, though the powers of all the worlds be arrayed against me. Alone and unaided I have, by the power of Thy might, arisen to proclaim Thy Cause, unafraid of the host of my oppressors.

To all that dwell on earth I cry aloud and say: "Fear ye God, O ye servants of God, and suffer not yourselves to be kept back from this pure Wine that hath flowed from the right hand of the throne of the mercy of your Lord, the Most Merciful. I swear by God! Better for you is what He possesseth than the things ye yourselves possess and the things ye have sought and are now seeking in this vain and empty life. Forsake the world, and set your faces towards the all-glorious Horizon. Whoso hath partaken of the wine of His remembrance will forget every other remembrance, and whoso hath recognized Him will rid himself of all attachment to this life and to all that pertaineth unto it."

I implore Thee, O my God and my Master, by Thy word through which they who have believed in Thy unity have soared up into the atmosphere of Thy knowledge, and they who are devoted to Thee have ascended into the heaven of Thy oneness, to inspire Thy loved ones with that which will assure their hearts in Thy Cause. Endue them with such steadfastness that nothing whatsoever will hinder them from turning towards Thee.

Thou art, verily, the Bountiful, the Munificent, the Forgiving, the Compassionate.

CXII

Thou beholdest, O my God, how bewildered in their drunkenness are Thy servants who have turned back from Thy beauty and caviled at what hath been sent down from the right hand of the throne of Thy majesty. Thou didst come, O my God, in the clouds of Thy spirit and Thine utterance, and lo, the entire creation shook and trembled, and the limbs of them who repudiated Thy testimonies were made to quiver, O Thou in Whose grasp is the lordship of all things!

Thou art He, O my God, Who hast summoned all men to turn in the direction of Thy mercy, and called them unto the horizon of Thy grace and bounties. None, however, heeded Thy call, except such as have forsaken all things save Thee, and hastened unto the Day-Spring of Thy beauty, and the Dawning-Place of Thine inspiration and Thy revelation.

Thou knowest, O my God, that none can be found on the face of the earth to remember Thee except them. Thou seest how the oppressors among Thy creatures have laid hold on them. Some, O my God, have shed their blood in Thy path, others have aban-

doned their homes and set their faces towards the
seat of Thy throne, and were hindered from step-
ping into the court of Thy great glory, while still
others have been cast into prison and are at the mercy
of the workers of iniquity.

I implore Thee, O Thou Who holdest in Thy
hands the reins of unconstrained power, to succor
them through the wondrous potency of Thy might.
Misery, O my Lord, hath taken hold on them in Thy
path, exalt them by the power of Thy sovereignty;
and weariness hath afflicted them in their love for
Thee, render them victorious, through Thy strength
and Thine omnipotence, over Thine enemies.

Aware as I am, O my God, that Thou hast decreed
for them that which excelleth whatsoever is in Thy
heaven and on Thy earth, I still cherish the desire
that Thou mayest behold them in Thy days exalted
and honored by Thy creatures. Supreme art Thou
over Thy creation. All are held within Thy grasp,
and lie prisoned in the hollow of Thy hand. No
God is there but Thee, the All-Powerful, the All-
Knowing, the All-Wise.

CXIII

Magnified be Thy name, O my God! I testify that
if Thy servants were to turn towards Thee with the

eyes Thou didst create in them and with the ears wherewith Thou didst endow them, they would all be carried away by a single word sent down from the right hand of the throne of Thy majesty. That word alone would suffice to brighten their faces, and to assure their hearts, and to cause their souls to soar up to the atmosphere of Thy great glory, and to ascend into the heaven of Thy sovereignty.

I pray Thee, O Thou Who art the Lord of all names and the Ruler of both earth and heaven, to grant that all who are dear to Thee may each become a cup of Thy mercy in Thy days, that they may quicken the hearts of Thy servants. Empower them also, O my God, to be as the rain that poureth down from the clouds of Thy grace, and as the winds that waft the vernal fragrances of Thy loving-kindness, that through them the soil of the hearts of Thy creatures may be clad with verdure, and may bring forth the things that will shed their fragrance over all Thy dominion, so that every one may perceive the sweet smell of the Robe of Thy Revelation. Potent art Thou to do what Thou willest.

The power of Thy might beareth me witness! Whoso hath drunk of the cup which the hand of Thy mercy hath borne round will strip himself of all things except Thee, and will be able, through a word of his mouth, to enrapture the souls of such of Thy servants as have slumbered on the bed of forgetfulness and negligence, and to cause them to turn their faces toward Thy most Great Sign, and seek from

Thee naught else except Thyself, and ask of Thee only what Thou hast determined for them by the pen of Thy judgment and hast prescribed in the Tablet of Thy decree.

Send down, then, O my God, through Thy Most Great Name, upon Thy loved ones what will, under all conditions, draw them nearer unto Thee. Thou art, verily, the Almighty, the All-Glorious, Whose help is implored by all men.

CXIV

Mine eyes are cheered, O my God, when I contemplate the tribulations that descend upon me from the heaven of Thy decree, and which have encompassed me on every side according to what Thy pen hath irrevocably established. I swear by Thy Self! Whatsoever is of Thee is well pleasing unto me, though it involve the bitterness of mine own death.

He Who was Thy Spirit (Jesus), O my God, withdrew all alone in the darkness of the night preceding His last day on earth, and falling on His face to the ground besought Thee saying: "If it be Thy will, O my Lord, my Well-Beloved, let this cup, through Thy grace and bounty, pass from me."

By Thy beauty, O Thou Who art the Lord of all names and the Creator of the heavens! I can smell

detachment

the fragrance of the words which, in His love for Thee, His lips have uttered, and can feel the glow of the fire that had inflamed His soul in its longing to behold Thy face and in its yearning after the Day-Spring of the light of Thy oneness, and the Dawning-Place of Thy transcendent unity.

As to me—and to this Thou art Thyself my witness—I call upon Thee saying: "I have no will of mine own, O my Lord, and my Master and my Ruler, before the indications of Thy will, and can have no purpose in the face of the revelation of Thy purpose. I swear by Thy glory! I wish only what Thou wishest, and cherish only what Thou cherishest. What I have chosen for myself is what Thou hast Thyself chosen for me, O Thou the Possessor of my soul!" Nay, I find myself to be altogether nothing when face to face with the manifold revelations of Thy names, how much less when confronted with the effulgent splendors of the light of Thine own Self. O miserable me! Were I to attempt merely to describe Thee, such an attempt would itself be an evidence of my impiety, and would attest my heedlessness in the face of the clear and resplendent tokens of Thy oneness. Who else except Thee can claim to be worthy of any notice in the face of Thine own revelation, and who is he that can be deemed sufficiently qualified to adequately praise Thee, or to pride himself on having befittingly described Thy glory? Nay—and to this Thou dost Thyself bear witness— it hath incontrovertibly been made evident that

Thou art the one God, the Incomparable, Whose help is implored by all men. From everlasting Thou wert alone, with none to describe Thee, and wilt abide for ever the same with no one else to equal or rival Thee. Were the existence of any co-equal with Thee to be recognized, how could it then be maintained that Thou art the Incomparable, or that Thy Godhead is immeasurably exalted above all peers or likeness? The contemplation of the highest minds that have recognized Thy unity failed to attain unto the comprehension of the One Thou hast created through the word of Thy commandment, how much more must it be powerless to soar into the atmosphere of the knowledge of Thine own Being. Every praise which any tongue or pen can recount, every imagination which any heart can devise, is debarred from the station which Thy most exalted Pen hath ordained, how much more must it fall short of the heights which Thou hast Thyself immensely exalted above the conception and the description of any creature. For the attempt of the evanescent to conceive the signs of the Uncreated is as the stirring of the drop before the tumult of Thy billowing oceans. Nay, forbid it, O my God, that I should thus venture to describe Thee, for every similitude and comparison must pertain to what is essentially created by Thee. How can then such similitude and comparison ever befit Thee, or reach up unto Thy Self?

By Thy glory, O my God! Though I recognize and firmly believe that no description which any ex-

cept Thyself can give of Thee can beseem Thy
grandeur, and that no glory ascribed to Thee by any
save Thyself can ever ascend into the atmosphere of
Thy presence, yet were I to hold my peace, and cease
to glorify Thee and to recount Thy wondrous glory,
my heart would be consumed, and my soul would
melt away.

My remembrance of Thee, O my God, quencheth
my thirst, and quieteth my heart. My soul delighteth in its communion with Thee, as the sucking child
delighteth itself in the breasts of Thy mercy; and my
heart panteth after Thee even as one sore athirst
panteth after the living waters of Thy bounty, O
Thou Who art the God of mercy, in Whose hand is
the lordship of all things!

I give thanks to Thee, O my God, that Thou hast
suffered me to remember Thee. What else but remembrance of Thee can give delight to my soul or
gladness to my heart? Communion with Thee en-
ableth me to dispense with the remembrance of all
Thy creatures, and my love for Thee empowereth
me to endure the harm which my oppressors inflict
upon me.

Send, therefore, unto my loved ones, O my God,
what will cheer their hearts, and illumine their faces,
and delight their souls. Thou knowest, O my Lord,
that their joy is to behold the exaltation of Thy Cause
and the glorification of Thy word. Do Thou unveil,
therefore, O my God, what will gladden their eyes,

and ordain for them the good of this world and of the world which is to come.

Thou art, verily, the God of power, of strength and of bounty.

CXV

Thou seest, O my God, how the wrongs committed by such of Thy creatures as have turned their backs to Thee have come in between Him in Whom Thy Godhead is manifest and Thy servants. Send down upon them, O my Lord, what will cause them to be busied with each others' concerns. Let, then, their violence be confined to their own selves, that the land and they that dwell therein may find peace.

One of Thy handmaidens, O my Lord, hath sought Thy face, and soared in the atmosphere of Thy pleasure. Withhold not from her, O my Lord, the things Thou didst ordain for the chosen ones among Thy handmaidens. Enable her, then, to be so attracted by Thine utterances that she will celebrate Thy praise amongst them.

Potent art Thou to do what pleaseth Thee. No God is there but Thee, the Almighty, Whose help is implored by all men.

CXVI

My God, my Well-Beloved! No place is there for any one to flee to when once Thy laws have been sent down, and no refuge can be found by any soul after the revelation of Thy commandments. Thou hast inspired the Pen with the mysteries of Thine eternity, and bidden it teach man that which he knoweth not, and caused him to partake of the living waters of truth from the cup of Thy Revelation and Thine inspiration.

No sooner, however, had the Pen traced upon the tablet one single letter of Thy hidden wisdom, than the voice of the lamentation of Thine ardent lovers was lifted up from all directions. Thereupon, there befell the just what hath caused the inmates of the tabernacle of Thy glory to weep and the dwellers of the cities of Thy revelation to groan.

Thou dost consider, O my God, how He Who is the Manifestation of Thy names is in these days threatened by the swords of Thine adversaries. In such a state He crieth out and summoneth all the inhabitants of Thine earth and the denizens of Thy heaven unto Thee.

Purify, O my God, the hearts of Thy creatures with the power of Thy sovereignty and might, that Thy words may sink deep into them. I know not what is in their hearts, O my God, nor can tell the thoughts they think of Thee. Methinks that they im-

agine that Thy purpose in calling them to Thine
all-highest horizon is to heighten the glory of Thy
majesty and power. For had they been satisfied that
Thou summonest them to that which will recreate
their hearts and immortalize their souls, they would
never have fled from Thy governance, nor deserted the
shadow of the tree of Thy oneness. Clear away, then,
the sight of Thy creatures, O my God, that they may
recognize Him Who showeth forth the Godhead as
One Who is sanctified from all that pertaineth unto
them, and Who, wholly for Thy sake, is summoning
them to the horizon of Thy unity, at a time when
every moment of His life is beset with peril. Had His
aim been the preservation of His own Self, He would
never have left it at the mercy of Thy foes.

I swear by Thy glory! I have accepted to be tried
by manifold adversities for no purpose except to re-
generate all that are in Thy heaven and on Thy earth.
Whoso hath loved Thee, can never feel attached to
his own self, except for the purpose of furthering
Thy Cause; and whoso hath recognized Thee can
recognize naught else except Thee, and can turn to
no one save Thee.

Enable Thy servants, O my God, to discover the
things Thou didst desire for them in Thy Kingdom.
Acquaint them, moreover, with what He Who is the
Origin of Thy most excellent titles hath, in His love
for Thee, been willing to bear for the sake of the
regeneration of their souls, that they may haste to
attain the River that is Life indeed, and turn their

faces in the direction of Thy Name, the Most Merciful. Abandon them not to themselves, O my God! Draw them, by Thy bountiful favor, to the heaven of Thine inspiration. They are but paupers, and Thou art the All-Possessing, the ever-Forgiving, the Most Compassionate.

CXVII

Glory to Thee, O my God! The first stirrings of the spring of Thy grace have appeared and clothed Thine earth with verdure. The clouds of the heaven of Thy bounty have rained their rain on this City within whose walls is imprisoned Him Whose desire is the salvation of Thy creatures. Through it the soil of this City hath been decked forth, and its trees clothed with foliage, and its inhabitants gladdened.

The hearts of Thy dear ones, however, will rejoice only at the Divine Springtime of Thy tender mercies, whereby the hearts are quickened, and the souls are renewed, and the trees of human existence bear their fruits.

The plants that have sprung forth, O my Lord, in the hearts of Thy loved ones have withered away. Send down upon them, from the clouds of Thy spirit, that which will cause the tender herbs of Thy knowledge and wisdom to grow within their breasts.

Rejoice, then, their hearts with the proclamation of
Thy Cause and the exaltation of Thy sovereignty.

Their eyes, O my Lord, are expectantly turned in
the direction of Thy bounty, and their faces are set
towards the horizon of Thy grace. Suffer them not,
through Thy bounty, to be deprived of Thy grace.
Potent art Thou, by Thy sovereign might, over all
things. No God is there but Thee, the Almighty, the
Help in Peril, the Self-Subsisting.

CXVIII

Thou seest, O my God, how Thy servants have
been cleaving fast to Thy names, and have been calling on them in the daytime and in the night season.
No sooner, however, had He been made manifest
through Whose word the kingdom of names and the
heaven of eternity were created, than they broke
away from Him and disbelieved in the greatest of
Thy signs. They finally banished Him from the land
of His birth, and caused Him to dwell within the
most desolate of Thy cities, though all the world had
been built up by Thee for His sake. Within this, the
Most Great Prison, He hath established His seat.
Though sore tried by trials, the like of which the eye
of creation hath not seen, He summoneth the people

unto Thee, O Thou Who art the Fashioner of the universe!

I beseech Thee, O Thou the Shaper of all the nations and the Quickener of every moldering bone, to graciously enable Thy servants to recognize Him Who is the Manifestation of Thy Self and the Revealer of Thy transcendent might, that they may cut down, by Thy power, all the idols of their corrupt inclinations, and enter beneath the shadow of Thine all-encompassing mercy, which, by virtue of Thy name, the Most Exalted, the All-Glorious, hath surpassed the entire creation.

I know not, O my God, how long will Thy creatures continue to slumber on the bed of forgetfulness and evil desires, and remain far removed from Thee and shut out from Thy presence. Draw them nearer, O my God, unto the scene of Thine effulgent glory, and enrapture their hearts with the sweet savors of Thine inspiration, through which they who adore Thy unity have soared on the wings of desire towards Thee, and they who are devoted to Thee have reached unto Him Who is the Dawning-Place of the Day-Star of Thy creation.

Cleave asunder, O my Lord, the veils that shut them out from Thee, that they may behold Thee shining above the horizon of Thy oneness and shedding Thy radiance from the dawning-place of Thy sovereignty. By Thy glory! Were they to discover the sweetness of Thy remembrance and apprehend the excellence of the things that are sent down upon them from the right hand of the throne of Thy majesty, they would cast away all that they possess, and would rush forth into the wilderness of their longing after Thee, that the glance of Thy loving-kindness may be directed towards them and the radiance of the Day-Star of Thy beauty may be shed upon them.

Let their hearts, O my Lord, be carried away by Thy remembrance, and their souls enriched by Thy riches, and their wills strengthened to proclaim Thy Cause amidst Thy creatures. Thou art, verily, the Great Giver, the Ever-Forgiving, the Most Compassionate.

CXIX

Lauded be Thy name, O my God! Thou seest how I have been sorely vexed among Thy servants, and beholdest the things that have befallen me in Thy path. Thou knowest full well that I have not spoken a word but by Thy leave, that my lips have never been opened except at Thy bidding and in accordance with Thy pleasure, that every breath I have breathed hath been animated with Thy praise and Thy remembrance, that I have summoned all men to naught else except that whereunto Thy chosen ones have through all eternity been summoned, and

that I have bidden them observe only the things that
would draw them nearer unto the Day-Spring of
Thy loving-kindness, and the Dawning-Place of Thy
favors, and the Horizon of Thy riches, and the
Manifestation of Thine inspiration and Thy revelation.

Thou art well aware, O my God, that I have not
failed in my duty towards Thy Cause. At all times
and under all conditions I have wafted, in every
direction, the breezes of Thine inspiration, and shed
abroad the sweet smell of the raiment of Thy mercy,
that haply Thy servants may discover its fragrance,
and through it be enabled to turn towards Thee.

I implore Thee, O my God, by the Lights of Thy
unity and the Repositories of Thy revelation, to send
down from the clouds of Thy mercy that which will
cleanse the hearts of all such as have turned towards
Thee. Blot out, then, from their hearts all that may
induce Thy servants to cavil at Thy Cause.

Thy will hath overruled my will, O my God, and
I have shown forth what hath grievously vexed me.
Have mercy, then, upon me, O Thou Who of all
those who show mercy art the Most Merciful!

Assist Thou Thy servants, O my God, to help Thy
Cause, and give them to drink what will quicken
their hearts in Thy realm, lest anything hinder them
from remembering Thee and from extolling Thy
virtues, that they may quit their homes in Thy name,
and summon all the multitudes unto Thee. Guard
their faces, O my God, from turning to any one save

Thee, and their ears from hearkening unto the sayings of all such as have turned away from Thy beauty and repudiated Thy signs.

Supreme art Thou over all things. There is none other God save Thee, the All-Knowing, the All-Wise.

CXX

Glorified art Thou, O Lord my God! Thou beholdest my low estate and the habitation wherein I dwell, and bearest witness unto my perplexity, my crying needs, my troubles, and the afflictions I suffer among Thy servants who recite Thy verses and repudiate their Revealer, who call on Thy names and cavil at their Creator, who seek to draw nigh unto Him Who is Thy Friend and put to death Him Who is the Best-Beloved of the worlds.

Open Thou their eyes, O my God, and My Master, that they may gaze on Thy beauty, or cause them to return unto the lowest abyss of the fire. Potent art Thou to do what Thou willest. Thou art, verily, the All-Glorious, the All-Wise.

The glory of Thy might, O my God, beareth me witness! Every time I attempt to remember Thee, I find myself overpowered by the sublimity of Thy station and the immensity of Thy might; and every time I hold my peace, lo, I am impelled by my love

for Thee and by the potency of Thy will, to unloose
my tongue and mention Thee. He who is poor and
needy, O my God, is calling for his Lord, the All-
Possessing; and he who is destitute of all strength
remembereth his Master, the All-Powerful. If He
deign to accept His servant's supplication, He is, verily, of unsurpassed bounteousness; and if He cast him
out, He is of those who judge equitably the best. He
indeed is acceptable, O my God, who hath set his
face towards Thee, and he is truly deprived who
hath been careless of the remembrance of Thee in
Thy days. Blessed is he that hath tasted of the sweetness of Thy remembrance and praise. Nothing, not
even the arising of all the peoples of the whole
world to assail him, can hinder such a man from
directing his steps towards the paths of Thy pleasure
and the ways of Thy Cause.

Look, then, O Thou Who art the Well-Beloved of
Bahá, upon the tears he sheddeth before Thee, and
behold the sighs which he uttereth, O Thou Who art
his heart's Desire! I swear by Thy might, and Thy
majesty and Thy glory! Were I to inherit from Thee
all the delights of Paradise, and to keep them in my
possession as long as Thine own Being endureth, and
were I to become, for less than a moment, careless
of the remembrance of Thee, I would, of a certainty,
cast them away from me and cease to consider them.
I am the one, O my God, who for love of Thee hath
forsaken the world and all its benefits, and willingly

accepted every tribulation for the sake of Thy remembrance.

I entreat Thee, O Thou Who art my Companion and my Best-Beloved, to lift the veil that hath come in between Thee and Thy servants, that they may recognize Thee with Thine own eye and rid themselves of all attachment to any one but Thee. Thou art, verily, the Almighty, the Ever-Forgiving, the Most Compassionate. No God is there beside Thee, the Most Exalted, the Self-Sufficing, the Self-Exalting, the All-Glorious, the All-Wise.

Praise be unto Thee, for Thou art, in truth, the Lord of earth and heaven.

CXXI

Praise be to Thee, O Lord my God! I am the one who hath sought the good pleasure of Thy will, and directed his steps towards the seat of Thy gracious favors. I am he who hath forsaken his all, who hath fled to Thee for shelter, who hath set his face towards the tabernacle of Thy revelation and the adored sanctuary of Thy glory. I beseech Thee, O my Lord, by Thy call whereby they who recognized Thy unity have sought the shadow of Thy most gracious providence, and the sincere have fled far from themselves unto Thy name, the Most Exalted, the All-Glorious,

through which Thy verses were sent down, and Thy
word fulfilled, and Thy proof manifested, and the
sun of Thy beauty risen, and Thy testimony established, and Thy signs uncovered,—I beseech Thee to
grant that I may be numbered with them that have
quaffed the wine that is life indeed from the hands
of Thy gracious providence, and have rid themselves,
in Thy path, of all attachment to Thy creatures, and
been so inebriated with Thy manifold wisdom that
they hastened to the field of sacrifice with Thy praise
on their lips and Thy remembrance in their hearts.
Send down, also, upon me, O my God, that which
will wash me from anything that is not of Thee, and
deliver me from Thine enemies who have disbelieved
in Thy signs.

Potent art Thou to do what Thou willest. No God
is there beside Thee, the Help in Peril, the Self-
Subsisting.

CXXII

Praise be to Thee, O Lord my God! Thou seest and
knowest that I have called upon Thy servants to
turn nowhere except in the direction of Thy bestowals, and have bidden them observe naught save
the things Thou didst prescribe in Thy Perspicuous
Book, the Book which hath been sent down according
to Thine inscrutable decree and irrevocable purpose.

I can utter no word, O my God, unless I be permitted by Thee, and can move in no direction until I obtain Thy sanction. It is Thou, O my God, Who hast called me into being through the power of Thy might, and hast endued me with Thy grace to manifest Thy Cause. Wherefore I have been subjected to such adversities that my tongue hath been hindered from extolling Thee and from magnifying Thy glory.

All praise be to Thee, O my God, for the things Thou didst ordain for me through Thy decree and by the power of Thy sovereignty. I beseech Thee that Thou wilt fortify both myself and them that love me in our love for Thee, and wilt keep us firm in Thy Cause. I swear by Thy might! O my God! Thy servant's shame is to be shut out as by a veil from Thee, and his glory is to know Thee. Armed with the power of Thy name nothing can ever hurt me, and with Thy love in my heart all the world's afflictions can in no wise alarm me.

Send down, therefore, O my Lord, upon me and upon my loved ones that which will protect us from the mischief of those that have repudiated Thy truth and disbelieved in Thy signs.

Thou art, verily, the All-Glorious, the Most Bountiful.

nov 4

Station of Believers

CXXIII

Glorified art Thou, O Lord my God! Thou hast, in Thine all highest Paradise, assigned unto Thy servants such stations that if any one of them were to be unveiled to men's eyes all who are in heaven and all who are on earth would be dumbfounded. By Thy might! Were kings to witness so great a glory they would, assuredly, rid themselves of their dominions and cleave to such of their subjects as have entered beneath the shadow of Thine immeasurable mercy and sought the shelter of Thine all-glorious name.

power of the name of God

I implore Thee, O Thou Who art the Beloved of the worlds and the Desire of all that have recognized Thee, by Thy name, through which Thou stirrest up whom Thou willest and drawest toward Thee whom Thou pleasest, to open the eyes of all that are dear to Thee, that haply they may not be veiled from Thee as the peoples of the earth are, but may outwardly perceive the signs and tokens of Thy power, and inwardly apprehend the things Thou didst ordain for them in the realms of Thy glory.

Potent art Thou to do Thy pleasure. Thou art the one alone Beloved in both this world and in the next. No God is there but Thee, the Most Exalted, the All-Glorious.

god

assistence to do the will of God

CXXIV

Glorified art Thou, O Lord my God! Every time I venture to make mention of Thee, I am held back by my mighty sins and grievous trespasses against Thee, and find myself wholly deprived of Thy grace, and utterly powerless to celebrate Thy praise. My great confidence in Thy bounty, however, reviveth my hope in Thee, and my certitude that Thou wilt bountifully deal with me emboldeneth me to extol Thee, and to ask of Thee the things Thou dost possess.

I implore Thee, O my God, by Thy mercy that hath surpassed all created things, and to which all that are immersed beneath the oceans of Thy names bear witness, not to abandon me unto my self, for my heart is prone to evil. Guard me, then, within the stronghold of Thy protection and the shelter of Thy care. I am he, O my God, whose only wish is what Thou hast determined by the power of Thy might. All I have chosen for myself is to be assisted by Thy gracious appointments and the ruling of Thy will, and to be aided with the tokens of Thy decree and judgment.

I beseech Thee, O Thou Who art the Beloved of the hearts which long for Thee, by the Manifestations of Thy Cause and the Day-Springs of Thine inspiration, and the Exponents of Thy majesty, and the Treasuries of Thy knowledge, not to suffer me to be deprived of Thy holy Habitation, Thy Fane and Thy Tabernacle. Aid me, O my Lord, to attain His hallowed court, and to circle round His person, and to stand humbly at His door.

Thou art He Whose power is from everlasting to everlasting. Nothing escapeth Thy knowledge. Thou art, verily, the God of power, the God of glory and wisdom.

Praised be God, the Lord of the worlds!

CXXV

O Thou the dread of Whom hath fallen upon all things, before the splendors of Whose face the countenances of all men are downcast, at the revelations of Whose sovereignty all necks have humbly bowed, to the ruling of Whose will all hearts have been subdued, the awfulness of Whose majesty hath caused the foundations of all things to tremble, and to the power of Whose authority the winds have been subjected! I beseech Thee by the compelling force of Thy Revelation, and by the power of Thy might, and by the exaltation of Thy word, and by the sublimity of Thy sovereignty, to number us with them whom the world hath been powerless to hinder from turning towards Thee.

Cause me, O my Lord, to be of those who, with

their substance and their own selves, have fought valiantly in Thy path. Write down, then, for me the recompense Thou didst ordain for them in the Tablet of Thy decree. Stablish me also on the seat of truth in Thy presence, and join me with the sincere among Thy servants.

I implore Thee, O my Lord, by Thy Messengers, and Thy Chosen Ones, and by Him through Whom Thou hast affixed Thy seal upon the Manifestations of Thy Cause among Thy creatures, and Whom Thou hast adorned with the ornament of Thine acceptance among all that dwell in Thy heaven and on Thy earth, to graciously assist me to attain unto what Thou hast ordained for Thy servants and bidden them observe in Thy Tablets. Wash away, then, my sins, O my God, by Thy grace and bounty, and reckon me among such as are not overtaken by fear nor put to grief.

Thou art, verily, the Almighty, the Help in Peril, the Self-Subsisting.

CXXVI

Glorified art Thou, O Lord my God! Thou art He the fire of Whose love hath set ablaze the hearts of them who have recognized Thy unity, and the splendors of Whose countenance have illuminated the

faces of such as have drawn nigh unto Thy court.
How plenteous, O my God, is the stream of Thy
knowledge! How sweet, O my Beloved, is the injury
which, in my love for Thee, and for the sake of Thy
pleasure, I suffer from the darts of the wicked doers!
How pleasing are the wounds which, in Thy path
and in order to proclaim Thy Faith, I sustain from
the swords of the infidels!

I beseech Thee, by Thy name through which Thou
turnest restlessness into tranquillity, fear into confidence, weakness into strength, and abasement into
glory, that Thou of Thy grace wilt aid me and Thy
servants to exalt Thy name, to deliver Thy Message,
and to proclaim Thy Cause, in such wise that we may
remain unmoved by either the assaults of the transgressors or the wrath of the infidels, O Thou Who art
my Well-Beloved!

I am, O my Lord, Thy handmaiden, who hath
hearkened to Thy call, and hastened unto Thee, flee-
ing from herself and resting her heart upon Thee. I
implore Thee, O my Lord, by Thy name out of which
all the treasures of the earth were brought forth, to
shield me from the hints of such as have disbelieved
in Thee and repudiated Thy truth.

Powerful art Thou to do what Thou pleasest. Thou
art, verily, the All-Knowing, the All-Wise.

CXXVII

All praise be to Thee, O Lord, my God! How mysterious the Fire which Thou hast enkindled within my heart! My very limbs testify to the intensity of its heat, and evince the consuming power of its flame. Should my bodily tongue ever attempt to describe Thee as the One Whose strength hath ever excelled the strength of the most mighty amongst men, the tongue of my heart would address me, saying: "These are but words which can only be adequate to such things as are of the same likeness and nature as themselves. But He, of a truth, is infinitely exalted above the mention of all His creatures."

The power of Thy might beareth me witness, O my Well-Beloved! Every limb of my body, methinks, is endowed with a tongue that glorifieth Thee and magnifieth Thy name. Armed with the power of Thy love, the hatred which moveth them that are against Thee can never alarm me; and with Thy praise on my lips, the rulings of Thy decree can in no wise fill me with sorrow. Fortify, therefore, Thy love within my breast, and suffer me to face the assaults which all the peoples of the earth may launch against me. I swear by Thee! Every hair of my head proclaimeth: "But for the adversities that befall me in Thy path, how could I ever taste the divine sweetness of Thy tenderness and love?"

Send down, therefore, O my Lord, upon me and

upon them that love me, that which will cause us to become steadfast in Thy Faith. Enable them, then, to become the Hands of Thy Cause amongst Thy servants, that they may scatter abroad Thy signs, and show forth Thy sovereignty. There is no God but Thee, Who art powerful to do whatsoever Thou willest. Thou art, in truth, the All-Glorious, the All-Praised.

CXXVIII

Praise be unto Thee, O my God! I am one of Thy servants, who hath believed on Thee and on Thy signs. Thou seest how I have set myself towards the door of Thy mercy, and turned my face in the direction of Thy loving-kindness. I beseech Thee, by Thy most excellent titles and Thy most exalted attributes, to open to my face the portals of Thy bestowals. Aid me, then, to do that which is good, O Thou Who art the Possessor of all names and attributes!

I am poor, O my Lord, and Thou art the Rich. I have set my face towards Thee, and detached myself from all but Thee. Deprive me not, I implore Thee, of the breezes of Thy tender mercy, and withhold not from me what Thou didst ordain for the chosen among Thy servants.

Remove the veil from mine eyes, O my Lord, that

I may recognize what Thou hast desired for Thy creatures, and discover, in all the manifestations of Thy handiwork, the revelations of Thine almighty power. Enrapture my soul, O my Lord, with Thy most mighty signs, and draw me out of the depths of my corrupt and evil desires. Write down, then, for me the good of this world and of the world to come. Potent art Thou to do what pleaseth Thee. No God is there but Thee, the All-Glorious, Whose help is sought by all men.

I yield Thee thanks, O my Lord, that Thou hast wakened me from my sleep, and stirred me up, and created in me the desire to perceive what most of Thy servants have failed to apprehend. Make me able, therefore, O my Lord, to behold, for love of Thee and for the sake of Thy pleasure, whatsoever Thou hast desired. Thou art He to the power of Whose might and sovereignty all things testify.

There is none other God but Thee, the Almighty, the Beneficent.

CXXIX

Praised be Thou, O my God! Thou seest how Thy righteous servants have fallen into the hands of the wicked doers, who have disbelieved in Thy name, the Unconstrained, and denied Thy majesty, and Thine unrestrained authority, and Thy strength, and Thy sovereign might. Their mouths utter what the mouths of the Jews uttered aforetime.

Put forth, therefore, out of the bosom of Thy glory, O my Lord, the hand of Thine omnipotence, and through it assist Thou Thy loved ones who, though sore-tried in Thy path with such trials as have caused the inmates of the kingdom of Thy Cause to groan, were not deterred from turning towards the horizon of Thy Revelation.

Set, then, the seal of Thine unerring protection on their hearts, O my Lord, lest perchance the remembrance of aught else except Thee enter therein. Make them able, moreover, to proclaim Thy name amidst Thy creatures, and supply them with the best of what Thou hast destined for such of Thy chosen ones as enjoy near access to Thee.

Potent art Thou to do Thy pleasure. Thou truly art the All-Glorious to whom all cry for help.

CXXX

Lauded be Thy name, O Lord my God! Thou seest how Thy servants have everywhere been compassed with tribulations, how their adversaries have all risen up against them and grievously wronged them. Thy glory beareth me witness! Were all the wicked doers of the earth to band themselves against us, and to cast us into a fire such as no man hath kindled, they would be powerless to distract our gaze from the horizon of Thy name, the Most Exalted, the Most High, and would fail to turn aside our hearts from the seat of Thine effulgent glory.

I swear by Thy might! The arrows that transfix us in Thy path are the ornaments of our temples, and the spears which pierce us in our love for Thee are as silk unto our bodies. By the glory of Thy might! Nothing whatsoever can beseem Thy servants except what the pen of Thine irrevocable decree hath traced in this priceless and exalted Tablet.

All praise be to Thy Self at all times and under all conditions. Thou art, verily, the God of knowledge and wisdom.

CXXXI

Praise be unto Thee, O my God! Thou seest how He Who is Thy Light hath been shut up in the fortress-town of 'Akká, and been sore oppressed by reason of what the hands of the wicked doers have wrought, whose corrupt desires have kept them back from turning towards Thee, O Thou Who art the King of all names!

I swear by Thy glory! Tribulations, however woeful, can never hinder me from remembering Thee or from celebrating Thy praise. Every vexation borne for love of Thee is a token of Thy mercy unto Thy creatures, and every ordeal suffered in Thy path is but a gift from Thee bestowed on Thy chosen ones. I testify that my countenance, which shineth above the Day-Spring of eternity, hath been irradiated by adversity, and my body hath been adorned by it before all who are in heaven and all who are on earth.

I pray Thee, by Thy Most Great Name, to aid all them that have believed on Thee and on Thy signs to be steadfast in Thy love and to set themselves towards the Dawning-Place of the Day-Star of Thy loving-kindness. Inspire them, then, O my God, with what will unloose their tongue to praise Thee, and will draw them nigh unto Thee in the life that now is and the life that is to come.

Thou truly art the Almighty, the All-Glorious, the Beneficent.

CXXXII

Glorified be Thy name, O Lord my God! I beseech Thee by Thy power that hath encompassed all created things, and by Thy sovereignty that hath transcended the entire creation, and by Thy Word which was hidden in Thy wisdom and whereby Thou didst create Thy heaven and Thy earth, both to enable us to be steadfast in our love for Thee and in our obedience to Thy pleasure, and to fix our gaze upon Thy face, and celebrate Thy glory. Empower us, then, O my God, to spread abroad Thy signs among Thy creatures, and to guard Thy Faith in Thy realm. Thou hast ever existed independently of the mention of any of Thy creatures, and wilt remain as Thou hast been for ever and ever.

In Thee I have placed my whole confidence, unto Thee I have turned my face, to the cord of Thy loving providence I have clung, and towards the shadow of Thy mercy I have hastened. Cast me not as one disappointed out of Thy door, O my God, and withhold not from me Thy grace, for Thee alone do I seek. No God is there beside Thee, the Ever-Forgiving, the Most Bountiful.

Praise be to Thee, O Thou Who art the Beloved of them that have known Thee!

CXXXIII

O Thou Whose tests are a healing medicine to such as are nigh unto Thee, Whose sword is the ardent desire of all them that love Thee, Whose dart is the dearest wish of those hearts that yearn after Thee, Whose decree is the sole hope of them that have recog-

nized Thy truth! I implore Thee, by Thy divine
sweetness and by the splendors of the glory of Thy
face, to send down upon us from Thy retreats on
high that which will enable us to draw nigh unto
Thee. Set, then, our feet firm, O my God, in Thy
Cause, and enlighten our hearts with the effulgence
of Thy knowledge, and illumine our breasts with the
brightness of Thy names.

CXXXIV

I am he, O my Lord, that hath set his face towards
Thee, and fixed his hope on the wonders of Thy grace
and the revelations of Thy bounty. I pray Thee that
Thou wilt not suffer me to turn away disappointed
from the door of Thy mercy, nor abandon me
to such of Thy creatures as have repudiated Thy
Cause.

I am, O my God, Thy servant and the son of Thy
servant. I have recognized Thy truth in Thy days,
and have directed my steps towards the shores of Thy
oneness, confessing Thy singleness, acknowledging
Thy unity, and hoping for Thy forgiveness and pardon. Powerful art Thou to do what Thou willest; no
God is there beside Thee, the All-Glorious, the Ever-
Forgiving.

CXXXV

Unto Thee be praise, O Lord my God! I testify that Thou art God, and that there is none other God besides Thee. Thou hast from eternity been immeasurably exalted above the praise of any one except Thee, and far above the description of any of Thy creatures. All created things have borne witness to Thy unity, and every dweller in Thy kingdom hath confessed Thy oneness. The essence of the apprehension of the assured among Thy creatures can never attain unto Thee, and the gem-like utterances with which Thy people have praised and glorified Thee can never hope to ascend unto the atmosphere of Thy holiness. For men's apprehension of Thee is but the apprehension of Thine own creation; how can it reach up to Thee? And all human praise and glorification of Thee pertain unto Thy servants; how can they be deemed worthy of the court of Thy oneness?

I swear by Thy glory! The quintessence of knowledge is powerless to comprehend Thy nature, and the inmost reality of every praise of Thee falleth short of the seat of Thy great glory and of Thine all-compelling power. Every utterance that seeketh to describe Thee, and every knowledge that attempteth to comprehend Thee, is but an expression of Thine own creating, and is begotten by Thy will, and fashioned in conformity with Thy purpose.

I implore Thee, O Thou Who art inscrutable to

all except Thee, and can be comprehended through naught else save Thyself, by the wrongs which He Who is the Day-Spring of Thy Cause hath suffered at the hands of the ignoble among Thy creatures, and by what hath befallen Him in Thy path, to grant that I may, at all times, be wholly dissolved in Thee, and fix my gaze upon the horizon of Thy will and be steadfast in Thy love.

I have, O my Lord, turned unto Thee according to what Thou hast commanded me in Thy Book, and have set my face towards the horizon of Thy loving-kindness even as Thou hast permitted me in Thy Tablets. Cast me not out of the door of Thy grace, I beseech Thee, and write down for me the recompense destined for him who hath entered Thy presence, and hath risen to serve Thee, and hath been carried away by the drops sprinkled upon him from the Ocean of Thy favors in Thy days, and by the splendors of the Day-Star of Thy gifts that have been shed upon him at the revelation of the light of Thy countenance.

Potent art Thou to do what pleaseth Thee. No God is there save Thee, the Help in Peril, the Self-Subsisting.

CXXXVI

Lauded be Thy Name, O Lord my God! I am Thy servant who hath laid hold on the cord of Thy tender mercies, and clung to the hem of Thy bounteousness. I entreat Thee by Thy name whereby Thou hast subjected all created things, both visible and invisible, and through which the breath that is life indeed was wafted over the entire creation, to strengthen me by Thy power which hath encompassed the heavens and the earth, and to guard me from all sickness and tribulation. I bear witness that Thou art the Lord of all names, and the Ordainer of all that may please Thee. There is none other God but Thee, the Almighty, the All-Knowing, the All-Wise.

Do Thou ordain for me, O my Lord, what will profit me in every world of Thy worlds. Supply me, then, with what Thou hast written down for the chosen ones among Thy creatures, whom neither the blame of the blamer, nor the clamor of the infidel, nor the estrangement of such as have withdrawn from Thee, hath deterred from turning towards Thee.

Thou, truly, art the Help in Peril through the power of Thy sovereignty. No God is there save Thee, the Almighty, the Most Powerful.

CXXXVII

Glorified art Thou, O my God! I yield Thee thanks that Thou hast made known unto me Him Who is the Day-Spring of Thy mercy, and the Dawning-Place of Thy grace, and the Repository of Thy Cause. I beseech Thee by Thy Name, through which the faces of them that are nigh unto Thee have turned white, and the hearts of such as are devoted to Thee have winged their flight towards Thee, to grant that I may, at all times and under all conditions, lay hold on Thy cord, and be rid of all attachment to any one except Thee, and may keep mine eyes directed towards the horizon of Thy Revelation, and may carry out what Thou hast prescribed unto me in Thy Tablets.

Attire, O my Lord, both my inner and outer being with the raiment of Thy favors and Thy loving-kindness. Keep me safe, then, from whatsoever may be abhorrent unto Thee, and graciously assist me and my kindred to obey Thee, and to shun whatsoever may stir up any evil or corrupt desire within me.

Thou, truly, art the Lord of all mankind, and the Possessor of this world and of the next. No God is there save Thee, the All-Knowing, the All-Wise.

CXXXVIII

O God, and the God of all Names, and Maker of the heavens! I entreat Thee by Thy Name through which He Who is the Day-Spring of Thy might and the Dawning-Place of Thy power hath been manifested, through which every solid thing hath been made to flow, and every dead corpse hath been quickened, and every moving spirit confirmed—I entreat Thee to enable me to rid myself of all attachment to any one but Thee, and to serve Thy Cause, and to wish what Thou didst wish through the power of Thy sovereignty, and to perform what is the good pleasure of Thy will.

I beseech Thee, moreover, O my God, to ordain for me what will make me rich enough to dispense with any one save Thee. Thou seest me, O my God, with my face turned towards Thee, and my hands clinging to the cord of Thy grace. Send down upon me Thy mercy, and write down for me what Thou hast written down for Thy chosen ones. Powerful art Thou to do what pleaseth Thee. No God is there but Thee, the Ever-Forgiving, the All-Bountiful.

CXXXIX

Glory be to Thee, O Thou Who hast, through the movement of Thy most august pen, subdued the concourse of Thy creation, and manifested the pearls of the ocean of Thy wisdom through the words which Thy tongue hath spoken before all who are in heaven and on earth. I testify that Thy might hath encompassed the whole universe, and Thy mercy surpassed all created things. The powers of the earth have never prevailed against Thee, nor hath the tumult of the nations frustrated Thy purpose. Thou hast revealed in Thy realm whatsoever Thou hadst desired through the power of Thy sovereignty, and hast ordained all things according to the good pleasure of Thy will. From eternity Thou hast inhabited the loftiest heights of Thy dominion and of Thine unfettered sovereignty, and wilt unto eternity continue to abide in the inaccessible retreats of Thy majesty and glory.

I implore Thee, by Thy Name through which the fragrance of the raiment of Thy presence was wafted, and the gentle winds of Thy bountiful grace passed over all created things, to graciously assist me, at all times and under all conditions, to serve Thy Cause, and to enable me to remember Thee and to extol Thy virtues. Let, then, Thine almighty arms enfold me, O my God, and ordain for me what beseemeth Thy bounty in every world of Thy worlds.

Thou beholdest, O my Lord, how I have set myself

towards the ocean of Thy grace and the adored sanctuary of Thy favors. Deny me not, I pray Thee, the drops which are sprinkled from the ocean of Thy gifts; neither do Thou withhold from me the out-pourings of the clouds of Thy tender mercies. I am he, O my God, that hath clung to the resplendent hem of Thy robe, and taken hold on Thy strong cord that none can sever. I testify that Thou hast created me, and nourished me, and brought me up, and fed me, and sustained me, that I may recognize Him Who is the Day-Spring of Thy signs, and the Revealer of Thy clear tokens. I offer unto Thee, therefore, most high praise, O Lord my God, that Thou hast suffered me to attain unto this most sublime station and this most august seat. Thou, truly, art the Great Giver, the Almighty, the All-Bountiful, the Ever-Forgiving, the Most Generous.

Illumine mine eyes, O my Lord, with the splendors of the horizon of Thy Revelation, and brighten my heart with the effulgence of the Day-Star of Thy knowledge and wisdom, that I may set myself wholly towards Thy face, and be rid of all attachment to any one except Thee, in such wise that the changes and chances of the world will be powerless to hinder me from recognizing Him Who is the Manifestation of Thine own Self, and the Revealer of Thy signs, and the Day-Spring of Thy Revelation, and the Reposi-tory of Thy Cause.

Thou art, verily, the Almighty, the Protector, the All-Glorious, the All-Wise.

CXL

Praised be Thou, O my God! This servant of Thine testifieth that naught else except Thee can ever express Thee, nor canst Thou be described by any one save Thyself. The thoughts of them that have recognized Thy reality, however much they may ascend towards the heaven of Thy praise, can never hope to pass beyond the bounds which, by Thy behest and decree, have been fixed within their own hearts. How can the creature who is as nothing comprehend Him Who is the Ancient of Days, or succeed in describing the full measure of His sovereignty, His glory, and His grandeur? Nay, and to this Thou Thyself dost witness, O Thou Who art the Governor of nations! Every created thing hath recognized its own impotence, and the power of Thy might, and hath confessed its own abasement and Thy great glory.

I beseech Thee by Thy Lastness which is the same as Thy Firstness, and by Thy Revelation which is identical with Thy Concealment, to grant that they who are dear to Thee, and their children, and their kindred, may become the revealers of Thy purity amidst Thy creatures, and the manifestations of Thy sanctity amongst Thy servants.

Thou art, verily, powerful to do Thy pleasure. Thou art, in truth, the Help in Peril, the Self-Subsisting.

steadfastness

CXLI

I give Thee thanks, O my God, for that Thou hast made me to be a target for the darts of Thine adversaries in Thy path. I offer Thee most high praise, O Thou Who art the Knower of the seen and unseen and the Lord of all being, that Thou hast suffered me to be cast into prison for love of Thee, and caused me to quaff the cup of woe, that I may reveal Thy Cause and glorify Thy word.

Which of my tribulations am I to recount before Thy face, O my Lord? Am I to recite before Thee what in days of old befell me at the hands of the workers of iniquity among Thy creatures, or to describe the vexations which have compassed me about in these days for the sake of Thy good pleasure?

Thanks be to Thee, O Thou the Lord of all names; and glory be to Thee, O Maker of the heavens, for all that I have sustained in these days at the hands of such of Thy servants as have transgressed against Thee, and of Thy people that have dealt frowardly towards Thee.

Number us, we implore Thee, with them who have stood fast in Thy Cause until their souls finally winged their flight unto the heaven of Thy grace and the atmosphere of Thy loving-kindness. Thou art, verily, the Ever-Forgiving, the Most Merciful.

CXLII

Glory be to Thee, O my God! My face hath been set towards Thy face, and my face is, verily, Thy face, and my call is Thy call, and my Revelation Thy Revelation, and my self Thy Self, and my Cause Thy Cause, and my behest Thy behest, and my Being Thy Being, and my sovereignty Thy sovereignty, and my glory Thy glory, and my power Thy power.

I implore Thee, O Thou Fashioner of the nations and the King of eternity, to guard Thy handmaidens within the tabernacle of Thy chastity, and to cancel such of their deeds as are unworthy of Thy days. Purge out, then, from them, O my God, all doubts and idle fancies, and sanctify them from whatsoever becometh not their kinship with Thee, O Thou Who art the Lord of names, and the Source of utterance. Thou art He in Whose grasp are the reins of the entire creation.

No God is there but Thee, the Almighty, the Most Exalted, the All-Glorious, the Self-Subsisting.

CXLIII

Glory be to Thee, O my God! I beg of Thee by Thy name, the Most Merciful, to protect Thy servants and Thy handmaidens when the tempests of trials pass over them, and Thy manifold tests assail them. Enable them, then, O my God, so to seek refuge within the stronghold of Thy love and of Thy Revelation, that neither Thine adversaries nor the wicked doers among Thy servants, who have broken Thy Covenant and Thy Testament, and turned away most disdainfully from the Day-Spring of Thine Essence and the Revealer of Thy glory, may prevail against them.

They themselves, O my Lord, have waited at the door of Thy grace. Do Thou open it to their faces with the keys of Thy bountiful favors. Potent art Thou to do what Thou willest, and to ordain what Thou pleasest. These are the ones, O my Lord, who have set their faces towards Thee, and turned unto Thy habitation. Do with them, therefore, as becometh Thy mercy, which hath surpassed the worlds.

CXLIV

O my God and my Master! I am Thy servant and the son of Thy servant. I have risen from my couch at this dawn-tide when the Day-Star of Thy oneness hath shone forth from the Day-Spring of Thy will, and hath shed its radiance upon the whole world,

according to what had been ordained in the Books of
Thy Decree.

Praise be unto Thee, O my God, that we have
wakened to the splendors of the light of Thy knowledge. Send down, then, upon us, O my Lord, what
will enable us to dispense with any one but Thee, and
will rid us of all attachment to aught except Thyself.
Write down, moreover, for me, and for such as are
dear to me, and for my kindred, man and woman
alike, the good of this world and the world to come.
Keep us safe, then, through Thine unfailing protection, O Thou the Beloved of the entire creation and
the Desire of the whole universe, from them whom
Thou hast made to be the manifestations of the Evil
Whisperer, who whisper in men's breasts. Potent art
Thou to do Thy pleasure. Thou art, verily, the Almighty, the Help in Peril, the Self-Subsisting.

Bless Thou, O Lord my God, Him Whom Thou
hast set over Thy most excellent Titles, and through
Whom Thou hast divided between the godly and the
wicked, and graciously aid us to do what Thou lovest
and desirest. Bless Thou, moreover, O my God, them
Who are Thy Words and Thy Letters, and them who
have set their faces towards Thee, and turned unto
Thy face, and hearkened to Thy Call.

Thou art, truly, the Lord and King of all men,
and art potent over all things.

CXLV

O God, my God! Be Thou not far from me, for tribulation upon tribulation hath gathered about me. O God, my God! Leave me not to myself, for the extreme of adversity hath come upon me. Out of the pure milk, drawn from the breasts of Thy loving-kindness, give me to drink, for my thirst hath utterly consumed me. Beneath the shadow of the wings of Thy mercy shelter me, for all mine adversaries with one consent have fallen upon me. Keep me near to the throne of Thy majesty, face to face with the revelation of the signs of Thy glory, for wretchedness hath grievously touched me. With the fruits of the Tree of Thine Eternity nourish me, for uttermost weakness hath overtaken me. From the cups of joy, proffered by the hands of Thy tender mercies, feed me, for manifold sorrows have laid mighty hold upon me. With the broidered robe of Thine omnipotent sovereignty attire me, for poverty hath altogether de-spoiled me. Lulled by the cooing of the Dove of Thine Eternity, suffer me to sleep, for woes at their blackest have befallen me. Before the throne of Thy oneness, amid the blaze of the beauty of Thy countenance, cause me to abide, for fear and trembling have violently crushed me. Beneath the ocean of Thy forgive-ness, faced with the restlessness of the leviathan of glory, immerse me, for my sins have utterly doomed me.

CXLVI

Forgiveness
Healing

Glory be to Thee, O Lord my God! I beg of Thee
by Thy Name through which He Who is Thy Beauty
hath been stablished upon the throne of Thy Cause,
and by Thy Name through which Thou changest all
things, and gatherest together all things, and callest
to account all things, and rewardest all things, and
preservest all things, and sustainest all things—I beg
of Thee to guard this handmaiden who hath fled for
refuge to Thee, and hath sought the shelter of Him
in Whom Thou Thyself art manifest, and hath put
her whole trust and confidence in Thee.

Family

She is sick, O my God, and hath entered beneath
the shadow of the Tree of Thy healing; afflicted, and
hath fled to the City of Thy protection; diseased, and
hath sought the Fountain-Head of Thy favors; sorely
vexed, and hath hasted to attain the Well-Spring of
Thy tranquillity; burdened with sin, and hath set her
face toward the court of Thy forgiveness.

Attire her, by Thy sovereignty and Thy loving-
kindness, O my God and my Beloved, with the raiment of Thy balm and Thy healing, and make her
quaff of the cup of Thy mercy and Thy favors. Protect her, moreover, from every affliction and ailment,
from all pain and sickness, and from whatsoever may
be abhorrent unto Thee.

Thou, in truth, art immensely exalted above all else

*power of
the Name
of God*

except Thyself. Thou art, verily, the Healer, the All-Sufficing, the Preserver, the Ever-Forgiving, the Most Merciful.

CXLVII

Thou art He, O my God, through Whose names the sick are healed and the ailing are restored, and the thirsty are given drink, and the sore-vexed are tranquillized, and the wayward are guided, and the abased are exalted, and the poor are enriched, and the ignorant are enlightened, and the gloomy are illumined, and the sorrowful are cheered, and the chilled are warmed, and the downtrodden are raised up. Through Thy name, O my God, all created things were stirred up, and the heavens were spread, and the earth was established, and the clouds were raised and made to rain upon the earth. This, verily, is a token of Thy grace unto all Thy creatures.

I implore Thee, therefore, by Thy name through which Thou didst manifest Thy Godhead, and didst exalt Thy Cause above all creation, and by each of Thy most excellent titles and most august attributes, and by all the virtues wherewith Thy transcendent and most exalted Being is extolled, to send down this night from the clouds of Thy mercy the rains of Thy healing upon this suckling, whom Thou hast related unto Thine all-glorious Self in the kingdom of Thy creation. Clothe him, then, O my God, by Thy grace, with the robe of well-being and health, and guard him, O my Beloved, from every affliction and disorder, and from whatever is obnoxious unto Thee. Thy might, verily, is equal to all things. Thou, in truth, art the Most Powerful, the Self-Subsisting. Send down, moreover, upon him, O my God, the good of this world and of the next, and the good of the former and latter generations. Thy might and Thy wisdom are, verily, equal unto this.

CXLVIII

Glory be to Thee, O Lord my God! I implore Thee by Thy Name, through which Thou didst lift up the ensigns of Thy guidance, and didst shed the radiance of Thy loving-kindness, and didst reveal the sovereignty of Thy Lordship; through which the lamp of Thy names hath appeared within the niche of Thine attributes, and He Who is the Tabernacle of Thy unity and the Manifestation of detachment hath shone forth; through which the ways of Thy guidance were made known, and the paths of Thy good pleasure were marked out; through which the foundations of error have been made to tremble, and the signs of wickedness have been abolished; through which the fountains of wisdom have burst forth, and the heavenly table hath been sent down; through which Thou didst preserve Thy servants and didst vouchsafe Thy healing; through which Thou didst show forth Thy tender mercies unto Thy servants and revealedst Thy forgiveness amidst Thy creatures —I implore Thee to keep safe him who hath held fast and returned unto Thee, and clung to Thy mercy, and seized the hem of Thy loving providence. Send down, then, upon him Thy healing, and make him whole, and endue him with a constancy vouchsafed by Thee, and a tranquillity bestowed by Thy highness.

Thou art, verily, the Healer, the Preserver, the Helper, the Almighty, the Powerful, the All-Glorious, the All-Knowing.

CXLIX

Glorified art Thou, O my God! I give praise to Thee, that Thou hast made me able so to reveal Thine utterances, and manifest Thy proofs and Thy testimonies, that every proof hath been made to circle round my will, and every testimony to compass my pleasure. Thou seest me, O my Lord, lying at the mercy of Thine adversaries, who have repudiated Thy signs, and refuted Thy testimony, and turned back from Thy beauty, and resolved to shed Thy blood. I beseech Thee, O Thou Who art the Lord of all names, by Thy name through which Thou hast subdued all created things, to graciously aid Thy servants and Thy loved ones to cleave steadfastly to Thy Cause. Give them, then, to drink what will quicken their hearts in Thy days. Enable them, moreover, O my Lord, to fix their gaze at all times upon Thy pleasure, and to yield Thee thanks for the evidences of Thine irrevocable decree. For Thou art, verily, praiseworthy in all that Thou hast done in the past, or wilt do in the future, and art to be obeyed in whatsoever Thou hast wished or wilt wish, and to be loved in all that Thou hast desired or wilt desire. Thou lookest upon them that are dear to Thee with the eyes of Thy loving-kindness, and sendest down for them only that which will profit them through Thy grace and Thy gifts.

We entreat Thee, O Thou Who art the Cloud of Bounty and the Succorer of the distressed, that Thou wilt aid us to remember Thee, and to make known Thy Cause, and to arise to help Thee. Though all weakness, we yet have clung to Thy Name, the Most Powerful, the Almighty.

Bless Thou, O my God, them that have stood fast in Thy Cause, and whom the evil suggestions of the workers of iniquity have failed to deter from turning towards Thy face, and who have hastened with their whole hearts toward Thy grace, until they finally quaffed the water that is life indeed from the hands of Thy bounty.

Potent art Thou to do Thy pleasure. No God is there save Thee, the Mighty, the Most Generous.

CL

I give praise to Thee, O my God, that the fragrance of Thy loving-kindness hath enraptured me, and the gentle winds of Thy mercy have inclined me in the direction of Thy bountiful favors. Make me to quaff, O my Lord, from the fingers of Thy bounteousness the living waters which have enabled every one that hath partaken of them to rid himself of all attachment to any one save Thee, and to soar into the atmosphere of detachment from all Thy creatures, and to fix his gaze upon Thy loving providence and Thy manifold gifts.

Make me ready, in all circumstances, O my Lord, to serve Thee and to set myself towards the adored sanctuary of Thy Revelation and of Thy Beauty. If it be Thy pleasure, make me to grow as a tender herb in the meadows of Thy grace, that the gentle winds of Thy will may stir me up and bend me into conformity with Thy pleasure, in such wise that my movement and my stillness may be wholly directed by Thee.

Thou art He, by Whose name the Hidden Secret was divulged, and the Well-Guarded Name was revealed, and the seals of the sealed-up Goblet were opened, shedding thereby its fragrance over all creation, whether of the past or of the future. He who was athirst, O my Lord, hath hasted to attain the living waters of Thy grace, and the wretched creature hath yearned to immerse himself beneath the ocean of Thy riches.

I swear by Thy glory, O Lord the Beloved of the world and the Desire of all them that have recognized Thee! I am sore afflicted by the grief of my separation from Thee, in the days when the Day-Star of Thy presence hath shed its radiance upon Thy people. Write down, then, for me the recompense decreed for such as have gazed on Thy face, and have, by Thy leave, gained admittance into the court of Thy throne, and have, at Thy bidding, met Thee face to face.

I implore Thee, O my Lord, by Thy name the splendors of which have encompassed the earth and the heavens, to enable me so to surrender my will to what Thou hast decreed in Thy Tablets, that I may cease to discover within me any desire except what Thou didst desire through the power of Thy sovereignty, and any will save what Thou didst destine for me by Thy will.

Whither shall I turn, O my God, powerless as I am to discover any other way except the way Thou didst set before Thy chosen Ones? All the atoms of the earth proclaim Thee to be God, and testify that there is none other God besides Thee. Thou hast from eternity been powerful to do what Thou hast willed, and to ordain what Thou hast pleased.

Do Thou destine for me, O my God, what will set me, at all times, towards Thee, and enable me to cleave continually to the cord of Thy grace, and to proclaim Thy name, and to look for whatsoever may flow down from Thy pen. I am poor and desolate, O my Lord, and Thou art the All-Possessing, the Most High. Have pity, then, upon me through the wonders of Thy mercy, and send down upon me, every moment of my life, the things wherewith Thou hast recreated the hearts of all Thy creatures who have recognized Thy unity, and of all Thy people who are wholly devoted to Thee.

Thou, verily, art the Almighty, the Most Exalted, the All-Knowing, the All-Wise.

CLI

Glorified art Thou, O my Lord! Thou beholdest my tribulations and all that hath befallen me at the hands of such of Thy servants as keep company with me, who have disbelieved in Thy most resplendent signs, and turned back from Thy most effulgent Beauty. I swear by Thy glory! Such are the troubles that vex me, that no pen in the entire creation can either reckon or describe them.

I implore Thee, O Thou Who art the King of names and the Creator of earth and heaven, so to assist me by Thy strengthening grace that nothing whatsoever will have the power to hinder me from remembering Thee, or celebrating Thy praise, or to keep me back from observing what Thou hast pre-scribed unto me in Thy Tablets, that I may so arise to serve Thee that with bared head I will hasten forth from my habitation, cry out in Thy name amidst Thy creatures, and proclaim Thy virtues among Thy servants. Having accomplished what Thou hadst de-creed, and delivered the thing Thou hadst written down, the wicked doers among Thy people would, then, compass me about and would do with me in Thy path as would please them.

In the love I bear to Thee, O my Lord, my heart longeth for Thee with a longing such as no heart hath known. Here am I with my body between Thy hands, and my spirit before Thy face. Do with them as it may please Thee, for the exaltation of Thy word, and the revelation of what hath been enshrined within the treasuries of Thy knowledge.

Potent art Thou to do what Thou willest, and able to ordain what Thou pleasest.

CLII

Lauded be Thy name, O my God! I can discover no one in Thy realm who can befittingly turn unto Thee, or is able to adequately hearken unto what hath gone out of the mouth of Thy will. I beseech Thee, therefore, O Thou Who art the Possessor of the entire creation and the King of the realm of Thine invention, graciously to aid Thy creatures to accomplish that which is pleasing and acceptable unto Thee, that they may arise to serve Thy Cause amidst Thy creatures, and to speak forth Thy praise before all who are in heaven and on earth.

Thou art He, O my Lord, Whose bounty hath surpassed all things, and Whose power hath transcended all things, and Whose mercy hath encompassed all things. Look, then, upon Thy people with the eyes of Thy tender mercies, and leave them not to themselves and to their corrupt desires in Thy days. How farsoever they may have strayed from Thee, and however grievously they have turned back from Thy face, yet Thou, in Thine essence, art the All-Bountiful, and, in Thine inmost spirit, art the Most Merciful. Deal with them according to the unrevealed tokens of Thy bounty and Thy gifts. Thou art, verily, the One to the power of Whose might all things have testified, and to Whose majesty and omnipotence the whole creation hath borne witness.

No God is there but Thee, the Help in Peril, the Self-Subsisting.

CLIII

My God, Thou Whom I adore and worship, Who art Most Powerful! I testify that no description by any created thing can ever reveal Thee, and no praise which any being is able to utter can express Thee. Neither the comprehension of any one in the whole world, nor the intelligence of any of its peoples, can, as it befitteth Thee, gain admittance into the court of Thy holiness, or unravel Thy mystery. What sin hath kept the inmates of the city of Thy names so far from Thine all-glorious Horizon, and deprived them of access to Thy most great Ocean? One single letter of Thy Book is the mother of all utterances, and a word therefrom the begetter of all creation. What ingratitude have Thy servants shown forth that Thou hast withheld them, one and all, from recognizing Thee? A drop out of the ocean of Thy mercy sufficeth to quench the flames of hell, and a spark of the fire of Thy love is enough to set ablaze a whole world.

O Thou Who art the All-Knowing! Wayward though we be, we still cling to Thy bounty; and though ignorant, we still set our faces toward the ocean of Thy wisdom. Thou art that All-Bountiful Who art not deterred by a multitude of sins from vouchsafing Thy bounty, and the flow of Whose gifts is not arrested by the withdrawal of the peoples of the world. From eternity the door of Thy grace hath remained wide open. A dewdrop out of the ocean of Thy mercy is able to adorn all things with the ornament of sanctity, and a sprinkling of the waters of Thy bounty can cause the entire creation to attain unto true wealth.

Lift not the veil, O Thou Who art the Concealer! From eternity the tokens of Thy bounty have encompassed the universe, and the splendors of Thy Most Great Name have been shed over all created things. Deny not Thy servants the wonders of Thy grace. Cause them to be made aware of Thee, that they may bear witness to Thy unity, and enable them to recognize Thee, that they may hasten towards Thee. Thy mercy hath embraced the whole creation, and Thy grace hath pervaded all things. From the billows of the ocean of Thy generosity the seas of eagerness and enthusiasm were revealed. Thou art what Thou art. Aught except Thee is unworthy of any mention unless it entereth beneath Thy shadow, and gaineth admittance into Thy court.

Whatever betide us, we beseech Thine ancient forgiveness, and seek Thine all-pervasive grace. Our hope is that Thou wilt deny no one Thy grace, and wilt deprive no soul of the ornament of fairness and justice. Thou art the King of all bounty, and the Lord of all favors, and supreme over all who are in heaven and on earth.

God answers prayer. steadfastness

CLIV

Dispel my grief by Thy bounty and Thy generosity, O God, my God, and banish mine anguish through Thy sovereignty and Thy might. Thou seest me, O my God, with my face set towards Thee at a time when sorrows have compassed me on every side. I implore Thee, O Thou Who art the Lord of all being, and overshadowest all things visible and invisible, by Thy Name whereby Thou hast subdued the hearts and the souls of men, and by the billows of the Ocean of Thy mercy and the splendors of the Day-Star of Thy bounty, to number me with them whom nothing whatsoever hath deterred from setting their faces toward Thee, O Thou Lord of all names and Maker of the heavens!

Thou beholdest, O my Lord, the things which have befallen me in Thy days. I entreat Thee, by Him Who is the Day-Spring of Thy names and the Dawning-Place of Thine attributes, to ordain for me what will enable me to arise to serve Thee and to extol Thy virtues. Thou art, verily, the Almighty, the Most Powerful, Who art wont to answer the prayers of all men!

resistance to serve

prayer for daily needs

And, finally, I beg of Thee by the light of Thy countenance to bless my affairs, and redeem my debts, and satisfy my needs. Thou art He to Whose power and to Whose dominion every tongue hath testified, and Whose majesty and Whose sovereignty every understanding heart hath acknowledged. No God is there but Thee, Who hearest and art ready to answer.

CLV

Create in me a pure heart, O my God, and renew a tranquil conscience within me, O my Hope! Through the spirit of power confirm Thou me in Thy Cause, O my Best-Beloved, and by the light of Thy glory reveal unto me Thy path, O Thou the Goal of my desire! Through the power of Thy transcendent might lift me up unto the heaven of Thy holiness, O Source of my being, and by the breezes of Thine eternity gladden me, O Thou Who art my God! Let Thine everlasting melodies breathe tranquillity on me, O my Companion, and let the riches of Thine ancient countenance deliver me from all except Thee, O my Master, and let the tidings of the revelation of Thine incorruptible Essence bring me joy, O Thou Who art the most manifest of the manifest and the most hidden of the hidden!

CLVI

I give praise to Thee, O my God, that Thou hast awakened me out of my sleep, and brought me forth after my disappearance, and raised me up from my slumber. I have wakened this morning with my face set toward the splendors of the Day-Star of Thy Revelation, through Which the heavens of Thy power and Thy majesty have been illumined, acknowledging Thy signs, believing in Thy Book, and holding fast unto Thy Cord.

I beseech Thee, by the potency of Thy will and the compelling power of Thy purpose, to make of what Thou didst reveal unto me in my sleep the surest foundation for the mansions of Thy love that are within the hearts of Thy loved ones, and the best instrument for the revelation of the tokens of Thy grace and Thy loving-kindness.

Do Thou ordain for me through Thy most exalted Pen, O my Lord, the good of this world and of the next. I testify that within Thy grasp are held the reins of all things. Thou changest them as Thou pleasest. No God is there save Thee, the Strong, the Faithful.

Thou art He Who changeth through His bidding abasement into glory, and weakness into strength, and powerlessness into might, and fear into calm, and doubt into certainty. No God is there but Thee, the Mighty, the Beneficent.

Thou disappointest no one who hath sought Thee, nor dost Thou keep back from Thee any one who hath desired Thee. Ordain Thou for me what becometh the heaven of Thy generosity, and the ocean of Thy bounty. Thou art, verily, the Almighty, the Most Powerful.

CLVII

My God, Whom I worship and adore! I bear witness unto Thy unity and Thy oneness, and acknowledge Thy gifts, both in the past and in the present. Thou art the All-Bountiful, the overflowing showers of Whose mercy have rained down upon high and low alike, and the splendors of Whose grace have been shed over both the obedient and the rebellious.

O God of mercy, before Whose door the quintessence of mercy hath bowed down, and round the sanctuary of Whose Cause loving-kindness, in its inmost spirit, hath circled, we beseech Thee, entreating Thine ancient grace, and seeking Thy present favor, that Thou mayest have mercy upon all who are the manifestations of the world of being, and to deny them not the outpourings of Thy grace in Thy days.

All are but poor and needy, and Thou, verily, art the All-Possessing, the All-Subduing, the All-Powerful.

CLVIII

I have wakened in Thy shelter, O my God, and it becometh him that seeketh that shelter to abide within the Sanctuary of Thy protection and the Stronghold of Thy defense. Illumine my inner being, O my Lord, with the splendors of the Day-Spring of Thy Revelation, even as Thou didst illumine my outer being with the morning light of Thy favor.

CLIX

O my God, the God of bounty and mercy! Thou art that King by Whose commanding word the whole creation hath been called into being; and Thou art that All-Bountiful One the doings of Whose servants have never hindered Him from showing forth His grace, nor have they frustrated the revelations of His bounty.

Suffer this servant, I beseech Thee, to attain unto that which is the cause of his salvation in every world of Thy worlds. Thou art, verily, the Almighty, the Most Powerful, the All-Knowing, the All-Wise.

CLX

My God, the Object of my adoration, the Goal of my desire, the All-Bountiful, the Most Compassionate! All life is of Thee and all power lieth within the grasp of Thine omnipotence. Whosoever Thou exaltest is raised above the angels, and attaineth the station: "Verily, We uplifted him to a place on high!"; and whosoever Thou dost abase is made lower than dust, nay, less than nothing.

O Divine Providence! Though wicked, sinful, and intemperate, we still seek from Thee a "seat of truth," and long to behold the countenance of the Omnipotent King. It is Thine to command, and all sovereignty belongeth to Thee, and the realm of might boweth before Thy behest. Everything Thou doest is pure justice, nay, the very essence of grace. One gleam from the splendors of Thy Name, the All-Merciful, sufficeth to banish and blot out every trace of sinfulness from the world, and a single breath from the breezes of the Day of Thy Revelation is enough to adorn all mankind with a fresh attire.

Vouchsafe Thy strength, O Almighty One, unto Thy weak creatures, and quicken them who are as dead, that haply they may find Thee, and may be led unto the ocean of Thy guidance, and may remain steadfast in Thy Cause. Should the fragrance of Thy praise be shed abroad by any of the divers tongues of the world, out of the East or out of the West, it would, verily, be prized and greatly cherished. If such tongues, however, be deprived of that fragrance, they assuredly would be unworthy of any mention, be they words or thoughts.

We beg of Thee, O Providence, to show Thy way unto all men, and to guide them aright. Thou art, verily, the Almighty, the Most Powerful, the All-Knowing, the All-Seeing.

CLXI

Praise be to Thee, O my God, inasmuch as Thou hast turned the faces of Thy servants towards the right-hand of the throne of Thy gifts, and hast caused them to be detached from all else besides Thee, that they may recognize Thy sovereignty and acknowledge Thy glory. I testify to the potency of Thy Cause, the pervasive influence of Thy decree, the immutability of Thy will, the endlessness of Thy purpose. All things lie prisoned within the grasp of Thy might, and the whole creation is destitute when brought face to face with the evidences of Thy wealth.

Deal Thou, therefore, O my God, my Beloved, my supreme Desire, with Thy servants and with all that were created by Thee as would beseem Thy beauty and Thy greatness, and would be worthy of Thy generosity and gifts. Thou art, in truth, He Whose mercy hath encompassed all the worlds, and Whose grace hath embraced all that dwell on earth and in heaven. Who is there that hath cried after Thee, and whose prayer hath remained unanswered? Where is he to be found who hath reached forth towards Thee, and whom Thou hast failed to approach? Who is he that can claim to have fixed his gaze upon Thee, and toward whom the eye of Thy loving-kindness hath not been directed? I bear witness that Thou hadst turned toward Thy servants ere they had turned toward Thee, and hadst remembered them ere they had remembered Thee. All grace is Thine, O Thou in Whose hand is the kingdom of Divine gifts and the source of every irrevocable decree.

Send down, therefore, O my God, upon all that seek Thee that which will entirely strip them of all that pertaineth not unto Thee, and will draw them nigh unto Thy Self. Assist them, by Thy grace, to love Thee and to conform unto that which shall please Thee. Grant, then, that they may go straight on in the path of Thy Cause, the path wherein have slipped the footsteps of the doubters among Thy people and the froward among Thy servants. Thou art, verily, the All-Powerful, the Almighty, the Most Great.

mercy

CLXII

Lauded and glorified art Thou, O my God! I entreat Thee by the sighing of Thy lovers and by the tears shed by them that long to behold Thee, not to withhold from me Thy tender mercies in Thy Day, nor to deprive me of the melodies of the Dove that extolleth Thy oneness before the light that shineth from Thy face. I am the one who is in misery, O God! Behold me cleaving fast to Thy Name, the All-Possessing. I am the one who is sure to perish; behold me clinging to Thy Name, the Imperishable. I implore Thee, therefore, by Thy Self, the Exalted, the Most High, not to abandon me unto mine own self and unto the desires of a corrupt inclination. Hold Thou my hand with the hand of Thy power, and deliver me from the depths of my fancies and idle imaginings, and cleanse me of all that is abhorrent unto Thee.

Cause me, then, to turn wholly unto Thee, to put my whole trust in Thee, to seek Thee as my Refuge, and to flee unto Thy face. Thou art, verily, He Who, through the power of His might, doeth whatsoever He desireth, and commandeth, through the potency of His will, whatsoever He chooseth. None can withstand the operation of Thy decree; none can divert the course of Thine appointment. Thou art, in truth, the Almighty, the All-Glorious, the Most Bountiful.

*power of the name
of God*

CLXIII

Lauded be Thy name, O Lord my God! Thou seest how I have turned myself toward Thee, and set my face in the direction of Thy grace and Thy gifts. I implore Thee, by Thy name through which Thou didst enable all them that have recognized Thy unity to partake of the wine of Thy mercy, and all such as have drawn nigh unto Thee to quaff the living waters of Thy loving-kindness, to rid me entirely of all vain imaginings, and to incline me in the direction of Thy grace, O Thou Who art the Lord of all men!

Graciously assist me, O my God, in the days of the Manifestation of Thy Cause and of the Day-Spring of Thy Revelation, to tear asunder the veils which have hindered me from recognizing Thee, and from immersing myself beneath the ocean of Thy knowledge. Hold Thou me with the hands of Thy power, and grant that I may be so carried away by the sweet melodies of the Dove of Thy oneness, that I will cease to regard in all creation any face except Thy face, O Thou the Goal of my desire, and will recognize in the visible world naught else save the evidences of Thy might, O Thou Who art the God of mercy!

I am but a wretched creature, O my Lord, and Thou art the All-Possessing, the Most High; and I am all weakness, and Thou art the Almighty, and the Supreme Ordainer in both the beginning and the

end. Withhold not from me the fragrances of Thy
Revelation, and shatter not my hopes in the outpourings which have been sent down out of the heaven
of Thy gifts. Ordain Thou for me, O my God, the
good of this world and the world to come, and grant
me what will profit me in every world of Thy worlds,
for I know not what will help or harm me. Thou, in
truth, art the All-Knowing, the All-Wise.

Have mercy, then, O my God, upon Thy servants
who are drowned in the midst of the ocean of evil
suggestions, and deliver them by the power of Thy
sovereignty, O Thou Who art the Lord of all names
and attributes! Thou art He Who from everlasting
hath ordained what hath pleased Thee, and will unto
everlasting abide the same. No God is there but Thee,
the Ever-Forgiving, the Most Merciful.

CLXIV

O God, my God! I have set out from my home,
holding fast unto the cord of Thy love, and I have
committed myself wholly to Thy care and Thy protection. I entreat Thee by Thy power through which
Thou didst protect Thy loved ones from the wayward
and the perverse, and from every contumacious oppressor, and every wicked doer who hath strayed far
from Thee, to keep me safe by Thy bounty and Thy

grace. Enable me, then, to return to my home by Thy power and Thy might. Thou art, truly, the Almighty, the Help in Peril, the Self-Subsisting.

CLXV

From the sweet-scented streams of Thine eternity give me to drink, O my God, and of the fruits of the tree of Thy being enable me to taste, O my Hope! From the crystal springs of Thy love suffer me to quaff, O my Glory, and beneath the shadow of Thine everlasting providence let me abide, O my Light! Within the meadows of Thy nearness, before Thy presence, make me able to roam, O my Beloved, and at the right hand of the throne of Thy mercy seat me, O my Desire! From the fragrant breezes of Thy joy let a breath pass over me, O my Goal, and into the heights of the paradise of Thy reality let me gain admission, O my Adored One! To the melodies of the dove of Thy oneness suffer me to hearken, O Resplendent One, and through the spirit of Thy power and Thy might quicken me, O my Provider! In the spirit of Thy love keep me steadfast, O my Succorer, and in the path of Thy good-pleasure set firm my steps, O my Maker! Within the garden of Thine immortality, before Thy countenance, let me abide for ever, O Thou Who art merciful unto me, and upon the seat of Thy glory stablish me, O Thou Who art my Possessor! To the heaven of Thy loving-kindness lift me up, O my Quickener, and unto the Day-Star of Thy guidance lead me, O Thou my Attractor! Before the revelations of Thine invisible spirit summon me to be present, O Thou Who art my Origin and my Highest Wish, and unto the essence of the fragrance of Thy beauty, which Thou wilt manifest, cause me to return, O Thou Who art my God!

Potent art Thou to do what pleaseth Thee. Thou art, verily, the Most Exalted, the All-Glorious, the All-Highest.

CLXVI

O Thou Whose face is the object of my adoration, Whose beauty is my sanctuary, Whose habitation is my goal, Whose praise is my hope, Whose providence is my companion, Whose love is the cause of my being, Whose mention is my solace, Whose nearness is my desire, Whose presence is my dearest wish and highest aspiration, I entreat Thee not to withhold from me the things Thou didst ordain for the chosen ones among Thy servants. Supply me, then, with the good of this world and of the next.

Thou, truly, art the King of all men. There is no God but Thee, the Ever-Forgiving, the Most Generous.

prayer for the dead to be read by one person while others stand from Kitáb-i-Aqdas

CLXVII

O my God! This is Thy servant and the son of Thy servant who hath believed in Thee and in Thy signs, and set his face towards Thee, wholly detached from all except Thee. Thou art, verily, of those who show mercy the most merciful.

Deal with him, O Thou Who forgivest the sins of men and concealest their faults, as beseemeth the heaven of Thy bounty and the ocean of Thy grace. Grant him admission within the precincts of Thy transcendent mercy that was before the foundation of earth and heaven. There is no God but Thee, the Ever-Forgiving, the Most Generous.

Let him, then, repeat six times the greeting "Alláh-u-Abhá," and then repeat nineteen times each of the following verses:

We all, verily, worship God.

We all, verily, bow down before God.

We all, verily, are devoted unto God.

We all, verily, give praise unto God.

We all, verily, yield thanks unto God.

We all, verily, are patient in God.

(If the dead be a woman, let him say:
This is Thy handmaiden and the daugh-
ter of Thy handmaiden, etc. . . .)
Prayer for the Dead.

CLXVIII

spiritual sustenance

O my Lord! Make Thy beauty to be my food, and
Thy presence my drink, and Thy pleasure my hope,
and praise of Thee my action, and remembrance of
Thee my companion, and the power of Thy sovereignty my succorer, and Thy habitation my home,
and my dwelling-place the seat Thou hast sanctified
from the limitations imposed upon them who are
shut out as by a veil from Thee.

Thou art, verily, the Almighty, the All-Glorious,
the Most Powerful.

CLXIX

Glory be to Thee, O Lord my God! Abase not him
whom Thou hast exalted through the power of Thine
everlasting sovereignty, and remove not far from
Thee him whom Thou hast caused to enter the tabernacle of Thine eternity. Wilt Thou cast away, O my

God, him whom Thou hast overshadowed with Thy Lordship, and wilt Thou turn away from Thee, O my Desire, him to whom Thou hast been a refuge? Canst Thou degrade him whom Thou hast uplifted, or forget him whom Thou didst enable to remember Thee?

Glorified, immensely glorified art Thou! Thou art He who from everlasting hath been the King of the entire creation and its Prime Mover, and Thou wilt to everlasting remain the Lord of all created things and their Ordainer. Glorified art Thou, O my God! If Thou ceasest to be merciful unto Thy servants, who, then, will show mercy unto them; and if Thou refusest to succor Thy loved ones, who is there that can succor them?

Glorified, immeasurably glorified art Thou! Thou art adored in Thy truth, and Thee do we all, verily, worship; and Thou art manifest in Thy justice, and to Thee do we all, verily, bear witness. Thou art, in truth, beloved in Thy grace. No God is there but Thee, the Help in Peril, the Self-Subsisting.

CLXX

Thy name is my healing, O my God, and remembrance of Thee is my remedy. Nearness to Thee is my hope, and love for Thee is my companion. Thy

mercy to me is my healing and my succor in both
this world and the world to come. Thou, verily, art
the All-Bountiful, the All-Knowing, the All-Wise.

CLXXI

O my God, my Master, the Goal of my desire!
This, Thy servant, seeketh to sleep in the shelter of
Thy mercy, and to repose beneath the canopy of
Thy grace, imploring Thy care and Thy protection.

I beg of Thee, O my Lord, by Thine eye that
sleepeth not, to guard mine eyes from beholding
aught beside Thee. Strengthen, then, their vision that
they may discern Thy signs, and behold the Horizon
of Thy Revelation. Thou art He before the revelations of Whose omnipotence the quintessence of
power hath trembled.

No God is there but Thee, the Almighty, the All-
Subduing, the Unconditioned.

CLXXII

How can I choose to sleep, O God, my God, when
the eyes of them that long for Thee are wakeful
because of their separation from Thee; and how can

I lie down to rest whilst the souls of Thy lovers are sore vexed in their remoteness from Thy presence?

I have committed, O my Lord, my spirit and my entire being into the right hand of Thy might and Thy protection, and I lay my head on my pillow through Thy power, and lift it up according to Thy will and Thy good-pleasure. Thou art, in truth, the Preserver, the Keeper, the Almighty, the Most Powerful.

By Thy might! I ask not, whether sleeping or waking, but that which Thou dost desire. I am Thy servant and in Thy hands. Do Thou graciously aid me to do what will shed forth the fragrance of Thy good pleasure. This, truly, is my hope and the hope of them that enjoy near access to Thee. Praised be Thou, O Lord of the worlds!

CLXXIII

My God, my Adored One, my King, my Desire! What tongue can voice my thanks to Thee? I was heedless, Thou didst awaken me. I had turned back from Thee, Thou didst graciously aid me to turn towards Thee. I was as one dead, Thou didst quicken me with the water of life. I was withered, Thou didst revive me with the heavenly stream of Thine utterance which hath flowed forth from the Pen of the All-Merciful.

O Divine Providence! All existence is begotten by Thy bounty; deprive it not of the waters of Thy generosity, neither do Thou withhold it from the ocean of Thy mercy. I beseech Thee to aid and assist me at all times and under all conditions, and seek from the heaven of Thy grace Thine ancient favor. Thou art, in truth, the Lord of bounty, and the Sovereign of the kingdom of eternity.

CLXXIV

O God, my God! I beg of Thee by the ocean of Thy healing, and by the splendors of the Day-Star of Thy grace, and by Thy Name through which Thou didst subdue Thy servants, and by the pervasive power of Thy most exalted Word and the potency of Thy most august Pen, and by Thy mercy that hath preceded the creation of all who are in heaven and on earth, to purge me with the waters of Thy bounty from every affliction and disorder, and from all weakness and feebleness.

Thou seest, O my Lord, Thy suppliant waiting at the door of Thy bounty, and him who hath set his hopes on Thee clinging to the cord of Thy generosity. Deny him not, I beseech Thee, the things he seeketh from the ocean of Thy grace and the Day-Star of Thy loving-kindness.

Powerful art Thou to do what pleaseth Thee. There is none other God save Thee, the Ever-Forgiving, the Most Generous.

CLXXV

I have risen this morning by Thy grace, O my God, and left my home trusting wholly in Thee, and committing myself to Thy care. Send down, then, upon me, out of the heaven of Thy mercy, a blessing from Thy side, and enable me to return home in safety even as Thou didst enable me to set out under Thy protection with my thoughts fixed steadfastly upon Thee.

There is none other God but Thee, the One, the Incomparable, the All-Knowing, the All-Wise.

CLXXVI

Praise be unto Thee, Who art my God and the God of all men, and my Desire and the Desire of all them that have recognized Thee, and my Beloved and the Beloved of such as have acknowledged Thy unity, and the Object of my adoration and of the adoration of them that have near access to Thee, and my Wish and the Wish of such as are wholly devoted to Thee, and my Hope and the Hope of them that have fixed their hearts upon Thee, and my Refuge and the Refuge of all such as have hastened towards Thee, and my Haven and the Haven of whosoever hath repaired unto Thee, and my Goal and the Goal of all them that have set themselves towards Thee, and my Object and the Object of those who have fixed their gaze upon Thee, and my Paradise and the Paradise of them that have ascended towards Thee, and my Lode-star and the Lode-star of all such as yearn after Thee, and my Joy and the Joy of all them that love Thee, and my Light and the Light of all such as have erred and asked to be forgiven by Thee, and my Exultation and the Exultation of all them that remember Thee, and my Stronghold and the Stronghold of all such as have fled to Thee, and my Sanctuary and the Sanctuary of all that dread Thee, and my Lord and the Lord of all such as dwell in the heavens and on the earth!

Unto Thee be praise for that Thou hast enraptured me by the sweetness of Thine utterances, and set me towards the horizon above which the splendors of the Day-Star of Thy face have shone, and caused me to turn unto Thee at a time when most of Thy creatures had broken off from Thee.

Thou art He, O my God, Who hath unlocked the

gate of heaven with the key of Thy Name, the Ever-Blessed, the All-Powerful, the All-Glorious, the Most Great, and hast summoned all mankind to the ocean of Thy presence. No sooner had Thy most sweet voice been raised, than all the inmates of the Kingdom of Names and the Concourse on high were stirred up. By Thy call the fragrance of the raiment of Thy Revelation was wafted over such of Thy creatures as have loved Thee, and such of Thy people as have yearned towards Thee. They rose up and rushed forth to attain the Ocean of Thy meeting, and the Horizon of Thy beauty, and the Tabernacle of Thy Revelation and Thy majesty, and the Sanctuary of Thy Presence and Thy glory. They were so inebriated with the wine of their reunion with Thee, that they rid themselves of all attachment to whatever they themselves and others possessed.

These are Thy servants whom the ascendancy of the oppressor hath failed to deter from fixing their eyes on the Tabernacle of Thy majesty, and whom the hosts of tyranny have been powerless to affright and divert their gaze from the Day-Spring of Thy signs and the Dawning-Place of Thy testimonies.

I swear by Thy glory, O Thou the Lord of all being and the Enlightener of all things visible and invisible! Whoso hath quaffed from the hands of Thy bounteousness the living waters of Thy love will never allow the things pertaining to Thy creatures to keep him back from Thee, neither will he be dismayed at the refusal of all the dwellers of Thy realm to acknowledge Thee. Before all who are in heaven and on earth such a man will cry aloud, and announce unto the people the tumult of the Ocean of Thy bounty and the splendors of the Luminaries of the heaven of Thy bestowals.

Happy indeed is the man that hath turned towards the sanctuary of Thy presence, and rid himself of all attachment to any one except Thyself. He is truly exalted who hath confessed Thy glory, and fixed his eyes upon the Day-Star of Thy loving-kindness. He is endued with understanding who is aware of Thy Revelation and hath acknowledged Thy manifold tokens, Thy signs, and Thy testimonies. He is a man of insight whose eyes have been illumined with the brightness of Thy face, and who, as soon as Thy call was raised, hath recognized Thee. He is a man of hearing who hath been led to hearken unto Thy speech, and to draw nigh unto the billowing ocean of Thine utterances.

Behold Thou this stranger, O my Lord, who hath hastened to attain his most exalted Home in the shelter of Thy shadowing mercy, and this ailing soul who hath set his face towards the ocean of Thy healing.

Look, then, O Thou my God Who settest my soul on fire, upon the tears I shed, and the sighs I utter, and the anguish that afflicteth my heart and the fire that consumeth my being. Thy glory beareth me witness, O Thou, the Light of the world! The fire of Thy love that burneth continually within me hath so inflamed me that whoever among Thy creatures approacheth me, and inclineth his inner ear towards me, cannot fail to hear its raging within each of my veins.

I am so carried away by the sweetness of Thine utterances, and so inebriated with the wine of Thy tender mercies, that my voice can never be stilled, nor can my suppliant hands any longer desist from being stretched out towards Thee. Thou seest, O my Lord, how mine eyes are fixed in the direction of Thy grace, and mine ears inclined towards the kingdom of Thine utterance, and my tongue unloosed to celebrate Thy praise, and my face set towards Thy face that surviveth all that hath been created by Thy word, and my hands raised up towards the heaven of Thy bounty and favor.

Wilt Thou keep back from Thee the stranger whom Thou didst call unto his most exalted Home beneath the shadow of the wings of Thy mercy, or cast away the wretched creature that hath hastened to attain the shores of the ocean of Thy wealth? Wilt Thou shut up the door of Thy grace to the face of Thy creatures after having opened it through the power of Thy might and of Thy sovereignty, or close the eyes of Thy people when Thou hast already commanded them to turn unto the Day-Spring of Thy Beauty and the Dawning-Place of the splendors of Thy countenance?

Nay, and to this Thy glory beareth me witness! Such is not my thought of Thee, nor the thought of those of Thy servants that have near access to Thyself, nor that of the sincere amongst Thy people.

Thou knowest, and seest, and hearest, O my Lord, that before every tree I am moved to lift up my voice to Thee, and before every stone I am impelled to sigh and lament. Hath it been Thy purpose in creating me, O my God, to touch me with tribulation, or to enable me to manifest Thy Cause in the kingdom of Thy creation?

Thou hearest, O my God, my sighs and my groaning, and beholdest my powerlessness, and my poverty, and my misery, and my woes, and my wretchedness. I swear by Thy might! I have wept with such a weeping that I have been unable to make mention of Thee, or to extol Thee, and cried with such a bitter cry that every mother in her bereavement was bewildered at me, and forgot her own anguish and the sighs she had uttered.

I implore Thee, O my Lord, by Thine Ark, through which the potency of Thy will was manifested and the energizing influences of Thy purpose were revealed, and which saileth on both land and sea through the power of Thy might, not to seize me in my mighty sins and great trespasses. I swear by Thy glory! The waters of Thy forgiveness and Thy mercy have emboldened me, as hath Thy dealing, in bygone ages, with the sincere among Thy chosen ones, and with such of Thy Messengers as have proclaimed Thy oneness.

I am well aware, O my Lord, that I have been so

carried away by the clear tokens of Thy loving-kindness, and so completely inebriated with the wine of Thine utterance, that whatever I behold I readily discover that it maketh Thee known unto me, and it remindeth me of Thy signs, and of Thy tokens, and of Thy testimonies. By Thy glory! Every time I lift up mine eyes unto Thy heaven, I call to mind Thy highness and Thy loftiness, and Thine incomparable glory and greatness; and every time I turn my gaze to Thine earth, I am made to recognize the evidences of Thy power and the tokens of Thy bounty. And when I behold the sea, I find that it speaketh to me of Thy majesty, and of the potency of Thy might, and of Thy sovereignty and Thy grandeur. And at whatever time I contemplate the mountains, I am led to discover the ensigns of Thy victory and the standards of Thine omnipotence.

I swear by Thy might, O Thou in Whose grasp are the reins of all mankind, and the destinies of the nations! I am so inflamed by my love for Thee, and so inebriated with the wine of Thy oneness, that I can hear from the whisper of the winds the sound of Thy glorification and praise, and can recognize in the murmur of the waters the voice that proclaimeth Thy virtues and Thine attributes, and can apprehend from the rustling of the leaves the mysteries that have been irrevocably ordained by Thee in Thy realm.

Glorified art Thou, O God of all names and Creator of the heavens! I render Thee thanks that

Thou hast made known unto Thy servants this Day whereon the river that is life indeed hath flowed forth from the fingers of Thy bounty, and the spring-time of Thy revelation and Thy presence hath appeared through Thy manifestation unto all who are in Thy heaven and all who are on Thy earth.

This is the Day, O my Lord, whose brightness Thou hast exalted above the brightness of the sun and the splendors thereof. I testify that the light it sheddeth proceedeth out of the glory of the light of Thy countenance, and is begotten by the radiance of the morn of Thy Revelation. This is the Day whereon the hopeless have been clothed with the raiment of confidence, and the sick attired with the robe of healing, and the poor drawn nigh unto the ocean of Thy riches.

I swear by Thy Beauty, O King of eternity Who sittest on Thy most glorious Throne! He Who is the Day-Spring of Thy signs and the Revealer of Thy clear tokens hath, notwithstanding the immensity of His wisdom and the loftiness of His knowledge, confessed His powerlessness to comprehend the least of Thine utterances, in their relation to Thy most exalted Pen,—how much more is He incapable of apprehending the nature of Thine all-glorious Self and of Thy most august Essence!

I cannot think, O my God, of any words wherewith to make mention of Thee, and know not how to express or extol Thee. Were I to attempt to describe Thee by Thy names, I would readily recognize that the kingdom of these names is itself created through the movement of Thy fingers, and trembleth for fear of Thee. And were I to venture to extol Thine attributes, I would be forced to admit that these attributes are Thine own creation, and lie within Thy grasp. It behooveth not Them Who are the Manifestations of these names and attributes to stand before the gate of the city of Thy Revelation, how much less to scale the heights whereon Thou didst stablish the throne of Thy majesty.

I swear by Thy might, O Thou Who art the King of names and the Maker of the heavens! Whatsoever hath been adorned with the robe of words is but Thy creation which hath been generated in Thy realm and begotten through the operation of Thy will, and is wholly unworthy of Thy highness and falleth short of Thine excellence.

And since it hath been demonstrated that Thy most august Self is immeasurably exalted above all that hath been created in the world of being, and is far above the reach and ken of the apprehension of Thy chosen Ones and Thy loved Ones, the splendors of the light of Thy unity are therefore manifested, and it becometh evident unto every one, whether free or bond, that Thou art One in Thine own Self, one in Thy Cause, and one in Thy Revelation. Great is the blessedness of the man who, in his love towards Thee, hath rid himself of all attachment from every one except Thyself, and hastened unto the horizon of Thy Revelation, and attained unto this Cup which Thou hast caused to excel all the seas of the earth.

I beg of Thee, O my God, by Thy power, and Thy might, and Thy sovereignty, which have embraced all who are in Thy heaven and on Thy earth, to make known unto Thy servants this luminous Way and this straight Path, that they may acknowledge Thy unity and Thy oneness, with a certainty which the vain imaginations of the doubters will not impair, nor the idle fancies of the wayward obscure. Illumine, O my Lord, the eyes of Thy servants, and brighten their hearts with the splendors of the light of Thy knowledge, that they may apprehend the greatness of this most sublime station, and recognize this most luminous Horizon, that haply the clamor of men may fail to deter them from turning their gaze towards the effulgent light of Thy unity, and to hinder them from setting their faces toward the Horizon of detachment.

This is the Day, O my Lord, which Thou didst announce unto all mankind as the Day whereon Thou wouldst reveal Thy Self, and shed Thy radiance, and shine brightly over all Thy creatures. Thou hast, moreover, entered into a covenant with them, in Thy Books, and Thy Scriptures, and Thy Scrolls, and Thy Tablets, concerning Him Who is the Day-Spring of Thy Revelation, and hast appointed the Bayán to be the Herald of this Most Great and all-glorious Manifestation, and this most resplendent and most sublime Appearance.

And when the world's horizon was illumined, and He Who is the Most Great Name was manifested, all disbelieved in Him and in His signs, except such as have been carried away by the sweetness of Thy glorification and praise. There befell Him what must remain inscrutable to everyone except Thee, Whose knowledge transcendeth all who are in Thy heaven and all who are on Thy earth.

Thou well knowest, O my God, that the Revealer of the Bayán (the Báb) hath commanded all mankind concerning Thy Cause, and Thy Revelation, and Thy Sovereignty. He hath said, and sweet is His speech: "Beware lest the Bayán and its Letters keep you back from Him Who is the Most Merciful and from His sovereignty." He, moreover, hath written: "Were He to produce no more than one verse, ye must not deny Him. Haste ye towards Him, that haply He may cause to descend upon you what He pleaseth, as a token of His grace unto you. He truly is the Possessor of His servants, and the King of creation."

Thou seest, then, O Thou Who art the Beloved of the world and the Revealer of the Most Great Name, how He hath come down with the kingdom of His signs, and in a manner that hath caused the atoms of the earth to testify that the whole world hath been filled with these signs. And yet, notwithstanding this most manifest and all-glorious Revelation, and these signs which none can appraise except Thee, O Thou the King of names, Thou beholdest how they have broken off from Him Who is the Day-Spring of Thine Essence, and have caviled at the One Who is the Fountain-Head of Thy wisdom and of Thine utterance. They were so seized with thirst for fame, that they rejected Thy tokens, and Thy testimonies, and Thy signs, which every man of insight perceiveth in whatsoever declareth Thy greatness, and Thy sovereignty, and acknowledgeth Thy Revelation and Thy might. They have so traduced Him as to cause the inmates of the all-glorious Tabernacle and the Concourse on high to lament, and have uttered such calumnies against Him that the souls of Thy chosen Ones and the hearts of them that are dear to Thee have melted. They have erred so grievously that they cast away Thy most resplendent signs, and clung to their idle fancies, O Thou Who art the Possessor of Names and the Lord of the Throne on high and of earth below!

Thou art, O my God and the Exultation of my heart, the One Who hath adorned Thy Tablet, of which none is aware except Thee, with the mention of this Day which Thou didst call after Thy name, that haply none may on that day be seen save Thy most august Self, and naught else be brought to mind except Thy most sweet remembrance.

No sooner had He revealed Himself than the foundations of the kindreds of the earth shook and trembled, and the learned swooned away, and the wise were bewildered, except such as have, through the power of Thy might, drawn nigh unto Thee, and

received the choice wine of Thy Revelation from the hand of Thy grace, and have quaffed it in Thy name, and exclaimed: "Praise be unto Thee, O Thou the Desire of the worlds! and glory be to Thee, O Thou Who art the Exultation of the hearts that pant after Thee!"

My God, my Master, my Highest Hope, and the Goal of my desire! Thou seest and hearest the sighing of this wronged One, from this darksome well which the vain imaginations of Thine adversaries have built, and from this blind pit which the idle fancies of the wicked among Thy creatures have digged. By Thy Beauty, O Thou Whose glory is uncovered to the face of men! I am not impatient in the troubles that touch me in my love for Thee, neither in the adversities which I suffer in Thy path. Nay, I have, by Thy power, chosen them for mine own self, and I glory in them amongst such of Thy creatures as enjoy near access to Thee, and those of Thy servants that are wholly devoted to Thy Self.

I beseech Thee, however, O Thou Who art the Enlightener of the world and the Lord of the nations, at this very moment when, with the hands of hope, I have clung to the hem of the raiment of Thy mercy and Thy bounty, to forgive Thy servants who have soared in the atmosphere of Thy nearness, and set their faces towards the splendors of the light of Thy countenance, and turned unto the horizon of Thy good pleasure, and approached the ocean of Thy mercy, and all their lives long have spoken

forth Thy praise, and have been inflamed with the
fire of their love for Thee. Do Thou ordain for them,
O Lord my God, both before and after their death,
what becometh the loftiness of Thy bounty and the
excellence of Thy loving-kindness.

Grant, O my Lord, that they who have ascended
unto Thee may repair unto Him Who is the most
exalted Companion, and abide beneath the shadow of
the Tabernacle of Thy majesty and the Sanctuary of
Thy glory. Sprinkle, O my Lord, upon them from
the ocean of Thy forgiveness what will make them
worthy to abide, so long as Thine own sovereignty endureth, within Thy most exalted kingdom and Thine
all-highest dominion. Potent art Thou to do what
pleaseth Thee.

Deny not Thy loved ones, O my Lord, the sweet
savors of this Day whereon the mysteries of Thy
name, the Self-Subsisting, were unraveled, and all
that had been enshrined within the treasuries of Thy
wisdom was revealed. This is the Day, O my Lord,
whereon every atom of the earth hath been made to
vibrate and to cry out: "O Thou Who art the
Revealer of signs and the King of creation! I, verily,
perceive the fragrance of Thy presence. Methinks
Thou hast revealed Thyself, and unlocked the door
of reunion with Thee before all who are in Thy
heaven and all who are on Thy earth. I am persuaded
through the fragrance of Thy robe, O my Lord, that
the world hath been honored through Thy presence,
and hath inhaled the sweet smell of Thy meeting. I

know not, however, O Thou the Beloved of the world and the Desire of the nations, the place wherein the throne of Thy majesty hath been established, nor the seat which hath been made Thy footstool, and been illumined with the splendors of the light of Thy face."

I swear by Thy glory, O Thou Who art the Lord of all being and the Possessor of all things visible and invisible! Every man of understanding hath been so bewildered at Thy knowledge, and every man endued with insight been so perplexed in his attempt to fathom the signs of Thy great glory, that all have recognized their powerlessness to visualize, and their impotence to soar into, the heaven wherefrom one of the Luminaries of the Manifestations of Thy knowledge and of the Day-Springs of Thy wisdom hath shone forth. Who is he that shall befittingly describe this most sublime station and this most august seat— the seat which, as decreed by Thee, transcendeth the comprehension of Thy creatures and the testimonies of Thy servants, and which hath everlastingly been hid from the understanding and the knowledge of men, and been closed with the seal of Thy name, the Self-Subsisting.

I swear by Thy glory and Thy sovereignty which overshadow the kingdoms of earth and of heaven! Were any of Thy chosen Ones and Thy Messengers to meditate on the manifold evidences of Thy most exalted Pen—a Pen which is driven by the fingers of Thy will—and were he to muse on its mysteries, and its tokens, and all that it showeth forth, he would be so perplexed that his tongue would fail to extol and describe Thee, and his heart would be utterly unable to understand Thee. For he would, at one time, discover that from this Pen there floweth out unto all created things the water that is life indeed, and that the Pen itself hath been named by Thee the trumpet whereby the dead speed out of their sepulchers. At another time he would find that there proceedeth from this Pen such fire as Thine own Revelation can kindle, and as He Who conversed with Thee (Moses) on Sinai hath perceived.

How marvelous, then, are the manifold tokens of Thy might, and how great are the diverse evidences of Thy power! The learned have, without exception, admitted their ignorance when confronted with the radiance of the Luminary of Thy knowledge; and the mighty have all confessed their impotence in the face of the billowing Ocean of Thy power; and the rich have one and all acknowledged their poverty before the effusions of the Treasuries of Thy wealth; and the worldly wise have each recognized their nothingness beside the splendors of the Light of Thy beauty; and the exalted have all witnessed unto their abasement when face to face with the effulgence of the Day-Star of Thy glory; and they who are in authority have borne witness to their own evanescence and to the evanescence of others, and discovered the eternity of Thy majesty, and of Thy sovereignty, and of Thy sublimity, and of Thy power.

My God, and the God of all things, and my King and the King of all things, and the Beloved of my soul, and the Goal of my desire! Thou knowest full well that I make mention of Thee, in this day, in the name of such of Thy creatures as have detached themselves from all except Thee, and I extol Thy virtues through the tongue of those of Thy people that have recognized Thy oneness, that haply there may pour out from the sighs which they utter in their love and their yearning for Thee what will melt away all that may hinder Thy servants from setting their faces towards the heaven of Thy knowledge and the kingdom of Thy signs.

This, then, O my God and the God of all names, and the Creator of earth and heaven, is the Day whereon He Whose heart gloweth with the flaming fire of Thy presence is calling upon Thee. Where can separation from Thee be found, O my God, so that reunion with Thee may be clearly recognized at the appearance of the Light of Thy unity, and the revelation of the splendors of the Sun of Thy oneness? I ask pardon of Thee, O my God, for all that hath been said, and for whatsoever hath flowed out, and is now flowing out from my Pen in Thy days. I testify that Thou hast decreed that the offering of prayer should befit not me, but Him Who hath, at Thy bidding and in conformity with Thy pleasure, preceded me. Rather hast Thou ordained that the revelation of verses should be specially attributed unto this mighty Manifestation, and to This Announcement that hath adorned the Scrolls of Thy majesty and Thy Tablet in which account is kept.

I render Thee thanks, O Thou Who hast lighted Thy fire within my soul, and cast the beams of Thy light into my heart, that Thou hast taught Thy servants how to make mention of Thee, and revealed unto them the ways whereby they can supplicate Thee, through Thy most holy and exalted tongue, and Thy most august and precious speech. But for Thy leave, who is there that could venture to express Thy might and Thy grandeur; and were it not for Thine instruction, who is the man that could discover the ways of Thy pleasure in the kingdom of Thy creation?

I beseech Thee, O God of bounty and King of all created things, to guard Thy servants from the imaginations which their hearts may devise. Raise them up, then, to such heights that their footsteps may slip not in the face of the evidences of Thy handiwork, which the manifold exigencies of Thy wisdom have ordained, and whose secrets Thou hast hid from the face of Thy people and Thy creatures. Withhold them not, O my Lord, from the ocean of Thy knowledge, neither do Thou deprive them of what Thou didst destine for such of Thy chosen ones as have near access to Thee, and those of Thy trusted ones as are wholly devoted to Thy Self. Supply them, then, from Thy sea of certainty with what will calm the agitation of their hearts. Turn, O Lord my God, the darkness of their fancies into the brightness of certitude, and cause them to arise, and to walk steadfastly in Thy straight Path, that haply Thy Book may not hinder them from recognizing Him Who is its Revealer, and Thy names from acknowledging the One Who is their Creator, and their Provider, and their Origin, and their King, and their Begetter, and their Destroyer, and their Glorifier, and their Abaser, and their Governor, and the Sovereign Protector of their Bearers.

Thou art the One, O my God and my Ruler, Who hast sent down Thy Book that Thou mayest manifest my Cause, and glorify my Word. Through it Thou didst enter into a Covenant, concerning me, with all that hath been created in Thy realm. Thou seest, O Beloved of the world, how the rebellious among Thy creatures have made of that Covenant a bulwark for themselves, and through it have withdrawn from Thy Beauty, and repudiated Thy signs.

Thou art He, O my God, Who hath commanded them in Thy great Book, and said: "Fear ye the Most Merciful, O people of the Bayán, and deny not Him for Whom I have ordained the Bayán to be one of the leaves of His Paradise. I, verily, esteem it as a gift from me unto Him. Were it His pleasure to accept it, He, truly, is the Most Bountiful; and if He cast it away and refuse to consider it, His verdict is just, and He, in very truth, is Praiseworthy in His acts, and meet to be obeyed in His behests. To none is given the right to cavil at Him."

Thou beholdest, therefore, O my God, how this

wronged one hath fallen into the hands of such as have denied Thy right, and broken off from Thy sovereignty. He, round whose person circleth Thy proof, and in whose name and on behalf of whose sovereignty Thy testimony crieth out unto all created things, hath suffered more grievously in his days than any pen can recount, and been so harassed that He Who is Thy Spirit (Jesus) lamented, and all the denizens of Thy Kingdom and all the inmates of Thy Tabernacle in the realms above cried with a great and bitter lamentation.

Should any one incline his inner ear, he would hear the cry and the wailing of all created things over what hath befallen Him Whom the world hath wronged, at the hands of them with whom Thou hast covenanted in the Day of Separation. Where is that fair-minded soul, O my God, who will judge equitably Thy Cause, and where is the man of insight to be found who will behold Thee with Thine own eyes? Is there any man of hearing who will hear Thee with Thine ears, or one endued with eloquence who will speak the truth in Thy days?

I swear by Thy glory, O Thou Who beholdest me from Thine all-glorious horizon, and hearest the voice of the Lote-Tree beyond which there is no passing! Should any one consider Thy Books which Thou didst name the Bayán, and ponder in his heart what hath been revealed therein, he would discover that each of these Books announceth my Revelation, and declareth my Name, and testifieth to my Self, and proclaimeth my Cause, and my Praise, and my Rising, and the radiance of my Glory. And yet, notwithstanding Thy proclamation, O my God, and in spite of the words Thou didst utter, O my Beloved, Thou hast seen and heard their calumnies against me, and their evil doings in my days.

I testify in my present state, O my Lord, and against the will of him who hath turned his back to Thee (Mírzá Yaḥyá), that Thou art God, and that there is none other God beside Thee. This, verily, is the Day wherewith Thy Scriptures, and Thy Books, and Thy Tablets, have been adorned. And He Who now speaketh is, in truth, the Well-guarded Treasure, and the Hidden Secret, and the Preserved Tablet, and the Impenetrable Mystery, and the Sealed Book. He, truly, is to be obeyed in whatsoever He commandeth, and decreeth, and revealeth, and is to be loved in everything He, through His sovereignty, enjoineth, and, through His power, ordaineth. Whoso will hesitate for less than the twinkling of an eye, hath, verily, denied Thy right, and repudiated all that Thou hast revealed in Thy Books, and in Thy Scriptures, and sent down with Thy chosen Ones, and Thy Prophets, and Thy Messengers, and the Trustees of Thy Revelation.

I beg of Thee, O Thou in Whose hands are the kingdoms of earth and heaven, and in Whose grasp lie all who dwell in the dominions of Thy Revelation and Thy creation, not to withhold the glance of Thy favors from such as have sustained tribulations in

Thy path, and tasted of the cup of woe in their love towards Thee, and have been cast into prison in Thy name, and endured what none of Thy creatures and Thy people have endured. They are Thy servants, O my Lord, who have responded to Thee as soon as Thou didst send out Thy summons, and have set their faces towards Thee when the light of Thy countenance was lifted upon them, and turned unto Thee at the time when Thy most exalted horizon shone forth with the brightness of Thy name through which all who are in Thy heaven and on Thy earth swooned away. Ordain for them, O my Lord, what Thou didst ordain for Thy chosen ones who have welcomed the darts of the infidels in Thy Cause and for love of Thee, and hasted to attain the orient of tribulation with Thy name on their lips and Thy remembrance in their hearts. Thou art the One, O my God, Who hath promised in Thy perspicuous utterances to remember them in Thy Book as a recompense for their works in Thy days.

Bless them, O my God, and ascribe unto them such glory as hath shone forth above the horizon of Thy will, and hath shed its splendors from the kingdom of Thine utterance. Immerse them, O my Lord, beneath the ocean of Thy mercy, and illumine them with the dawning light of Thy Revelation. Forgive, then, O my God, their fathers and their mothers, by Thy favor, and Thy bounty, and Thy tender mercies. Send, then, upon them from the right hand of Thy most exalted Paradise the fragrance of the robe of

Thine all-glorious Beauty. Potent art Thou to do what
pleaseth Thee. Thou, verily, art the Governor, the
Ordainer, the All-Bountiful, the Ever-Forgiving, the
Most Generous.

Praise be unto Thee, O Thou the Beloved of the
world, and the Adored of the hearts of them that
have recognized Thee.

CLXXVII

I beseech Thee, O my God, by Thy mighty Sign,
and by the revelation of Thy grace amongst men, to
cast me not away from the gate of the city of Thy
presence, and to disappoint not the hopes I have set
on the manifestations of Thy grace amidst Thy
creatures. Thou seest me, O my God, holding to Thy
Name, the Most Holy, the Most Luminous, the Most
Mighty, the Most Great, the Most Exalted, the Most
Glorious and clinging to the hem of the robe to which
have clung all in this world and in the world to come.

I beseech Thee, O my God, by Thy most sweet
Voice and by Thy most exalted Word, to draw me
ever nearer to the threshold of Thy door, and to suffer me not to be far removed from the shadow of
Thy mercy and the canopy of Thy bounty. Thou
seest me, O my God, holding to Thy Name, the Most
Holy, the Most Luminous, the Most Mighty, the

Most Great, the Most Exalted, the Most Glorious, and clinging to the hem of the robe to which have clung all in this world and in the world to come.

I beseech Thee, O my God, by the splendor of Thy luminous brow and the brightness of the light of Thy countenance, which shineth from the all-highest horizon, to attract me by the fragrance of Thy raiment, and make me drink of the choice wine of Thine utterance. Thou seest me, O my God, holding to Thy Name, the Most Holy, the Most Luminous, the Most Mighty, the Most Great, the Most Exalted, the Most Glorious, and clinging to the hem of the robe to which have clung all in this world and in the world to come.

I beseech Thee, O my God, by Thy hair which moveth across Thy face, even as Thy most exalted pen moveth across the pages of Thy Tablets, shedding the musk of hidden meanings over the kingdom of Thy creation, so to raise me up to serve Thy Cause that I shall not fall back, nor be hindered by the suggestions of them who have caviled at Thy signs and turned away from Thy face. Thou seest me, O my God, holding to Thy Name, the Most Holy, the Most Luminous, the Most Mighty, the Most Great, the Most Exalted, the Most Glorious, and clinging to the hem of the robe to which have clung all in this world and in the world to come.

I beseech Thee, O my God, by Thy Name which Thou hast made the King of Names, by which all who are in heaven and all who are on earth have been enraptured, to enable me to gaze on the Day-Star of Thy Beauty, and to supply me with the wine of Thine utterance. Thou seest me, O my God, holding to Thy Name, the Most Holy, the Most Luminous, the Most Mighty, the Most Great, the Most Exalted, the Most Glorious, and clinging to the hem of the robe to which have clung all in this world and in the world to come.

I beseech Thee, O my God, by the Tabernacle of Thy majesty upon the loftiest summits, and the Canopy of Thy Revelation on the highest hills, to graciously aid me to do what Thy will hath desired and Thy purpose hath manifested. Thou seest me, O my God, holding to Thy Name, the Most Holy, the Most Luminous, the Most Mighty, the Most Great, the Most Exalted, the Most Glorious, and clinging to the hem of the robe to which have clung all in this world and in the world to come.

I beseech Thee, O my God, by Thy Beauty that shineth forth above the horizon of eternity, a Beauty before which as soon as it revealeth itself the kingdom of beauty boweth down in worship, magnifying it in ringing tones, to grant that I may die to all that I possess and live to whatsoever belongeth unto Thee. Thou seest me, O my God, holding to Thy Name, the Most Holy, the Most Luminous, the Most Mighty, the Most Great, the Most Exalted, the Most Glorious, and clinging to the hem of the robe to which have clung all in this world and in the world to come.

I beseech Thee, O my God, by the Manifestation

of Thy Name, the Well-Beloved, through Whom the hearts of Thy lovers were consumed and the souls of all that dwell on earth have soared aloft, to aid me to remember Thee amongst Thy creatures, and to extol Thee amidst Thy people. Thou seest me, O my God, holding to Thy Name, the Most Holy, the Most Luminous, the Most Mighty, the Most Great, the Most Exalted, the Most Glorious, and clinging to the hem of the robe to which have clung all in this world and in the world to come.

I beseech Thee, O my God, by the rustling of the Divine Lote-Tree and the murmur of the breezes of Thine utterance in the kingdom of Thy names, to remove me far from whatsoever Thy will abhorreth, and draw me nigh unto the station wherein He Who is the Day-Spring of Thy signs hath shone forth. Thou seest me, O my God, holding to Thy Name, the Most Holy, the Most Luminous, the Most Mighty, the Most Great, the Most Exalted, the Most Glorious, and clinging to the hem of the robe to which have clung all in this world and in the world to come.

I beseech Thee, O my God, by that Letter which, as soon as it proceeded out of the mouth of Thy will, hath caused the oceans to surge, and the winds to blow, and the fruits to be revealed, and the trees to spring forth, and all past traces to vanish, and all veils to be rent asunder, and them who are devoted to Thee to hasten unto the light of the countenance of their Lord, the Unconstrained, to make known unto me what lay hid in the treasuries of Thy knowledge and concealed within the repositories of Thy wisdom. Thou seest me, O my God, holding to Thy Name, the Most Holy, the Most Luminous, the Most Mighty, the Most Great, the Most Exalted, the Most Glorious, and clinging to the hem of the robe to which have clung all in this world and in the world to come.

I beseech Thee, O my God, by the fire of Thy love which drove sleep from the eyes of Thy chosen ones and Thy loved ones, and by their remembrance and praise of Thee at the hour of dawn, to number me with such as have attained unto that which Thou hast sent down in Thy Book and manifested through Thy will. Thou seest me, O my God, holding to Thy Name, the Most Holy, the Most Luminous, the Most Mighty, the Most Great, the Most Exalted, the Most Glorious, and clinging to the hem of the robe to which have clung all in this world and in the world to come.

I beseech Thee, O my God, by the light of Thy countenance which impelled them who are nigh unto Thee to meet the darts of Thy decree, and such as are devoted to Thee to face the swords of Thine enemies in Thy path, to write down for me with Thy most exalted Pen what Thou hast written down for Thy trusted ones and Thy chosen ones. Thou seest me, O my God, holding to Thy Name, the Most Holy, the Most Luminous, the Most Mighty, the Most Great, the Most Exalted, the Most Glorious, and clinging to the hem of the robe to which have clung all in this world and in the world to come.

I beseech Thee, O my God, by Thy Name through which Thou hast hearkened unto the call of Thy lovers, and the sighs of them that long for Thee, and the cry of them that enjoy near access to Thee, and the groaning of them that are devoted to Thee, and through which Thou hast fulfilled the wishes of them that have set their hopes on Thee, and hast granted them their desires, through Thy grace and Thy favors, and by Thy Name through which the ocean of forgiveness surged before Thy face, and the clouds of Thy generosity rained upon Thy servants, to write down for every one who hath turned unto Thee, and observed the fast prescribed by Thee, the recompense decreed for such as speak not except by Thy leave, and who forsook all that they possessed in Thy path and for love of Thee.

I beseech Thee, O my Lord, by Thyself, and by Thy signs, and Thy clear tokens, and the shining light of the Day-Star of Thy Beauty, and Thy Branches, to cancel the trespasses of those who have held fast to Thy laws, and have observed what Thou hast prescribed unto them in Thy Book. Thou seest me, O my God, holding to Thy Name, the Most Holy, the Most Luminous, the Most Mighty, the Most Great, the Most Exalted, the Most Glorious, and clinging to the hem of the robe to which have clung all in this world and in the world to come.

CLXXVIII

Praised be Thou, O Lord my God! I supplicate Thee by Him Whom Thou hast called into being, Whose Revelation Thou hast ordained to be Thine own Revelation and His Concealment Thine own Concealment. Through His Firstness Thou hast confirmed Thine own Firstness, and through His Lastness Thou hast affirmed Thine own Lastness. Through the power of His might and the influence of His sovereignty the mighty have apprehended Thine omnipotence, and through His glory they who are endowed with authority have acknowledged Thy majesty and greatness. Through His supreme ascendancy Thy transcendent sovereignty and all-encompassing dominion have been recognized, and through His will Thine own will hath been revealed. Through the light of His countenance the splendors of Thine own face have shone forth, and through His Cause Thine own Cause hath been made manifest. Through the generative power of His utterance the whole earth hath been made the recipient of the wondrous signs and tokens of Thy sovereignty, and the heavens have been filled with the revelations of Thine incomparable majesty, and the seas have been enriched with the sacred pearls of Thine omniscience and wisdom, and the trees adorned with the fruits of Thy knowledge. Through Him all things have sung Thy praise, and all the eyes have been turned in the direction of

Thy mercy. Through Him the faces of all have been set towards the splendors of the light of Thy countenance, and the souls of all have been inclined unto the revelations of Thy divine greatness.

How great is Thy power! How exalted Thy sovereignty! How lofty Thy might! How excellent Thy majesty! How supreme is Thy grandeur—a grandeur which He Who is Thy Manifestation hath made known and wherewith Thou hast invested Him as a sign of Thy generosity and bountiful favor. I bear witness, O my God, that through Him Thy most resplendent signs have been uncovered, and Thy mercy hath encompassed the entire creation. But for Him, how could the Celestial Dove have uttered its songs or the Heavenly Nightingale, according to the decree of God, have warbled its melody?

I testify that no sooner had the First Word proceeded, through the potency of Thy will and purpose, out of His mouth, and the First Call gone forth from His lips than the whole creation was revolutionized, and all that are in the heavens and all that are on earth were stirred to the depths. Through that Word the realities of all created things were shaken, were divided, separated, scattered, combined and reunited, disclosing, in both the contingent world and the heavenly kingdom, entities of a new creation, and revealing, in the unseen realms, the signs and tokens of Thy unity and oneness. Through that Call Thou didst announce unto all Thy servants the advent of

Thy most great Revelation and the appearance of
Thy most perfect Cause.

No sooner had that Revelation been unveiled to
men's eyes than the signs of universal discord appeared among the peoples of the world, and commo-
tion seized the dwellers of earth and heaven, and the
foundations of all things were shaken. The forces of
dissension were released, the meaning of the Word
was unfolded, and every several atom in all created
things acquired its own distinct and separate char-
acter. Hell was made to blaze, and the delights of
Paradise were uncovered to men's eyes. Blessed is the
man that turneth towards Thee, and woe betide him
who standeth aloof from Thee, who denieth Thee and
repudiateth Thy signs in this Revelation wherein the
faces of the exponents of denial have turned black
and the faces of the exponents of truthfulness have
turned white, O Thou Who art the Possessor of all
names and attributes, Who holdest in Thy grasp the
empire of whatever hath been created in heaven and
on earth!

Praise be to Thee, therefore, O my God—such
praise as Thou didst ascribe to Thine own Self, and
which none except Thee can either comprehend or
reckon. Thou art He, O my Lord, Who hath made
known His own Self unto me, at a time when Thy
servants have failed to recognize Thee—servants who,
by virtue of the ties that bind them to Thee, have
been ruling over all that dwell on earth and have been
vaunting themselves over its peoples. Were I, O my

God, to exercise from pole to pole supreme dominion over the earth, and were I to be offered all the treasures it containeth, and were I to expend them in Thy path, I would still be powerless to attain unto this station, unless I were assisted and strengthened by Thee. And were I to glorify Thee, O my God, so long as the glory of Thy majesty endureth and the influence of Thy sovereignty and power will last, such a glorification could never be compared with any of the praises which Thou, as a token of Thy grace, hast taught me, and wherewith Thou hast bidden me to extol Thy virtues. If such be the excellence of each one of the praises which Thou hast taught me, how immeasurably greater must be the excellence of the station of the One Who hath known Thee, Who hath entered Thy Presence, and pursued steadfastly the path of Thy Cause!

I have clearly perceived, and I am wholly persuaded, that Thou hast from everlasting been immeasurably exalted above the mention of all beings, and wilt continue unto everlasting to remain far above the conception of Thy creatures. None can befittingly praise Thee except Thine own Self and such as are like unto Thee. Thou hast, verily, been at all times, and wilt everlastingly continue to remain, immensely exalted beyond and above all comparison and likeness, above all imagination of parity or resemblance. Having, thus, recognized Thee as One Who is incomparable, and Whose nature none can possess, it becometh incontrovertibly evident that whosoever may praise Thee, his praise can befit only such as are of his own nature, and are subject to his own limitations, and it can in no wise adequately describe the sublimity of Thy sovereignty, nor scale the heights of Thy majesty and holiness. How sweet, therefore, is the praise Thou givest to Thine own Self, and the description Thou givest of Thine own Being!

I testify, O my God, that Thou hast, from eternity, sent down upon Thy servants naught else except that which can cause them to soar up and be drawn near unto Thee, and to ascend into the heaven of Thy transcendent oneness. Thou hast established Thy bounds among them, and ordained them to stand among Thy creatures as evidences of Thy justice and as signs of Thy mercy, and to be the stronghold of Thy protection amongst Thy people, that no man may in Thy realm transgress against his neighbor. How great is the blessedness of him who, for love of Thy beauty and for the sake of Thy pleasure, hath curbed the desires of a corrupt inclination and observed the precepts laid down by Thy most exalted Pen! He, in truth, is to be numbered with them that have attained unto all good, and followed the way of guidance.

I beseech Thee, O my Lord, by Thy Name through which Thou hast enabled Thy servants and Thy people to know Thee, through which Thou hast drawn the hearts of those who have recognized Thee towards the resplendent court of Thy oneness, and the souls

of Thy favored ones unto the Day-Spring of Thy
unity,—I beseech Thee to grant that I may be assisted
to observe the fast wholly for Thy sake, O Thou Who
art full of majesty and glory! Empower me, then,
O my God, to be reckoned among them that have
clung to Thy laws and precepts for the sake of Thee
alone, their eyes fixed on Thy face. These, indeed,
are they whose wine is all that hath proceeded out
of the mouth of Thy primal will, whose pure beverage is Thine enthralling call, whose heavenly River is
Thy love, whose Paradise is entrance into Thy presence and reunion with Thee. For Thou hast been
their Beginning and their End, and their Highest
Hope, and their Supreme Desire. Blinded be the eye
that gazeth on whatsoever may displease Thee, and
confounded be the soul that seeketh the things that
are contrary to Thy will.

Deign, O my God, I implore Thee, by Thy Self
and by them, to accept, through Thy grace and Thy
loving-kindness, the works we have performed, however much they fall short of the loftiness of Thy state
and the sublimity of Thy station, O Thou Who art
most dear to the hearts that long for Thee, and the
Healer of the souls that have recognized Thee! Rain
down, therefore, upon us from the heaven of Thy
mercy and the clouds of Thy gracious providence
that which will cleanse us from the faintest trace of
evil and corrupt desires, and will draw us nearer unto
Him Who is the Manifestation of Thy most exalted
and all-glorious Self. Thou art, verily, the Lord of

this world and of the next, and art powerful to do all things.

Do Thou bless, O Lord my God, the Primal Point, through Whom the point of creation hath been made to revolve in both the visible and invisible worlds, Whom Thou hast designated as the One whereunto should return whatsoever must return unto Thee, and as the Revealer of whatsoever may be manifested by Thee. Do Thou also bless such of His Letters as have not turned away from Thee, who have been firmly established in Thy love, and clung steadfastly to Thy good-pleasure. Bless Thou, likewise, as long as Thine own Self endureth and Thine own Essence doth last, them that have suffered martyrdom in Thy path. Thou art, verily, the Ever-Forgiving, the Most Merciful.

Moreover, I beseech Thee, O my God, by Him Whom Thou hast announced unto us in all Thy Tablets and Thy Books and Thy Scrolls and Thy Scriptures, through Whom the kingdom of names hath been convulsed, and all that lay hid in the breasts of them that have followed their evil and corrupt desires hath been revealed,—I beseech Thee to strengthen us in our love for Him, to make us steadfast in His Cause, to help us befriend His loved ones and challenge His enemies. Shield us, then, O my God, from the mischief wrought by them that have denied Thy presence, and turned away from Thy face, and resolved to put an end to the life of Him Who is the Manifestation of Thine own Self.

O my God and my Master! Thou knowest how they have disgraced Thy Cause and dishonored Thee among Thy creatures, how they have joined Thine enemies, that they may undermine Thy Revelation and injure Thee. Lay hold on them with the power of Thy wrath and might, O my God, and expose their shameful acts and their wickedness, that whatever is hid in their breasts may be revealed unto the people that dwell within Thy land, O Thou Who art the Inflictor of trials, the Fashioner of nations, and the Bestower of favors! No God is there beside Thee, the All-Glorious, the Most Bountiful.

CLXXIX

Praised be Thou, O Lord my God! The tongues of all created things testify to Thy sovereignty and Thine omnipotence, and proclaim mine own poverty and my wretchedness when face to face with the revelations of Thy wealth. Look, then, O my God, upon this sinner whose gaze hath, at all times, been fixed upon the source of Thy forgiveness, and whose eyes have been bent upon the horizon of Thy grace and Thy gifts.

Ever since the day Thou didst create me at Thy bidding, O my God, and didst arouse me through the gentle winds of Thy tender mercies, I have refused

to turn to any one except Thee, and have, through
the power of Thy sovereignty and Thy might, arisen
to face Thine enemies, and have summoned all mankind unto the shores of the ocean of Thy oneness and
the heaven of Thine all-glorious unity. I have sought,
all my days, not to guard myself from the mischief
of the rebellious among Thy creatures, but rather to
exalt Thy name amidst Thy people. I have, thereby,
suffered what none of Thy creatures hath suffered.

How many the days, O my God, which I have
spent in utter loneliness with the transgressors
amongst Thy servants, and how many the nights, O
my Best-Beloved, during which I lay a captive in the
hands of the wayward amidst Thy creatures! In the
midst of my troubles and tribulations I have continued to celebrate Thy praise before all who are in
Thy heaven and on Thy earth, and have not ceased
to extol Thy wondrous glory in the kingdoms of Thy
Revelation and of Thy creation, though all that I
have been capable of showing forth hath fallen short
of the greatness and the majesty of Thy oneness, and
is unworthy of Thine exaltation and of Thine omnipotence.

I swear by Thy glory, O Thou Who art the one
alone Beloved! I find myself to be only nothing before
the habitation of Thy great glory. Every time I attempt to extol any one of Thy virtues, my heart
restraineth me, for naught but Thee is able to soar
into the atmosphere of the kingdom of Thy nearness,
or reach up to the heaven of Thy presence.

Thy might beareth me witness! I am well aware
that were I to bow myself before a handful of dust,
from now until the end that hath no end, in acknowledgment of its relationship to Thy name, the Fashioner, I would still find myself far removed from that
dust, and incapable of approaching it, and would discover that such an adoration can in no wise befit it,
nor transcend the limitations to which I myself have
been subjected. And were I to arise to serve one of
Thy servants, and to wait at his door so long as Thine
own kingdom endureth and Thine omnipotence will
last, as a sign of my acknowledgment of the tie that
bindeth him to Thy name, the Creator, I would,
likewise,—and to this Thy glory beareth me witness
—have to confess my complete failure to do him
adequate service, and my deprivation of what can
truly befit his station. And this for the reason that
I recognize in them naught else except the bond that
bindeth them to Thy names and Thine attributes.
How can, then, such a man succeed in befittingly extolling the One through a motion of Whose finger all
the names and their kingdom were called into being,
and all the attributes and their dominion were created,
and Who, through yet another motion of that same
finger, hath united the letters B and E (Be) and knit
them together, manifesting thereby what the highest
thoughts of Thy chosen ones who enjoy near access
to Thee are unable to grasp, and what the profoundest wisdom of those of Thy loved ones that are wholly
devoted to Thee are powerless to fathom.

I swear by Thy glory, O Beloved of my soul! I am bewildered when I contemplate the tokens of Thy handiwork, and the evidences of Thy might, and find myself completely unable to unravel the mystery of the least of Thy signs, how much more to apprehend Thine own Self. I beseech Thee, therefore, O my God, by Thy Name through which Thou hast caused all such as love Thee to soar in the atmosphere of Thy will, and hast guided all them that yearn after Thee into the Paradise of Thy nearness and Thy presence, to waft from the heaven of Thy loving-kindness the fragrance of certainty upon the needy among Thy loved ones, in these days when the tempests of trials have compassed them on every side, and so grievously assailed them that the souls of men have been troubled and the foundations of all beings have trembled at what hath been sent down unto them from the heaven of Thine irrevocable Purpose. They were so shaken that the lamp of their love for Thee and of their remembrance of Thee was ready to be extinguished in the recess of their hearts. Powerful art Thou to do what pleaseth Thee. Thou, in truth, art the Ever-Forgiving, the Most Generous.

Thou givest ear, O my God and my Master, to the sighing of them that are dear to Thee, and hearest from all sides their cry, by reason of what hath befallen them at the hands of those whose hearts have been deprived of the sweet savors of Thy love. There is none either to befriend or to succor them, nor can anything deter their enemies from harming them.

Unrestrained, they do what they wish, and deal with them as they please.

Give, therefore, O my Lord, the wonders of Thine aid to Thy loved ones, who have sought no helper except Thee, and have turned to none save Thyself, and whose eyes have expectantly awaited to behold the wonders of Thy favors and Thy gifts. Have pity, then, upon them, O my God, through the incomparable tokens of Thy mercy, and shelter them within the stronghold of Thy protection and Thy loving-kindness. Thou art the One, O my Lord, Who from everlasting hath been the Refuge of the fearful, and the Haven of the needy. Withhold not, I beseech Thee, from these feeble creatures the matchless tokens of Thy bounteousness and generosity, and leave them not to the mercy of them whose essence hath been solely created of the fire of Thy wrath and of Thine anger, and who have never discovered the fragrance of compassion and equity, and who have been so deluded by the deceitfulness of the world that they have denied Thy proof, and joined partners with Thee, and repudiated Thy signs, and shed the blood of those who are dear to Thee, and have been trusted by Thee. I swear by Thy might, O my Beloved! They have committed what no man before them hath committed, and have thereby deserved Thy wrath and the scourge of Thine anger. Lay hold on them by the power of Thy sovereignty, and set over them such as will have no mercy upon them, unless they return unto Thee, and enter beneath the shadow of Thy loving-kindness, and are forgiven by Thee. Thou hast from everlasting been supreme over all things, and wilt unto everlasting remain the same. Thou, truly, art the Almighty, the Most Exalted, the Equitable, the All-Wise.

Glorified art Thou, O Lord my God! Look Thou upon this wronged one, who hath been sorely afflicted by the oppressors among Thy creatures and the infidels among Thine enemies, though he himself hath refused to breathe a single breath but by Thy leave and at Thy bidding. I lay asleep on my couch, O my God, when lo, the gentle winds of Thy grace and Thy loving-kindness passed over me, and wakened me through the power of Thy sovereignty and Thy gifts, and bade me arise before Thy servants, and speak forth Thy praise, and glorify Thy word. Thereupon most of Thy people reviled me. I swear by Thy glory, O my God! I never thought that they would show forth such deeds, aware as I am that Thou hast Thyself announced this Revelation unto them in the Scrolls of Thy commandment and the Tablets of Thy decree, and hast covenanted with them concerning this youth in every word sent down by Thee unto Thy creatures and Thy people.

I am bewildered, therefore, O my God, and know not how to act toward them. Every time I hold my peace, and cease to extol Thy wondrous virtues, Thy Spirit impelleth me to cry out before all who are in Thy heaven and on Thy earth; and every time I am still, the breaths wafted from the right hand of Thy

will and purpose pass over me, and stir me up, and
I find myself to be as a leaf which lieth at the mercy
of the winds of Thy decree, and is carried away
whithersoever Thou dost permit or command it.
Every man of insight who considereth what hath been
revealed by me, will be persuaded that Thy Cause is
not in my hands, but in Thy hands, and will recognize that the reins of power are held not in my grasp
but in Thy grasp, and are subject to Thy sovereign
might. And yet, Thou seest, O my God, how the
inhabitants of Thy realm have arrayed themselves
against me, and inflict upon me every moment of
my life what causeth the realities of Thy chosen ones
and trusted ones to tremble.

I entreat Thee, therefore, O my God, by Thy
Name through which Thou hast guided Thy lovers
to the living waters of Thy grace and Thy favors, and
attracted them that long for Thee to the Paradise of
Thy nearness and Thy presence, to open the eyes of
Thy people that they may recognize in this Revelation the manifestation of Thy transcendent unity,
and the dawning of the lights of Thy countenance
and Thy beauty. Cleanse them, then, O my God,
from all idle fancies and vain imaginations, that they
may inhale the fragrances of sanctity from the robe
of Thy Revelation and Thy commandment, that
haply they may cease to inflict upon me what will
deprive their souls of the fragrances of the manifold
tokens of Thy mercy, that are wafted in the days of
Him Who is the Manifestation of Thyself, and the

Day-Spring of Thy Cause, and that they may not perpetrate what will call down Thy wrath and anger.

Thou well knowest, O my God, that I was regarded as one of the people of the Bayán, and consorted with them with love and fellowship, and summoned them to Thee in the daytime and in the night season, through the wonders of Thy Revelation and Thine inspiration, and sustained at their hands what the inmates of the cities of Thine invention are powerless to recount. I swear by Thy might, O my Beloved! Every morning I waken to find that I am made a target for the darts of their envy, and every night, when I lie down to rest, I discover that I have fallen a victim to the spears of their hate. Though Thou hast made known unto me the secrets of their hearts, and hast set me above them, I have refused to uncover their deeds, and have dealt patiently with them, mindful of the time which Thou hast fixed. And when Thy promise came to pass, and the set time was fulfilled, Thou didst lift, to an imperceptible degree, the veil of concealment, and lo, all the inmates of the kingdoms of Thy Revelation and of Thy creation shook and trembled, except those who were created by Thee, through the fire of Thy love, and the breath of Thine eagerness, and the water of Thy loving-kindness, and the clay of Thy grace. These are they who are glorified by the Concourse on high and the denizens of the Cities of eternity.

I give praise to Thee, therefore, O my God, that Thou hast preserved them that have acknowledged

Thy unity, and hast destroyed them that have joined partners with Thee, and hast divided the one from the other through yet another word that hath proceeded out of the mouth of Thy will, and flowed down from the pen of Thy purpose. Thereby have Thy servants, who were created through the word of Thy commandment, and were begotten by Thy will, caviled at me, and so fiercely opposed me that they repudiated Thee, and have rejected Thy signs, and have risen up against Thee.

Thy glory beareth me witness, O my Beloved! My pen is powerless to describe what their hands have wrought against Him Who is the Manifestation of Thy Cause, and the Day-Spring of Thy Revelation, and the Dawning-Place of Thine inspiration. For all this I give praise to Thee. I swear by Thy glory, O my God! My heart yearneth after the things ordained by Thee in the heaven of Thy decree and the kingdom of Thine appointment. For whatsoever befalleth me in Thy path is the beloved of my soul and the goal of my desire. This, verily, is to be ascribed to naught except Thy power and Thy might.

I am the one, O my God, who, through the love I bear to Thee, hath been able to dispense with all who are in heaven and on earth. Armed with this love, I am afraid of no one, though all the peoples of the world unite to hurt me. Oh, that my blood could, this very moment, be shed on the face of the earth before Thee, and Thou wouldst behold me in the condition in which Thou didst behold such of

Thy servants as have drawn nigh unto Thee, and those of Thy righteous creatures as have been chosen by Thee!

I give Thee thanks, O my God, that Thou hast decided through the power of Thy decree, and wilt continue to decide through Thine irrevocable appointment and purpose. I entreat Thee, O my Beloved, by Thy Name through which Thou didst lift up the ensigns of Thy Cause, and shed the splendors of the light of Thy countenance, to send down upon me and upon such of Thy servants as are wholly devoted to Thee all the good Thou hast ordained in Thy Tablets. Establish us, then, upon the seats of truth in Thy presence, O Thou in Whose hands is the kingdom of all things!

Thou art, verily, the Almighty, the All-Glorious, the Most Merciful.

CLXXX

The praise which hath dawned from Thy most august Self, and the glory which hath shone forth from Thy most effulgent Beauty, rest upon Thee, O Thou Who art the Manifestation of Grandeur, and the King of Eternity, and the Lord of all who are in heaven and on earth! I testify that through Thee the sovereignty of God and His dominion, and the

majesty of God and His grandeur, were revealed, and
the Day-Stars of ancient splendor have shed their
radiance in the heaven of Thine irrevocable decree,
and the Beauty of the Unseen hath shone forth above
the horizon of creation. I testify, moreover, that with
but a movement of Thy Pen Thine injunction "Be
Thou" hath been enforced, and God's hidden Secret
hath been divulged, and all created things have been
called into being, and all the Revelations have been
sent down.

I bear witness, moreover, that through Thy beauty
the beauty of the Adored One hath been unveiled,
and through Thy face the face of the Desired One
hath shone forth, and that through a word from Thee
Thou hast decided between all created things, causing
them who are devoted to Thee to ascend unto the
summit of glory, and the infidels to fall into the
lowest abyss.

I bear witness that he who hath known Thee hath
known God, and he who hath attained unto Thy
presence hath attained unto the presence of God.
Great, therefore, is the blessedness of him who hath
believed in Thee, and in Thy signs, and hath humbled himself before Thy sovereignty, and hath been
honored with meeting Thee, and hath attained the
good pleasure of Thy will, and circled around Thee,
and stood before Thy throne. Woe betide him that
hath transgressed against Thee, and hath denied Thee,
and repudiated Thy signs, and gainsaid Thy sovereignty, and risen up against Thee, and waxed proud

before Thy face, and hath disputed Thy testimonies, and fled from Thy rule and Thy dominion, and been numbered with the infidels whose names have been inscribed by the fingers of Thy behest upon Thy holy Tablets.

Waft, then, unto me, O my God and my Beloved, from the right hand of Thy mercy and Thy loving-kindness, the holy breaths of Thy favors, that they may draw me away from myself and from the world unto the courts of Thy nearness and Thy presence. Potent art Thou to do what pleaseth Thee. Thou, truly, hast been supreme over all things.

The remembrance of God and His praise, and the glory of God and His splendor, rest upon Thee, O Thou who art His Beauty! I bear witness that the eye of creation hath never gazed upon one wronged like Thee. Thou wast immersed all the days of Thy life beneath an ocean of tribulations. At one time Thou wast in chains and fetters; at another Thou wast threatened by the sword of Thine enemies. Yet, despite all this, Thou didst enjoin upon all men to observe what had been prescribed unto Thee by Him Who is the All-Knowing, the All-Wise.

May my spirit be a sacrifice to the wrongs Thou didst suffer, and my soul be a ransom for the adversities Thou didst sustain. I beseech God, by Thee and by them whose faces have been illumined with the splendors of the light of Thy countenance, and who, for love of Thee, have observed all whereunto they were bidden, to remove the veils that have come in between Thee and Thy creatures, and to supply me with the good of this world and the world to come. Thou art, in truth, the Almighty, the Most Exalted, the All-Glorious, the Ever-Forgiving, the Most Compassionate.

Bless Thou, O Lord my God, the Divine Lote-Tree and its leaves, and its boughs, and its branches, and its stems, and its offshoots, as long as Thy most excellent titles will endure and Thy most august attributes will last. Protect it, then, from the mischief of the aggressor and the hosts of tyranny. Thou art, in truth, the Almighty, the Most Powerful. Bless Thou, also, O Lord my God, Thy servants and Thy handmaidens who have attained unto Thee. Thou, truly, art the All-Bountiful, Whose grace is infinite. No God is there save Thee, the Ever-Forgiving, the Most Generous.

The Tablet of Visitation.

CLXXXI

I bear witness, O my God, that Thou hast created me to know Thee and to worship Thee. I testify, at this moment, to my powerlessness and to Thy might, to my poverty and to Thy wealth.

There is none other God but Thee, the Help in Peril, the Self-Subsisting.

> Short obligatory prayer, to be recited once in twenty-four hours, at noon.

CLXXXII

> Whoso wisheth to pray, let him wash his hands, and while he washeth, let him say:

Strengthen my hand, O my God, that it may take hold of Thy Book with such steadfastness that the hosts of the world shall have no power over it. Guard it, then, from meddling with whatsoever doth not belong unto it. Thou art, verily, the Almighty, the Most Powerful.

> And while washing his face, let him say:

I have turned my face unto Thee, O my Lord! Illumine it with the light of Thy countenance. Protect it, then, from turning to anyone but Thee.

Then let him stand up, and facing the
Qiblih (Point of Adoration, i.e., Bahjí,
'Akká), let him say:

God testifieth that there is none other God but
Him. His are the kingdoms of Revelation and of creation. He, in truth, hath manifested Him Who is the
Day-Spring of Revelation, Who conversed on Sinai,
through Whom the Supreme Horizon hath been made
to shine, and the Lote-Tree beyond which there is
no passing hath spoken, and through Whom the call
hath been proclaimed unto all who are in heaven and
on earth: "Lo, the All-Possessing is come. Earth and
heaven, glory and dominion are God's, the Lord of
all men, and the Possessor of the Throne on high and
of earth below!"

Let him, then, bend down, with hands
resting on the knees, and say:

Exalted art Thou above my praise and the praise
of anyone beside me, above my description and the
description of all who are in heaven and all who are
on earth!

Then, standing with open hands, palms
upward toward the face, let him say:

Disappoint not, O my God, him that hath, with
beseeching fingers, clung to the hem of Thy mercy
and Thy grace, O Thou Who of those who show
mercy art the Most Merciful!

Let him, then, be seated and say:

I bear witness to Thy unity and Thy oneness, and that Thou art God, and that there is none other God beside Thee. Thou hast, verily, revealed Thy Cause, fulfilled Thy Covenant, and opened wide the door of Thy grace to all that dwell in heaven and on earth. Blessing and peace, salutation and glory, rest upon Thy loved ones, whom the changes and chances of the world have not deterred from turning unto Thee, and who have given their all, in the hope of obtaining that which is with Thee. Thou art, in truth, the Ever-Forgiving, the All-Bountiful.

(If anyone choose to recite instead of the long verse these words: "God testifieth that there is none other God but Him, the Help in Peril, the Self-Subsisting," it would be sufficient. And likewise, it would suffice were he, while seated, to choose to recite these words: "I bear witness to Thy unity and Thy oneness, and that Thou art God, and that there is none other God beside Thee.")

Medium obligatory prayer, to be recited daily, in the morning, at noon, and in the evening.

CLXXXIII

Whoso wisheth to recite this prayer, let
him stand up and turn unto God, and,
as he standeth in his place, let him gaze
to the right and to the left, as if await-
ing the mercy of his Lord, the Most
Merciful, the Compassionate. Then
let him say:

O Thou Who art the Lord of all names and the
Maker of the heavens! I beseech Thee by them Who
are the Day-Springs of Thine invisible Essence, the
Most Exalted, the All-Glorious, to make of my
prayer a fire that will burn away the veils which have
shut me out from Thy beauty, and a light that will
lead me unto the ocean of Thy Presence.

Let him then raise his hands in supplication toward God—blessed and exalted be He—and say:

O Thou the Desire of the world and the Beloved
of the nations! Thou seest me turning toward Thee,
and rid of all attachment to anyone save Thee, and
clinging to Thy cord, through whose movement the
whole creation hath been stirred up. I am Thy servant, O my Lord, and the son of Thy servant. Behold
me standing ready to do Thy will and Thy desire, and
wishing naught else except Thy good pleasure. I implore Thee by the Ocean of Thy mercy and the Day-
Star of Thy grace to do with Thy servant as Thou

willest and pleasest. By Thy might which is far above
all mention and praise! Whatsoever is revealed by
Thee is the desire of my heart and the beloved of
my soul. O God, my God! Look not upon my hopes
and my doings, nay rather look upon Thy will that
hath encompassed the heavens and the earth. By Thy
Most Great Name, O Thou Lord of all nations! I
have desired only what Thou didst desire, and love
only what Thou dost love.

> Let him then kneel, and bowing his
> forehead to the ground, let him say:

Exalted art Thou above the description of anyone
save Thyself, and the comprehension of aught else
except Thee.

> Let him then stand and say:

Make my prayer, O my Lord, a fountain of living
waters whereby I may live as long as Thy sovereignty
endureth, and may make mention of Thee in every
world of Thy worlds.

> Let him again raise his hands in sup-
> plication, and say:

O Thou in separation from Whom hearts and souls
have melted, and by the fire of Whose love the whole
world hath been set aflame! I implore Thee by Thy
Name through which Thou hast subdued the whole
creation, not to withhold from me that which is with
Thee, O Thou Who rulest over all men! Thou seest,

O my Lord, this stranger hastening to his most exalted home beneath the canopy of Thy majesty and within the precincts of Thy mercy; and this transgressor seeking the ocean of Thy forgiveness; and this lowly one the court of Thy glory; and this poor creature the orient of Thy wealth. Thine is the authority to command whatsoever Thou willest. I bear witness that Thou art to be praised in Thy doings, and to be obeyed in Thy behests, and to remain unconstrained in Thy bidding.

> Let him then raise his hands, and repeat three times the Greatest Name. Let him then bend down with hands resting on the knees before God— blessed and exalted be He—and say:

Thou seest, O my God, how my spirit hath been stirred up within my limbs and members, in its longing to worship Thee, and in its yearning to remember Thee and extol Thee; how it testifieth to that whereunto the Tongue of Thy Commandment hath testified in the kingdom of Thine utterance and the heaven of Thy knowledge. I love, in this state, O my Lord, to beg of Thee all that is with Thee, that I may demonstrate my poverty, and magnify Thy bounty and Thy riches, and may declare my powerlessness, and manifest Thy power and Thy might.

> Let him then stand and raise his hands twice in supplication, and say:

There is no God but Thee, the Almighty, the All-Bountiful. There is no God but Thee, the Ordainer, both in the beginning and in the end. O God, my God! Thy forgiveness hath emboldened me, and Thy mercy hath strengthened me, and Thy call hath awakened me, and Thy grace hath raised me up and led me unto Thee. Who, otherwise, am I that I should dare to stand at the gate of the city of Thy nearness, or set my face toward the lights that are shining from the heaven of Thy will? Thou seest, O my Lord, this wretched creature knocking at the door of Thy grace, and this evanescent soul seeking the river of everlasting life from the hands of Thy bounty. Thine is the command at all times, O Thou Who art the Lord of all names; and mine is resignation and willing submission to Thy will, O Creator of the heavens!

Let him then raise his hands thrice, and say:

Greater is God than every great one!

Let him then kneel and, bowing his forehead to the ground, say:

Too high art Thou for the praise of those who are nigh unto Thee to ascend unto the heaven of Thy nearness, or for the birds of the hearts of them who are devoted to Thee to attain to the door of Thy gate. I testify that Thou hast been sanctified above all attributes and holy above all names. No God is there but Thee, the Most Exalted, the All-Glorious.

Let him then seat himself and say:

I testify unto that whereunto have testified all created things, and the Concourse on high, and the inmates of the all-highest Paradise, and beyond them the Tongue of Grandeur itself from the all-glorious Horizon, that Thou art God, that there is no God but Thee, and that He Who hath been manifested is the Hidden Mystery, the Treasured Symbol, through Whom the letters B and E (Be) have been joined and knit together. I testify that it is He Whose name hath been set down by the Pen of the Most High, and Who hath been mentioned in the Books of God, the Lord of the Throne on high and of earth below.

Let him then stand erect and say:

O Lord of all being and Possessor of all things visible and invisible! Thou dost perceive my tears and the sighs I utter, and hearest my groaning, and my wailing, and the lamentation of my heart. By Thy might! My trespasses have kept me back from drawing nigh unto Thee; and my sins have held me far from the court of Thy holiness. Thy love, O my Lord, hath enriched me, and separation from Thee hath destroyed me, and remoteness from Thee hath consumed me. I entreat Thee by Thy footsteps in this wilderness, and by the words "Here am I. Here am I" which Thy chosen Ones have uttered in this immensity, and by the breaths of Thy Revelation, and the gentle winds of the Dawn of Thy Manifestation, to ordain that I may gaze on Thy beauty and observe whatsoever is in Thy Book.

Let him then repeat the Greatest Name thrice, and bend down with hands resting on the knees, and say:

Praise be to Thee, O my God, that Thou hast aided me to remember Thee and to praise Thee, and hast made known unto me Him Who is the Day-Spring of Thy signs, and hast caused me to bow down before Thy Lordship, and humble myself before Thy Godhead, and to acknowledge that which hath been uttered by the Tongue of Thy grandeur.

Let him then rise and say:

O God, my God! My back is bowed by the burden of my sins, and my heedlessness hath destroyed me. Whenever I ponder my evil doings and Thy benevolence, my heart melteth within me, and my blood boileth in my veins. By Thy Beauty, O Thou the Desire of the world! I blush to lift up my face to Thee, and my longing hands are ashamed to stretch forth toward the heaven of Thy bounty. Thou seest, O my God, how my tears prevent me from remembering Thee and from extolling Thy virtues, O Thou the Lord of the Throne on high and of earth below! I implore Thee by the signs of Thy Kingdom and the mysteries of Thy Dominion to do with Thy loved ones as becometh Thy bounty, O Lord of all being, and is worthy of Thy grace, O King of the seen and the unseen!

Let him then repeat the Greatest Name
thrice, and kneel with his forehead to
the ground, and say:

Praise be unto Thee, O our God, that Thou hast
sent down unto us that which draweth us nigh unto
Thee, and supplieth us with every good thing sent
down by Thee in Thy Books and Thy Scriptures.
Protect us, we beseech Thee, O my Lord, from the
hosts of idle fancies and vain imaginations. Thou, in
truth, art the Mighty, the All-Knowing.

Let him then raise his head, and seat
himself, and say:

I testify, O my God, to that whereunto Thy
chosen Ones have testified, and acknowledge that
which the inmates of the all-highest Paradise and
those who have circled round Thy mighty Throne
have acknowledged. The kingdoms of earth and
heaven are Thine, O Lord of the worlds!

Long obligatory prayer, to be recited
once in twenty-four hours.

CLXXXIV

Since Thou hast, O my God, established Thyself
upon the throne of Thy transcendent unity, and ascended the mercy seat of Thy oneness, it befitteth
Thee to blot out from the hearts of all beings whatsoever may keep them back from gaining admittance
into the sanctuary of Thy Divine mysteries, and may
shut them out from the tabernacle of Thy Divinity,
that all hearts may mirror Thy beauty, and may reveal Thee, and speak of Thee, and that all created
things may show forth the tokens of Thy most august
sovereignty, and shed the splendors of the light of
Thy most holy governance, and that all who are in
heaven and on earth may laud and magnify Thy
unity, and give Thee glory, for having manifested
Thy Self unto them through Him Who is the
Revealer of Thy oneness.

Divest, then, Thy servants, O my God, of the
garments of self and desire, or grant that the eyes
of Thy people may be lifted up to such heights that
they will discern in their desires naught except the
stirring of the gentle winds of Thine eternal glory,
and may recognize in their own selves nothing but
the revelation of Thine own merciful Self, that the
earth and all that is therein may be cleansed of whatever is alien to Thee, or anything that manifesteth
aught save Thy Self. All this can be fulfilled throughout Thy dominion by Thy word of command, "Be,"

and it is! Nay, even swifter than this, and yet the people understand not.

Glorified, immeasurably glorified art Thou, O my Beloved! I swear by Thy glory! I recognize this very moment that Thou hast granted all for which I have supplicated Thee, in this blessed night which, as decreed by Thee, calleth to remembrance Him Who was the Companion of Thy beauty and the Beholder of Thy face, ere I had been mentioned by Thee, or called into being within the court of Thy holiness. I perceive that Thou hast made all things to be the manifestations of Thy behest, and the revelations of Thy handiwork, and the repositories of Thy knowledge, and the treasuries of Thy wisdom. I recognize, moreover, that were any of the revelations of Thy names and Thine attributes to be withheld, though it be the weight of a grain of mustard seed, from whatsoever hath been created by Thy power and begotten by Thy might, the foundations of Thine everlasting handiwork would thereby be made incomplete, and the gems of Thy Divine wisdom would become imperfect. For the letters of negation, no matter how far they may be removed from the holy fragrances of Thy knowledge, and however forgetful they may become of the wondrous splendors of the dawning light of Thy beauty, which are shed from the heaven of Thy majesty, must needs exist in Thy realm, so that the words which affirm Thee may thereby be exalted.

Thy might beareth me witness, O my Well-

Beloved! The entire creation hath been called into being to exalt Thy triumph and to establish Thine ascendancy, and all the bounds that have been set by Thee are but the signs of Thy sovereignty, and proclaim the power of Thy might. How great, how very great, are the revelations of Thy wondrous power in all things! They are such that the lowliest among Thy creatures hath been made by Thee a manifestation of Thy most august attribute, and the most contemptible token of Thy handiwork hath been chosen as a recipient of Thy most mighty name. Poverty, as decreed by Thee, hath been made the means for the revelation of Thy riches, and abasement a path leading to Thy glory, and sinfulness a cause for the exercise of Thy forgiveness. By them Thou hast demonstrated that to Thee belong Thy most excellent titles, and unto Thee pertain the wonders of Thy most exalted attributes.

Since Thou hast purposed, O my God, to cause all created things to enter into the tabernacle of Thy transcendent grace and favor, and to waft over the entire creation the fragrances of the raiment of Thy glorious unity, and to look upon all things with the eyes of Thy bounty and Thy oneness, I beseech Thee, therefore, by Thy love, which Thou hast made to be the mainspring of the revelations of Thine eternal holiness, and the flame that gloweth within the hearts of such of Thy creatures as yearn towards Thee, to create, this very moment, for those of Thy people who are wholly devoted to Thee, and for such of

Thy loved ones as love Thee, out of the essence of Thy bounty and Thy generosity, and from the inmost spirit of Thy grace and Thy glory, Thy Paradise of transcendent holiness, and to exalt it above everything except Thee, and to sanctify it from aught else save Thyself. Create, moreover, within it, O my God, out of the lights shed by Thy throne, handmaidens who will intone the melodies of Thy wondrous and most sweet invention, that they may magnify Thy name with such words as have not been heard by any of Thy creatures, be they the inmates of Thy heaven or the dwellers of Thine earth, nor been comprehended by any of Thy people. Unlock, then, the gates of this Paradise to the faces of Thy loved ones, that haply they may enter them in Thy name, and by the power of Thy sovereignty, that thereby the sovereign bounties vouchsafed by Thee unto Thy chosen ones and the transcendent gifts granted unto Thy trusted ones be perfected, that they may extol Thy virtues with such melodies as none can either intone or describe, and that none of Thy people may conceive the design of appearing in the guise of any of Thy chosen ones, or of emulating the example of Thy loved ones, and that none may fail to discern between Thy friends and Thine enemies, or to distinguish them that are devoted to Thee from such as stubbornly oppose Thee. Potent art Thou to do what Thou willest, and powerful and supreme art Thou over all things.

Exalted, immeasurably exalted art Thou, O my

Beloved, above the strivings of any of Thy creatures, however learned, to know Thee; exalted, immensely exalted art Thou above every human attempt, no matter how searching, to describe Thee! For the highest thought of men, however deep their contemplation, can never hope to outsoar the limitations imposed upon Thy creation, nor ascend beyond the state of the contingent world, nor break the bounds irrevocably set for it by Thee. How can, then, a thing that hath been created by Thy will that overruleth the whole of creation, a thing that is itself a part of the contingent world, have the power to soar into the holy atmosphere of Thy knowledge, or reach unto the seat of Thy transcendent power?

High, immeasurably high art Thou above the endeavors of the evanescent creature to soar unto the throne of Thine eternity, or of the poor and wretched to attain the summit of Thine all-sufficing glory! From eternity Thou didst Thyself describe Thine own Self unto Thy Self, and extol, in Thine own Essence, Thine Essence unto Thine Essence. I swear by Thy glory, O my Best-Beloved! Who is there besides Thee that can claim to know Thee, and who save Thyself can make fitting mention of Thee? Thou art He Who, from eternity, abode in His realm, in the glory of His transcendent unity, and the splendors of His holy grandeur. Were any one except Thee to be deemed worthy of mention, in all the kingdoms of Thy creation, from the highest realms of immortality down to the level of this nether world, how could it, then, be demonstrated that Thou art established upon the throne of Thy unity, and how could the wondrous virtues of Thy oneness and Thy singleness be glorified?

I bear witness, this very moment, to what Thou hast testified for Thine own Self, ere Thou hadst created the heavens and the earth, that Thou art God, and that there is none other God besides Thee. Thou hast from everlasting been potent, through the Manifestations of Thy might, to reveal the signs of Thy power, and Thou hast ever made known, through the Day-Springs of Thy knowledge, the words of Thy wisdom. No one besides Thee hath ever been found worthy to be mentioned before the Tabernacle of Thy unity, and none except Thyself hath proved himself capable of being praised within the hallowed court of Thy oneness.

Praise be to Thee, O my God, that Thou hast revealed Thy favors and Thy bounties; and glory be to Thee, O my Beloved, that Thou hast manifested the Day-Star of Thy loving-kindness and Thy tender mercies. I yield Thee such thanks as can direct the steps of the wayward towards the splendors of the morning light of Thy guidance, and enable those who yearn towards Thee to attain the seat of the revelation of the effulgence of Thy beauty. I yield Thee such thanks as can cause the sick to draw nigh unto the waters of Thy healing, and can help those who are far from Thee to approach the living fountain of Thy presence. I yield Thee such thanks as can divest

the bodies of Thy servants of the garments of mor-
tality and abasement, and attire them in the robes of
Thine eternity and Thy glory, and lead the poor unto
the shores of Thy holiness and all sufficient riches. I
yield Thee such thanks as can enable the Heavenly
Dove to warble forth, upon the branches of the Lote-
Tree of Immortality, her song: "Verily, Thou art
God. No God is there besides Thee. From eternity
Thou hast been exalted above the praise of aught
else but Thee, and been high above the description of
any one except Thyself." I yield Thee such thanks
as can cause the Nightingale of Glory to pour forth
its melody in the highest heaven: "'Alí (the Báb),
in truth, is Thy servant, Whom Thou hast singled out
from among Thy Messengers and Thy chosen Ones,
and made Him to be the Manifestation of Thyself in
all that pertaineth unto Thee, and that concerneth
the revelation of Thine attributes and the evidences of
Thy names." I yield Thee such thanks as can stir up
all things to extol Thee, and to glorify Thine Essence,
and can unloose the tongues of all beings to magnify
the sovereignty of Thy beauty. I yield Thee such
thanks as can fill the heavens and the earth with the
signs of Thy transcendent Essence, and assist all created things to enter the Tabernacle of Thy nearness
and Thy presence. I yield Thee such thanks as can
make every created thing to be a book that shall
speak of Thee, and a scroll that shall unfold Thy
praise. I yield Thee such thanks as can establish the
Manifestations of Thy sovereignty upon the throne

of Thy governance, and set up the Exponents of Thy
glory upon the seat of Thy Divinity. I yield Thee
such thanks as can make the corrupt tree to bring
forth good fruit through the holy breaths of Thy
favors, and revive the bodies of all beings with the
gentle winds of Thy transcendent grace. I yield Thee
such thanks as can cause the signs of Thine exalted
singleness to be sent down out of the heaven of Thy
holy unity. I yield Thee such thanks as can teach
all things the realities of Thy knowledge and the
essence of Thy wisdom, and will not withhold the
wretched creatures from the doors of Thy mercy and
Thy bountiful favor. I yield Thee such thanks as can
enable all who are in heaven and on earth to dispense
with all created things, through the treasuries of
Thine all-sufficing riches, and can aid all created
things to reach unto the summit of Thine almighty
favors. I yield Thee such thanks as can assist the hearts
of Thine ardent lovers to soar into the atmosphere of
nearness to Thee, and of longing for Thee, and kindle
the Light of Lights within the land of 'Iráq. I yield
Thee such thanks as can detach them that are nigh
unto Thee from all created things, and draw them to
the throne of Thy names and Thine attributes. I yield
Thee such thanks as can cause Thee to forgive all sins
and trespasses, and to fulfill the needs of the peoples
of all religions, and to waft the fragrances of pardon
over the entire creation. I yield Thee such thanks as
can enable them that recognize Thy unity to scale the
heights of Thy love, and cause such as are devoted

to Thee to ascend unto the Paradise of Thy presence. I yield Thee such thanks as can satisfy the wants of all such as seek Thee, and realize the aims of them that have recognized Thee. I yield Thee such thanks as can blot out from the hearts of men all suggestions of limitations, and inscribe the signs of Thy unity. I yield Thee such thanks as that with which Thou didst from eternity glorify Thine own Self, and didst exalt it above all peers, rivals, and comparisons, O Thou in Whose hands are the heavens of grace and of bounty, and the kingdoms of glory and of majesty!

Lauded be Thy name, O Lord my God, and my Master! Thou bearest witness, and seest, and knowest the things that have befallen Thy loved ones in Thy days, and the continual trials, and the successive tribulations, and the incessant afflictions, which have been sent down upon Thine elect. Such hath been their plight that the earth became too strait for them, and they were encompassed by the evidences of Thy wrath and the signs of Thy fear in every land, and the doors of Thy mercy and Thy loving-kindness were shut against them, and the garden of their hearts was deprived of the overflowing showers of Thy grace and Thy bountiful favors. Wilt Thou withhold, O my God, from such as love Thee the wonders of Thine ascendancy and triumph? Wilt Thou shatter, O my Beloved, the hopes which they who are devoted to Thee have fixed on Thy manifold bounties and gifts? Wilt Thou keep back, O my Master, those that have recognized Thee from the

shores of Thy sanctified knowledge, or wilt Thou
cease to rain down upon the hearts of such as desire
Thee the showers of Thy transcendent grace? No,
no, and to this Thy glory beareth me witness! I
testify this very moment that Thy mercy hath surpassed all created things, and Thy loving-kindness
encompassed all that are in heaven and all that are
on earth. From everlasting the doors of Thy generosity were open to the faces of Thy servants, and the
gentle winds of Thy grace were wafted over the
hearts of Thy creatures, and the overflowing rains of
Thy bounty were showered upon Thy people and
the dwellers of Thy realm.

I know full well Thou hast delayed to manifest
Thy triumph in the kingdom of creation by reason
of Thy knowledge which embraceth both the mysteries of Thy decree, and the hidden things ordained
behind the veils of Thine irrevocable purpose, that
thereby those who have entered beneath the shadow
of Thy transcendent mercy may be separated from
those who have dealt disdainfully with Thee, and
turned back from Thy presence at the time when
Thou didst manifest Thy most exalted Beauty.

Exalted, immeasurably exalted art Thou, therefore, O my Beloved! Forasmuch as Thou hast divided,
in Thy realm, Thy loved ones from Thine enemies,
and hast perfected Thy most weighty testimony and
Thy most infallible Proof unto all who are in heaven
and on earth, have mercy, then, upon those who
were brought low in Thy land, by reason of what

hath befallen them in Thy path. Exalt them, then, O my God, through the power of Thy might and the potency of Thy will, and raise them up to proclaim Thy Cause through Thine omnipotent sovereignty and purpose.

I swear by Thy glory! My sole purpose in showing forth Thine ascendancy hath been to glorify Thy Cause, and to magnify Thy word. I am persuaded that if Thou wert to delay to send down Thy victory and to demonstrate Thy power, the signs of Thy sovereignty would assuredly perish in Thy land, and the tokens of Thy rule would be blotted out throughout Thy dominion.

My breast is straitened, O my God, and sorrows and vexations have compassed me round, for I hear among Thy servants every praise except Thy wondrous praise, and behold amidst Thy people the evidences of all things save the evidences of what Thou hast prescribed unto them by Thy behest, and destined for them through Thy sovereign will, and ordained unto them by Thine overruling decree. They have strayed so far from Thee that should any of Thy loved ones deliver unto them the wondrous tokens of Thy unity, and the gem-like utterances that attest Thy transcendent oneness, they would thrust their fingers into their ears, and would cavil at him and mock him. All this hast Thou set down through Thine all-encompassing sovereignty, and apprehended through Thine omnipotent supremacy.

Glorified, immeasurably glorified art Thou, O my

Master! Look, then, upon the hearts which, in their love for Thee, have been transfixed by the darts of Thine enemies, and the heads which were borne on spears for the sake of the exaltation of Thy Cause and the glorification of Thy name. Have pity, then, upon those hearts which have been consumed by the fire of Thy love, and been touched by such tribulations as are known only unto Thee.

All laud and honor to Thee, O my God! Thou well knowest the things which, for a score of years, have happened in Thy days, and have continued to happen until this hour. No man can reckon, nor can any tongue tell, what hath befallen Thy chosen ones during all this time. They could obtain no shelter, nor find any refuge in which they could abide in safety. Turn, then, O my God, their fear into the evidences of Thy peace and Thy security, and their abasement into the sovereignty of Thy glory, and their poverty into Thine all-sufficient riches, and their distress into the wonders of Thy perfect tranquillity. Vouchsafe unto them the fragrances of Thy might and Thy mercy, and send down upon them, out of Thy marvelous loving-kindness, what will enable them to dispense with all except Thee, and will detach them from aught save Thyself, that the sovereignty of Thy oneness may be revealed and the supremacy of Thy grace and Thy bounty demonstrated.

Wilt Thou not, O my God, look upon the tears which Thy loved ones have shed? Wilt Thou not pity, O my Beloved, the eyes which have been dimmed by reason of their separation from Thee, and because of the cessation of the signs of Thy victory? Wilt Thou not behold, O my Master, the hearts wherein have beaten the wings of the dove of longing and love for Thee? By Thy glory! Things have come to such a pass that hope hath well nigh been banished from the hearts of Thy chosen ones, and the breaths of despair are ready to seize them, by reason of what hath befallen them in Thy days.

Behold me, then, O my God, how I have fled from myself unto Thee, and have abandoned my own being that I may attain unto the splendors of the light of Thy Being, and have forsaken all that keepeth me back from Thee, and maketh me forgetful of Thee, in order that I may inhale the fragrances of Thy presence and Thy remembrance. Behold how I have stepped upon the dust of the city of Thy forgiveness and Thy bounty, and dwelt within the precincts of Thy transcendent mercy, and have besought Thee, through the sovereignty of Him Who is Thy Remembrance and Who hath appeared in the robe of Thy most pure and most august Beauty, to send down, in the course of this year, upon Thy loved ones what will enable them to dispense with any one except Thee, and will set them free to recognize the evidences of Thy sovereign will and all-conquering purpose, in such wise that they will seek only what Thou didst wish for them through Thy bidding, and will desire naught except what Thou didst desire for them through Thy will. Sanctify, then, their eyes, O my

God, that they may behold the light of Thy Beauty,
and purge their ears, that they may listen to the melodies of the Dove of Thy transcendent oneness. Flood,
then, their hearts with the wonders of Thy love, and
preserve their tongues from mentioning any one save
Thee, and guard their faces from turning to aught
else except Thyself. Potent art Thou to do what
pleaseth Thee. Thou, verily, art the Almighty, the
Help in Peril, the Self-Subsisting.

fund Protect, moreover, O my Beloved, through Thy
love for them and through the love they bear to Thee,
this servant, who hath sacrificed his all for Thee, and
expended whatsoever Thou hast given him in the
path of Thy love and Thy good pleasure, and preserve
him from all that Thou abhorrest, and from whatsoever may hinder him from entering into the Tabernacle of Thy holy sovereignty, and from attaining
the seat of Thy transcendent oneness. Number him,
then, O my God, with such as have allowed nothing
whatever to deter them from beholding Thy beauty,
or from meditating on the wondrous evidences of
Thine everlasting handiwork, that he may have fellowship with none except Thee, and turn to naught
save Thyself, and discover in whatever hath been
created by Thee in the kingdoms of earth and heaven
nothing but Thy wondrous Beauty and the revelation
of the splendors of Thy face, and be so immersed beneath the billowing oceans of Thine overruling providence and the surging seas of Thy holy unity, that he
will forget every mention except the mention of Thy

transcendent oneness, and banish from his soul the traces of all evil suggestions, O Thou in Whose hands are the kingdoms of all names and attributes!

Lauded be Thy name, O Thou Who art the Goal of my desire! I swear by Thy glory! How great is my wish to attain unto a detachment so complete that were there to appear before me those countenances which are hid within the chambers of chastity, and the beauty of which Thou didst veil from the eyes of the entire creation, and whose faces Thou didst sanctify from the sight of all beings, and were they to unveil themselves in all the glory of the splendors of Thine incomparable beauty, I would refuse to look upon them, and would behold them solely for the purpose of discerning the mysteries of Thy handiwork, which have perplexed the minds of such as have drawn nigh unto Thee, and awed the souls of all them that have recognized Thee. I would, by Thy power and Thy might, soar to such heights that nothing whatsoever would have the power to keep me back from the manifold evidences of Thy transcendent dominion, nor would any earthly scheme shut me out from the manifestations of Thy Divine holiness.

Glorified, immeasurably glorified art Thou, O my God, and my Beloved, and my Master, and my Desire! Shatter not the hopes of this lowly one to attain the shores of Thy glory, and deprive not this wretched creature of the immensities of Thy riches, and cast not away this suppliant from the doors of Thy grace, and Thy bounty, and Thy gifts. Have mercy, then, upon this poor and desolate soul who hath sought no friend but Thee, and no companion except Thee, and no comforter save Thee, and no beloved apart from Thee, nor cherished any desire but Thyself.

Cast, then, upon me, O my God, the glances of Thy mercy, and forgive me my trespasses and the trespasses of them that are dear to Thee, and which come in between us and the revelation of Thy triumph and Thy grace. Cancel Thou, moreover, our sins which have shut off our faces from the splendors of the Day-Star of Thy favors. Powerful art Thou to do Thy pleasure. Thou ordainest what Thou willest, and art not asked of what Thou wishest through the power of Thy sovereignty, nor canst Thou be frustrated in whatsoever Thou prescribest through Thine irrevocable decree. No God is there save Thee, the Almighty, the Most Powerful, the Ever-living, the Most Compassionate.

INDEX

341

Progressive Revelation p. 50-51